Queen of Hearts:

The Story of Anna Sipl Meyers

Edited by Leita Kaldi Davis

The Queen of Hearts is the card of beauty, magnetism, affection and indispensable sister, the beloved daughter. If she did not have that inevitable negative side to deal with, this would be the most desirable card. The Queen of Heart natives are talented in some artistic line, even if it's just in their appreciation of beauty and art. They are often intense and dramatic and can be domineering in the family. They are also capable of deep devotion and loyalty. They have a strong streak of religion or spirituality and are often influenced by strong-minded women. The Queen of Hearts has the ability to reach others through her innate leadership abilities, powerful communication skills and strong business sense. The level of success achieved is predicated on her ability to keep emotional reactions in check. She may find a simple home life only part of her personal expression.

The Cards of Life

For my granddaughter, Aspen

and all the wonderful women in my life: Oma, Mami,

my lovely girl, Bridgett, and my baby, Leah

Contents

Foreword

When I met Anna Sipl Meyers in Las Vegas years ago, and mentioned that I had lived in Hungary, she told me that she spoke some Hungarian, that she had learned it as a child in a concentration camp on the border between what was then Yugoslavia and Hungary, during World War II. I did a double take, wondering if I had heard correctly. Then she said, "*Egy kicsi kenyere*" and laughed. "That's actually all I know." I knew that it meant "Please, a little bread." I instantly wanted to know more about this lovely blonde woman with hazel eyes and an alluring figure, who was a multi-millionaire, proprietor of prime properties in Las Vegas and Lake Tahoe. What had her journey been like, from surviving the hell of war to ruling a small empire.

I got the opportunity to track the road of her life when Anna asked me to edit a series of autobiographical interviews conducted by the Oral History Research Center of the University of Nevada Las Vegas. Claytee White, who interviewed Anna, told me that most oral histories can be captured in a two-hour session, but because of Anna's boundless life experiences, many sessions over almost a year had been required. The Research Center will catalogue her story and bind two copies for their archives. But Anna wanted a book. I agreed to take on the task, now knowing what a daunting literary endeavor it would be, organizing 300 pages of chronologically scattered notes. Nor did I know how much I would enjoy learning about Anna's life – from dancing the polka to murder on the Strip.

Idyllic stories of Anna's childhood in the German village of Krindijia on the Danube River changed dramatically into horror stories of concentration camps, barely surviving years of extreme suffering, along with her mother, grandmother and older brother, Michael, who had been crippled by polio as a baby.

As part of my research into Anna's past, I learned that in the early part of World War II, Marshal Josip Broz Tito formed "Tito's Partisans," officially the Yugoslav National Liberation Army, a highly effective anti-Axis resistance movement. Following the collapse of the German occupation of Yugoslavia towards the end of the war, Tito took vengeance on German Swabians. He brutally eradicated most of the Danube Swabian population by expulsions, starvation and mass executions. Anna bitterly says that Tito was their Hitler. Between August 1945 and May 1946, in the village of Krindija in Slavonia, where Anna and her family lived, the German population there disappeared almost overnight. They were sent to the death camp in Gakowa. In the 1950s, Anna and her family escaped from the camp and joined the refugee exodus to Austria, desperately hoping to find her father there.

Only in recent years have reports of the atrocities committed by Tito's Partisans during the postwar years been published. In *Leidensweg der Donauschwaben min Konnunistischen Jugoslawien,* (Passion of the Germans in Communist Yugoslavia: People's murder of the Donauschwaben. People's Loss – Names – Figures – Donauschwabisches Archiv – 1994), Anna came across a report by Anna Blechl, a midwife from Batschsentiwan near Apati on the Danube, known to Anna's people at the time of their expulsion. Blechl writes of helping a woman deliver her baby during her stay at Brestowatz. She also wrote of the women and teenage girls who came to her for help after Russian soldiers or Partisans had raped them.

Recalling painful memories for the purpose of recording her own history, Anna draws upon an outstanding publication by Hans Kopp, who shared her childhood experience in Batschentiwan: The Last Generation -

<u>Forgotten and Left to Die: The Postwar Memoirs of a Child: The History of</u> <u>the Danube Swabians in Word and Pictures</u> (<u>Die Letzte Generation</u> <u>Vergessen und dem Tod Überlassen</u>), written in German and English, a volume of 400 pages, with more than 1,400 pictures, documents and maps, copyrighted in 1999 and published in 2003. Among the dozens of names listed in Kopp's acknowledgements, Anna is mentioned.

By chance, Anna met Maria Kopp, Hans' niece, in Cleveland, Ohio, many years after both families emigrated to the United States. When she took Maria home with her, Anna's mother tearfully recalled braiding her hair when she was a little girl. They were grief-stricken to hear that Maria's parents had been murdered. Anna later reunited with Hans Kopp and his brother. Among Kopp's illustrations in his book, Anna saw a sketch of his parents standing in front of a barred cellar window, now a prison, and felt her heart stop when she recognized that window as the one her mother had been flung through as punishment by the Partisans.

After struggling for years in Austria, Anna's father applied to emigrate to the United States. They were refused asylum twice, the first time because of Oma's age -- she was in her fifties -- and again because of Michael's infirmity. When the father used a Yugoslav instead of German spelling of their name, they were finally accepted.

Their immigrant story describes the typical hurdles faced by refugees from all over the world. They battled prejudice and poverty, while the father worked beyond his strength to gain a foothold in the new world. Anna describes their unique personalities, marked by values of frugality and honesty, their generosity in extending a hand to relatives who came later, raising their children to be not only principled citizens, but to nurture some of their European culture through music and dancing, cooking and festivals.

Anna struggled through many misfortunes as she grew up, but clung to family values to define her ambitious determination to prosper. In her twenties, she worked as a teller in a small bank in Kent, Ohio, where my husband, Robert Davis, met her. He couldn't believe her entrepreneurial genius when, years later, he went to Las Vegas to help her with cash control in her casino.

Some of Anna's dreams were dashed -- the white wedding dress, the higher education -- but many were realized, especially her rise to success in Las Vegas as the only woman to own a hotel/casino in a world ruled by men. She socialized with the noteworthy and the notorious, gentlemen and thugs. She cared for the homeless and the derelicts, bore the scorn of the Country Club set who ended up celebrating her. She'd be the first to admit that she can't spell, but she certainly can count, and repair an elevator, and tar a roof in the pouring rain in high heels and an elegant suit.

Anna's story is extraordinary. She is an icon of womanly strength honed in hardship, who cultivated wisdom based on what she made of her experiences. Her philosophy has always been "Whether you call it work or play depends on your attitude." She rose from a child who begged for a bit of bread to a queen who built her own throne.

Leita Kaldi Davis
Editor
2017 Recipient, Lillian Carter Award
Bradenton, Florida

Childhood: A Reverie

I was born Anna Sippl on April 26, 1943, in Krindija, Yugoslavia, now Croatia, near the Danube. My family was part of the ethnic German population that was persecuted, massacred or expelled by Tito's Partisans to the neighboring village of Gakowa, which became a concentration camp.

My godmother, Anna Wittman, would reminisce about our life when I was a child, before the war, and when I grew up and was in danger of forgetting. I was named after her. All girls took the names of their godmothers. They were the keepers of our oral history. What my mother, my brother and I wrote before they passed away is so beautifully put that, you know, I'm going to reveal it to you.

*   *   *

My mother, Magdalena, was a handsome woman with a crown of dark braids and dark eyes. My father, Josef, was a strong man, not so tall, with hazel eyes and large, capable hands. My brother, Michael, was three years older than me. He had had polio at eighteen months and walked with small crutches that my father had made for him, one leg dangling. But that didn't stop him from hopping around the farm or playing with his toddling sister.

Krindija had 1500 German speaking people. Nobody learned Croatian until they went to school, but the war came before I was old enough to go to school, so I never learned it. One of my relatives, Matis Stoltz, wrote a book on Krindija that has maps of where everybody lived, along with a history of how our people came to settle there, and what life was like. I have a beautiful box about three inches deep that was hand carved by my Michael years later, when he was in Austria, and I put that big book in there for safe keeping.

Krindija had been settled by Germans as long ago as 1689 from various parts of the Austrian Empire. They had cultivated the Danube River basin, and turned it into rich farmland. All the houses were made of clay and straw, similar to adobe. Michael and I would watch the men make molds of wood and press the material into them. After drying, they'd come out like bricks. Roofs were made of wooden beams covered with red clay tiles. Our house was on a narrow plot, maybe three acres. It had an entrance at the side and a small "mud room" where people took off their boots and shoes. That led into the kitchen where there was also a bed, though the second room was the bedroom. The main room, or family room, might have a bed in it, too. There was no electricity, so we had kerosene lamps and a wrought iron coal stove. When a couple got married, they'd usually live with the bride's or the groom's parents for a while, depending on who had more room or who might need their help.

Everybody had their own vegetable gardens, fruit trees and grapevines. They made their own wine and plum brandy called *slivovitz,* as well as cherry brandy, and men took great pride in them. We always had things like wine and brandy and cookies in the house for company. Drunkenness was rare, because so much work went into making brandy that the men would not waste it. The only smoking I ever saw was a pipe, a luxury that a man might smoke once in a while.

Every farmer's life is dictated by four seasons. There was spring planting, and sometimes spring lettuce and radishes bloomed in June. Cherries and peaches started ripening at the beginning of July. By fall we had an abundance of everything. My father harvested wheat and took it to a miller in town to turn it into flour. The miller usually took a portion of the wheat as payment. There was a small general store in the town for staples, but my father rarely had cash to shop there.

Dried beans were a staple throughout the winter and, of course, we had lots of pickles and sauerkraut. My mother buried carrots, root vegetables, cabbage, parsnips, rutabaga and potatoes on a bed of straw deep in the earth and them covered them with more straw and earth. They never froze in their warm beds, and we lived on them when nothing else was growing.

We never threw away food. Scraps went to a compost pile or to the pigs. Slaughtering was usually done in the winter, because there was no refrigeration.

2

Families would get together to slaughter a pig and then make sausage. Michael and I would watch in fascinated horror as one of the men slit the screaming pig's throat and the snow turned red all around them, though they'd catch as much blood as possible for blood sausages. Then they'd hang it from a tree and slice open the stomach, and we watched with wide eyes as its guts spilled out. Women would preserve meat by canning or smoking it in small smoke houses attached to the house, which also held an oven where women baked bread.

We had a couple of pigs and one horse named Zoltan. Father made a wooden carriage with a metal band around the wooden wheel and a long pole to secure him. Michael and I loved to ride in the carriage, looking down upon Sultan's broad back, while my father coaxed him on in a gentle voice.

We had cats to keep the mice away, and a dog that was really a pet. Mother raised a few chickens, duck and geese in the yard, so we didn't eat poultry very often. When we did, mother would cut the head off a chicken and it would run around the yard squirting blood everywhere. She'd throw this chicken into boiling water, and it stank like something I'll never forget. Then she'd let Michael and I help pick off all the feathers. She saved those feathers to make down pillows (*duhood)* and quilts that were actually large pouches stuffed with feathers. No matter how cold it was outside, we'd stay warm as toast under those quilts. In the spring, Mother would take apart the pillows and quilts, wash and dry the feathers, and restuff them. She had to be careful not to do this on a windy day.

People were very clean about their things. They may not have taken a bath but once a week, but they "washed up" every day. Every morning the women aired out all the bedding, taking it outside or to an open window. No matter how cold it might be, they would air out that bedding before making the bed again.

Once a week, my mother would wash clothes in a big pot and a scrub board. She boiled white things, using the sun to bleach them. In winter time Michael and I found it hilarious to see frozen clothing flapping from the line like icy scarecrows, and bedding hanging like white boards.

My grandmother, Oma, who was my mother's mother, taught me how to make lace. It was common for girls to learn these skills. I learned how to crochet and knit when I was five years old. Through the years, as our family was buffeted on the winds of war from shore to shore, I kept a bedspread made of little crocheted squares. I also have a pair of crocheted slippers that my mother made for me before she died. At Christmas she would make everybody a pair of crocheted slippers. They were wonderful! She would cut a footprint in a heavier fabric like leather or suede and sew it on the bottoms for soles, and add a tie that went around the slipper to make a little tassel. Men didn't get tassels; only women did. My mother always adamantly said, "Use a dark color, because you're going to be sorry; it's going to show all the stains if you make it light." But I always wanted to have pink ones, and the last ones she made for me were pink, and I still have them.

Shoes were custom made by a shoemaker like my cousin, Frank Wittman. He learned the trade by going outside of Krindija to one of the larger cities, instead of learning as an apprentice. He would draw an outline of our feet and create a pair of plain, solid shoes that children would be expected to wear until they couldn't fit their feet into them any more.

Tailors made men's clothing, not women's. There was only one tailor in town, Willy Wittman who made jackets and work pants, usually from hemp. Zippers were very expensive, so women made buttonholes on their sewing machines. Some women had a Pfaff, a German foot-pedaled sewing machine, and even Singer machines. They were considered a real luxury, almost the equivalent of having a car.

My godmother told me that there were some Jewish people nearby who had a car and drove it into town. Nobody in Krindija had a car. If a car ever drove into town, it would cause a sensation. When I was a child I never ever dreamed that I would have a car. That would be like a fairy tale. If I had ever told anyone I dreamed about a car, they'd think I was crazy. We were taught to be content and grateful for what we had.

4

My grandmother made clothing for herself, me and my brother. Oma's husband, my grandfather, had died quite young of a malady I didn't understand, so she spent much of her time with us. Those who could afford it might buy fabric from the general store, but most people had a weaving loom for sheep's wool. They also spun hemp into yarn for men's clothing. Because they were so well made, clothes lasted for a long time. The most common way of cleaning was to hang them outdoors inside out to air. A woman never came into the house without putting on an apron that would have been made of remnants from discarded material.

Some families were very large. My father had twelve siblings. There was no birth control, so people didn't have all those children by choice, but they were considered as assets, as they would grow up to help in the fields.

There was a schoolhouse in the village where we were taught through four grades, with one teacher for each grade. After that, we helped our parents work the land. The schoolhouse had a wooden floor. Stone or brick floors were rare; the most common floors were made of mud treated with cow dung and earth. We wore outside shoes outside, slippers inside, and wooden clogs in the garden.

If someone wanted to teach school, or learn another profession, they'd have to go to Oseiak or one of the larger towns to learn that skill. Another relative of mine, Tony Wittman, went off to school in one of the larger towns and became a doctor.

Education was rarely thought about or encouraged. We accepted the fact that we were only going to get four years of education. The schoolhouse was also used as a church on Sundays until, later on, all the people in town got together and built a very nice church. My father helped build it and I have a picture of him way up high near the roof. The biggest festival we ever had was for the blessing of the church. Many people from other towns came for the celebration. Everybody was dressed in their Sunday best – women in white and men in black. All the women wore the same style -- long white skirts gathered at the waist and a shawl.

People took good care of their possessions, even the plow used to till the soil.

5

When that plow was put away, it was cleaned and dried to make sure it didn't rust, and protected and covered, even the leather bands that were put around the horse's bridle.

In our small village everybody knew each other. If a kid stole cherries off someone's tree, the whole town would know about it. We all had cherry trees -- sour cherries, white cherries and black cherries. We also had apricots and peaches, apples and pears. We had joyful festivals at harvest time to celebrate our abundance.

Festivals began by going to church, to Catholic mass, after which there was a procession through town, carrying the cross with altar boys on each side of the priest, to the feast, following the aroma of lamb or a pig turning on a spit, fruit pies and bread fresh from the oven, tables laden with bounty of the harvest.

Someone would be playing the accordion, a mouth organ or a guitar, a brass horn or clarinet. Musicians taught each other through the generations. People danced, women whirling around in long white skirts with aprons and blouses with puffy sleeves, with men dressed in black suits and hats. Kids would frolic around their mother's skirts or laugh together as they imitated their parents dance steps. Michael would stomp around on his crutches in time with the music, as I giggled and clapped for him. Beside the festivals, music was our best entertainment on Saturday night and Sunday afternoon. People would stroll around, showing off their gardens, and women would sing. For one hour on Sunday we'd listen to music broadcast on the radio. We were happy. We were so happy we never thought of anything that might make us unhappy.

And then the War came to our village.

Surviving the War

Though I was only two years old, and didn't fully understand what was happening to us, I've had vivid flashes of painful memories that would stay with me throughout my life. As I grew older, my mother, Oma and my godmother told me stories that formed a context around my childhood recollections of how the war devastated our lives.

On March 1, 1945 Tito's military police, the Partisans, started to drive people out of their homes and confiscate their property. We were summoned to the town square at gun point, and everyone huddled together, anxiously watching the guards, wondering if they intended to kill us all. Hours passed as we waited, paralyzed with fear, until night fell. My brother, Michael, who was five, sat close to me. We were shivering with cold. Neither of us really understood what was going on around us, but I felt that Michael was struggling to uphold his role as my big brother, trying to protect and comfort me. As darkness fell, I tried to sleep, but couldn't, fretting restlessly, terrified at what would happen to us. Next day, however, they sent us home!

We were elated, deluding ourselves that the Partisans would not really force us out of our homes. Then the townsfolk heard that Germans in the Banat region had been driven from their homes and forced into concentration camps, and that the Partisans had selected some people for forced labor details, but we could not imagine that happening to us, clinging to a stubborn illusion.

The town crier and the Partisans came numerous times, ordering us to leave our homes, until they finally threatened physical harm, and we had to prepare to go. My mother did not want to take a lot of belongings. She worried that, if we left our home, our father would not be able to find us. But Mami and Oma were forced to pack necessities that we might need, wherever we might be going, into pillow cases, as we had no suitcases, and load them into a wheelbarrow. I begged Mami to bring my doll, my *Mama Pupen,* that Oma had made especially for me, her *engelkind,* out of rags, with buttons for eyes, sheep wool for hair and miniscule crocheted slippers, but Mami refused, saying we didn't have room for such trifles. We took overcoats, blankets and as much food as we could carry. She sewed some of our most precious photographs into the hem of her skirt, but she couldn't take all of them, and still believed that we would return to our house. Our house that had been built by my father and relatives, that was meant to be passed on from one generation to the next, built with all the love that one can put into labor. More than a hundred years ago, my family had established themselves in Krindija. They settled on raw pieces of land, cut down trees into building lumber to construct their home. At first, a shelter was built from damp wood, just enough to keep out the elements. With only a hand saw and an axe, they steadfastly built a house that the wind would not penetrate. They hand dug a foundation and cultivated the soil. They planted a cornucopia of fruit trees from seeds that were shared amongst neighbors and relatives. They tended those trees from season to season until finally, after half a dozen years, the fruit could be picked. Anticipation of the first bite spurred the Harvest Festival. Now, outside this hardy orchard and building so painstakingly built, a town crier was ordering us to abandon our home!

Animals that my parents had helped birth would be left with strangers. All the chickens in the yard that had hatched on our watch, and roamed free, eating out of our hands, and we had names for all of them, including the cocky rooster. Mami fed Zoltan, our horse, for the last time, then she untied him and hoped he could find his own food and water. Clothes created from the spinning wheel, sweaters that took many hours to knit, were left behind.

After Mami and Oma had loaded whatever we could carry into a wheelbarrow, as we walked away from our home, our dog started barking frantically, and strangers tried to hold him on a rope as he struggled to run after us. I'll always remember the desperate look in his eyes as he watched us walk away. Michael was sobbing, with his face buried in Mami's skirt and, as Oma dragged me away, I wailed. What would happen to Zoltan, our cats, chickens, pigs and ducks? Who would eat the fruit from the budding trees? Who would eat the mulberries from the tree that I had climbed so often to pick berries?

When would we come back home? Oma told me to be quiet, fearing I would aggravate the Partisan guards around us.

The final expulsion of our people happened on March 15, 1945. An estimated 3,500 citizens began their slow march out of town, as the Partisans herded them at gun point. Mami struggled to push the heavy wheelbarrow, as did many other women in our dismal procession. Babies were crying and toddlers like me were whining, but neighbors grouped together trying to help each other as we trudged slowly down the road, away from our town. My father's father, a grandparent I scarcely remember, trailed along with us. He had been a widower for many years, was nearly blind, and had always been a very quiet man, a phantom in my memory.

When we reached the neighboring town of Doroslo, a Hungarian town that had been settled by Germans, we discovered that everyone there with a German name had been forced out of their homes. We continued on to Stapar, where we had traded with the townspeople, buying their products in exchange for our produce. The townsfolk had always been friendly good neighbors, so we expected they would give us water and let us rest for a while. We were all shocked when, instead of finding a welcome, a gang of teen-agers met us, cursing us as Germans, and throwing stones at us. Surely, we thought, their parents would punish the boys and make up for their abuse. As we hurried away from the young thugs, we came upon their parents, standing outside their houses or looking from their windows with the same hate-filled expressions. We recognized many of them, and were horrified at their betrayal.

Long lines of people, exhausted and hot, with no water, crept along the dusty road, children crying, old people leaving their belongings by the side of the road, because they could no longer carry them. Whoever stopped was brutally beaten by the Partisans. We had to sleep in a roadside ditch that night.

The next day we trailed into Filipowa, a Roman Catholic town whose citizens had fled or were forced from their homes. The Partisans crowded us into empty rooms where we slept on the floor. We children snooped through other houses that still had furnishings, but Oma warned us not to touch anything and to stay far away from the guards.

Several days later, we were marched to the town of Gakowa, one of the main internment camps that Germans people had been herded into, as they had been in Krindija, Filipowa Miletitsch and Brestowatz. The communist government of Yugoslavia turned the towns of Jarek, Gakowa and Kruschiwl, among several others, into extermination camps.

Gakowa was a typical *donauschwaben* (Danube Schwabian) town located northeast of Krindija near the Hungarian border. It had been a beautiful town until it was turned into a concentration camp where 17,000 inmates died of starvation, typhus, dysentery and malaria. They were buried in mass graves on the outskirts of town, including hundreds from our beloved Krindijia.

Though many guards patrolled the Gakowa camp, we were usually allowed to move about during the day. Children sneaked away in search of food they might find in nearby orchards. Even I, small as I was, would steal away with Mami to a nearby Hungarian settlement to beg for food. Whenever we met a Hungarian farmer, she would have me hold out my tiny hand and plead in Hungarian, *"Egy kicsi kenyere,"* -- a little bread, please.

Tito, in his delirious hatred for the Germans, came up with another way of getting rid of us. He loaded us into cattle cars, packed like sardines and shipped us off to Germany. Some people tried looking through the cracks in the seams of the cars, but could not see enough to guess where we were. We waited anxiously to be released from the suffocating car. Hours passed with no activity except for people elbowing their way to the hole they carved in the bottom of the car to relieve themselves. Hours turned into days, as we stopped at several stations only to be turned away by Germans who did not want any more refugees and wouldn't open the train doors. Europe was awash with refugees fleeing war ruins that had been their homes.

The locomotive would fire up and cars banged into each other as we slowly moved on. We had no idea where we were headed. One day, the train slowed down and finally stopped. The car doors opened and we were permitted to go outside. Fresh air! People stretched their legs, lifted their arms to the sky, breathed deeply, rejoicing in this moment of grace. Fields of grass stretched out on both sides of the train, and people saw a house far in the distance that filled them with melancholy. All too soon, we were beckoned back to the cars, the doors closed and we started to chug off again. Mami shouted that my grandfather wasn't there! Did he get on the wrong car? After the train's slow start, it stopped again. Guards opened the doors and asked if anyone knew an old man who might be missing. We got off the train and Oma saw my grandfather lying by the side of the tracks. He had been run over by the train. Women grabbed Michael and me and buried our faces in their skirts before we could catch a glimpse of grandfather. They buried him in a shallow grave nearby. Oma and Mami sobbed, wondering if he had chosen to end his life. We returned to the train and resumed our journey for several more hours, huddled together in shock and grief. When the train finally stopped, we were back at the same place in Yugoslavia where we had started.

We ended up back in the Gakowa camp, starving, exhausted, returning to our one cup of *einbrennsuppe* a day. Ordinarily, it would be made with brown flour, fat, vegetables and noodles. But the Gakowa soup was more or less empty boiled water, with a few occasional wormy peas floating on top. Years later, Michael, would not eat *einbrennsuppe* no matter how good it was, because it reminded him of those horrible years in Gakowa.

During the summer, children, old men and women were forced to work in the fields at gun point, and were promised an extra ration of bread. One day, when my mother was sent to work, she took my brother and me with her, but she became so tired that she stopped on the wayside to rest. A Partisan approached her and told her to get up. She told him she couldn't walk anymore. He replied, "Well, then I'm going to shoot you and your kids." My mother responded, "Shoot me first so I don't see my children die." The Partisan took pity on her. My mother was twenty-four years old, with jet black hair in a braided bun that she had never cut. However, malnutrition made her beautiful hair fall out, and so did ours. We all had lice, and had to have our hair shorn. Bald, we all looked the same, which was very humiliating for women, especially for teenage girls.

My grandmother worked in the fields, too, hoping for an extra crumb of bread for us, her children and grandchildren. She was relatively young, in her late forties, but the deprivations of war had taken their toll on her. Still, she struggled every day to take care of us in every way possible, if only by holding us in her arms or giving us a bit of food that she pretended she didn't want.

Grandmothers were the unsung heroines of our ordeal. Hans Kopp, whose experiences in Krindjia and Gakowa were very similar to mine, eulogizes them in his book, The Last Generation - Forgotten and Left to Die: The Postwar Memoirs of a Child: The History of the Danube Swabians in Word and Pictures.

During the fight for survival, the women, in particular the grandmothers, became heroines day in and day out. They were the ones that had to look after the children, go begging, find food in the fields, collect herbs, maybe soap, make clothes from pleated skirts that they took apart and reworked for a better use of the material. They had to cook. They were bakers, nurses, caretakers, healers and supporters both morally and spiritually. … If it had not been for our grandmothers who fought so courageously for the survival of their grandchildren, many of us would not be here today. Only they knew how painful it was to see their grandchildren starve day in and day out and watch them die. They were the ones that gave the last piece of bread to their grandchildren and sacrificed their own lives to save the lives of their children. The colossal hardship, the big worries and agony and the despair these women had to endure, and indeed did so admirably, must be considered as one of the greatest achievements on the face of this Earth. I was there to witness their monumental, heroic and unselfish deeds.

We might well erect a monument to honor the greatest grandmothers of all, the grandmothers of the death camps.

*   *   *

The cruelest camp commander was a Partisan by the name of Grabic, nicknamed Suco. He took office in September of 1945. He ordered the separation of families, just to harass and demoralize our people and inflict as much confusion and suffering as possible. He separated people into three groups—those who were capable of working beginning at the age of fourteen, women with children, and older and sick people. He also separated children from grandparents. We were fortunate not to be affected by many of those orders. Many families, however, suffered severely under the separations, especially the helpless old people. They were not only poorly fed, but they were rarely fed, and they soon perished. Suco would order brutal punishments of people for even the most insignificant matters that he would deem criminal, like begging for food. His captives would be bound and pushed down cellar stairs where they were imprisoned, with no sanitary installations whatsoever, living on watery soup or nothing. My mother endured this cruel ordeal several times. Once she told me that after she was pushed down the stairs, she found herself in the cellar where she tried to see in the dim light, and she saw a figure in the corner. She finally made out that it was another human being who had hung himself.

Many people not only suffered bumps and bruises, but also broken bones from falling down the stairs, and some never saw day light again. But even that punishment could not stop them from trying to beg for food again after they were released. Desperate, they did not care if they died at the hands of the Partisans; they felt doomed to die of starvation if they did not go begging. Consequently, the flow of beggars continued and, despite the consequences, several young men became escape artists from this hell. Again and again, people went out of the camp to seek food, and prayed each time that they wouldn't get caught and end up in the cellar. Suco was directly responsible for the death of many hundreds of innocent men, women and children.

Several priests like Monsignor Dobler, Father Grubler, Father Johler, and a couple of Catholic nuns made an effort to hold school classes for us in the camp, but their attempts were in vain, and were soon abandoned, because the children did not have the energy to learn anything. Another reason they failed was that the Partisans would disperse any kind of gathering. Going to church was forbidden, so priests held masses in different houses throughout the town, although it became more and more difficult. As sacramental wafers, the priests used cornbread when available. All our people were Catholic. None of them were Jewish. I didn't even know that there was another religion until I was older. During that terrible winter of starvation, people died in droves, while women kept praying the rosary, either in supplication for the living, or benediction for the dead.

The prejudice that Tito felt for us was, I think, a hatred of Germans that was tinged with jealousy of our achievements in farming and establishing an enviable life style in what he considered to be his domain. Like many Yugoslavs, he probably resented our prosperity and independence, and thought that gave us an air of superiority. We nurtured that sense of ourselves, in fact. My father always proudly told us, "You are German; you are not Yugoslavian." He was adamant about that. When the war progressed across Europe and Hitler's Third Reich was winning, Tito was on Hitler's side. Tito was as ruthless as Hitler. He remained in power for many years, and I feel that he should have been tried and executed as a war criminal.

As people began to starve to death, those who had any strength found their way at night to nearby orchards and fields, where they would steal whatever they could – fruit, vegetables, nuts, sometimes a bit of wheat or corn left by the harvesting machines. Oma would grind the bits of grain with a stone and boil them.

To stay alive became a daily fight for young and old. Only people who had the perseverance to fend for themselves, who were able to obtain food in whatever way possible would have a realistic chance to survive. About three weeks before Christmas my mother decided to go on a begging trip to one of her usual places. She wanted to

14

find some food, so we would have something special to fill our bellies on the approaching holiday. On her way back to Gakowa, the Partisans captured her. All the food she had been given was taken away from her and she was thrown into the cellar of the town hotel, the *gasthaus*. An announcement was broadcast that people who were caught that night would be sentenced to the firing squad. When we heard this terrible news, my brother and I ran to the hotel to see what would happen to our mother. I do not remember how long we waited there with others whose relatives were among the people to be executed. But we begged and pleaded so pathetically that my mother was miraculously released.

Sometimes the Partisans gave us hard stale corn bread that the women would soak to make it edible. We ate it gratefully, as if it were cake. We watched wagons roll into the camp filled with food, and especially bread, but it was all for the Partisans. We could only dream of eating it. On one rare occasion, a person who had been sleeping in the same room with us went begging and I found under her bed a rectangular wooden box about the size of a bread loaf, and inside of it was sort of a bluish red jelly. I crawled under the bed and tasted it. How could I resist? As I licked my finger, I fantasized about how good that would be on bread. Of course, I was caught and severely punished for stealing. Principles were not compromised under any circumstance.

In 1946, along with many other diseases that spread among us, a terrible typhus epidemic broke out. The hospital was actually nothing more than a house set up to separate people infected with typhus from the rest. There was no real help there, no medical care. Most people died a short time after they were brought there, especially the old ones who had no one to take care of them. The cemetery filled up, and men had to dig mass graves to bury hundreds of bodies there. The stench of death was everywhere, even beyond Gakowa.

Two years passed in this manner. Homeless, hungry, wearing rags, begging and stealing, struggling to stay alive.

Escape to Austria

My mother and Oma decided to try to escape to Austria, which was neutral at that time. I was four and my brother was seven. Young as I was, I remember almost everything.

European borders changed continually. Our region of Yugoslavia had previously been Austria-Hungary. My mother was born in Krindija -- the same place as my birthplace -- but her birth certificate says Austria-Hungary, while mine reads Yugoslavia.

Croatians and Yugoslavians were jealous of Germans who lived in their midst, because we developed the best farm land and trades, which they could see when they came to our towns. Germans were elite, more disciplined, cleaner, more educated and skilled people. Even though none of us had more than four years of schooling, it was more than most Yugoslavs had, and it was enough for us to thrive. We developed ingenuity and resourcefulness and made the most of what we had to work with. I always marveled at the ingenuity of my father.

When he was given options by Tito, along with all German men, to join the Partisans, the Yugoslavian Army, or the German Army, my father naturally joined the German army. My mother had no idea where he was sent, but he didn't come home for a long time, and then we were forced out of our home. Once we were in Gakowa, my mother basically gave up hope that she would ever see my father again. At that time, there were women who were getting mail out. Later, we learned that many women had been raped and abused for those favors, but that was something my mother never talked about.

Women persisted in coming to her saying, "Listen, we're getting these letters out; we're writing to an Austrian boarding house in Tyrol that has a bunch of German soldiers in it. Do you want us to look for your husband?"

My mother replied, "No, he's dead. I have not heard from him in over two years."

By this time, Germany had lost the war, and she despaired of any possibility that he could be alive. She gave in to depression, as we all did. We were skin and bones, our hair was falling out, we were covered with lice, suffering from malnutrition, barely clinging to life.

The women who had access to mail knew my father's name and they inquired about him, in spite of my mother's reticence. It took a very long time for letters to be sent back and forth, but eventually those women came back and told my mother they had found her husband. We rejoiced, screaming and hugging each other, elated by a ray of hope.

My father began to send us letters, but he had no money to enclose. Even though he had been paid as a soldier, it was barely enough for him to survive. Now that the war was more or less over, he was living in a boarding house in Austria. Though he was a stone mason by profession, he did any work he could get, including sweeping streets. He had always been a hard-working, resourceful man. After some months, we were amazed when my father sent us some money.

We immediately planned our escape. Mami and Oma decided we would walk more than a hundred kilometers from the camp to the Austrian border. In planning our marathon "hike," we had no plastic containers, aluminum foil or plastic wrap, no paper towels or toilet paper. We took rags instead torn from worn-out clothes. We cut off all the buttons that were made of bone or shell and put them in our button jar. If you were lucky enough to have a zipper, you removed the thread and saved every zipper, but we had no zippers. We packed a glass bottle for water. We weren't in the desert, after all, so there was a possibility of finding a well. Some people were lucky enough to have a bottle with a cork in it, but most bottles were protected by weaving, similar to what we see around an Italian bottle of Chianti. Bottles were precious. Nobody ever threw away a bottle, and people would even pass them down to their children. We had one bottle of water for four of us to walk a hundred kilometers.

The night of our escape finally came. In the darkness, we paid off a Partisan guard, and went off into the fields, walking north to the Austrian border. My mother carried my brother on her back, along with clothing and bare necessities, like bread and water. Oma carried me, although the fields weren't muddy, so I could walk most of the time until I became too tired. One day, after carrying me for a while, Oma said, "I have to let you down and leave you here; I can't carry you anymore." I cried out in terror, though I quickly realized she was joking; she would never abandon me.

Fortunately, it was spring and the weather was decent, but that meant there were no vegetables in any of the gardens we passed, not even a potato or a root that we might have boiled to take along with us. On our trek we begged farmers to let us stay in their barns, but they often refused us, so we sneaked into their barns and slept on the hay. We knew that farmers get up early, so we had to wake up before the sun rose and get out of the barn, terrified that they would run after us with a pitchfork. We understood that they wanted to protect their possessions and their families. Europe was crawling with refugees, and we were not welcome. Although they saw two children and two women, they were suspicious. In some cases, though, farmers were kind enough to give us milk.

It took us more than a week to get to the Austrian border. Once we arrived there, we were directed to a Red Cross hospital, where we hoped to meet my father. We were emaciated, sick with scurvy. When they did different tests on me, they would say, "Oh, you had rheumatic fever." I'd reply, "I had everything." We had worms, the little, short white ones, tapeworms that looked like a two- or three-foot long earthworms. We were so sick, and at the Red Cross hospital they tried to nurture us back to health. We stayed there for several months.

I will never forget the day that my father found us. He stood at the bottom of a big staircase with my mother and brother. I ran down those stairs into my father's arms. I had been only about eight months old the last time I'd seen him, and obviously I did not remember him, but he certainly remembered me, and I was overjoyed to be in his loving arms. We were overwhelmed at the prospect of starting a new life!

Shortly thereafter we received a letter from some relatives in the Graz area. Communication was very difficult in those days; there were only letters. (By the way,

Graz, Austria is where Arnold Schwarzenegger is from and, also by the way, one of my relatives is married to one of his relatives.)

Graz was not a small town, but on its outskirts, in Sading, Foitzbach and Köflach, lived some of our family members. After all, there were 1,500 of us in our extended family. I wonder if there had been intermarriage, with that many relatives living there for so long, isolated in their communities. My father somehow figured out where our people were and so we headed in their direction. We hoped to stay with them, but they were leasing the land where they lived, share cropping. Their landlord would not let us stay there, so we slept in a barn again.

Every day we walked across green rolling hills and through forests. I can still smell the damp pines of the forests. Blueberries were growing, so we picked them all day, then my father would go into town and trade them for whatever he could get. He seldom got money, but bartered for something else, like bread.

We found my father's sister, my aunt Dante Sieber. in Köflach. She and two adult children were living in one small room with a stove, a small table and chairs, a bunk bed on one side, a regular bed on the other, and just enough walking space in between. They were on the third floor of a commercial building, in a room that was really an attic, with open rafters. The owners lived in their *gasthaus* next door, and there were two small stores downstairs. Wooden stairs led to the second floor where other people resided.

There was enough room on the third floor for another living space, and my father asked the *gasthaus* owner if he could build an apartment for us there. The owner agreed to buy the materials and my father contributed his labor that was worth a few months rent. We wound up with a two-room apartment in the attic.

In the first room my father placed a wrought iron stove with a baking oven. We also had one single bed that was like a military cot, with metal rings that held it together, and a small table, a corner hand-carved Bavarian bench, a rectangular table and two extra chairs. In the second room where my parents slept, he placed two single beds together and another small bed for me. We were delighted to have straw mattresses.

There was a toilet on the second floor, a long room where there was a hole in the floor with rounded corners. We thought this was special because there was a cylinder below the hole, unlike the outhouses that we had used in the past that opened into the earth. A piece of wood like a step in front of the bench seat was ideal for someone like me, because my feet didn't reach the ground, so I could balance and go to the bathroom by myself. In that bathroom, many times I encountered those dreaded tapeworms that had not yet left my body. One horrible day, when I saw a two-foot long tapeworm hanging from me, I ran screaming to my aunt who pulled it out. I prayed that would be the last one.

Of course, there was no running water in the toilet that was shared by more than a dozen tenants. We got water from a pump at the *gasthaus* next door. We had to walk down the stairs, around the front of the building, past a gated area that connected the two properties, around the far side of the *gasthaus* into the back yard to get to the wrought iron pump with a stiff, creaking handle. We would fill our buckets and then go all the way around and up three flights of stairs to our attic. We used the water to flush the toilet, to cook, bathe and drink. We had two buckets; that's all we could afford. We were a two-bucket family! When times improved, we eventually bought a white glazed tub that measured seventeen by thirty-six inches, maybe twelve inches high. On Saturday night we filled the tub with heated water that required many long trips to the well. My father was the first to take a bath, then my mother, then my brother, and I was the last to take a bath. In the same water! (The reason I know the tub's dimensions is because that tub is in my backyard right now. It was our most prized possession and we took it with us when we came to the United States. It was packed into a crate that held the tub and whatever bedding or other things we brought with us. When I found it in my parents' garage after they died, I had to bring it home with me.)

Saturday was bath day for everybody. After our baths, we had to carry the water from the tub and pour it down the toilet on the second floor, if the toilet was not occupied. With all the people using it, however, it was usually occupied. Sometimes people threw the water out the window.

In Köflach, my father was able to find a job as a stonemason. He got a bicycle to get to his job, a prize possession, though most people walked. My grandfather, Nicolas Shrekhause, my mother's brother, had taught him masonry, though when we lived in Krindija, my father also worked in a hemp factory. I have a picture of him with about two dozen people holding large rolls of hemp.

It was very difficult for refugees to find work. There was one person in town who could afford to have a maid, and my mother and grandmother worked for her for a while. Then they got a job at the local lumber yard, loading lumber onto railroad cars. I have a picture of them hefting heavy sixteen-feet long boards, one at either end. Typical of my family, whatever it took, they were just happy to have work.

Laundry was a real chore, as there was no running water, but an aqueduct flowed from a river through Köflach that narrowed into a pool. In this hidden spot, we would take off our clothes and rinse them thoroughly in the pool. If they had stains, we'd scrub them against the stone and rinse them again. Women had such strong hands because of such work. (Even today, when we hand-wash clothes, we realize just how much strength it takes to wring them out.) They even washed linens by hand in the stream, scrubbing them on a washboard, then they boiled the whites and hung them on a line to dry, where the sunshine bleached them, just as they had done back in Krindija. I was always amazed that they came out snow white. Neighbors surreptitiously spied on each others' clothes lines, as extremely white laundry was almost a status symbol.

Sunday afternoons were special for us kids. Living on the third floor, we would hang out of our window that overlooked the street. Week-day traffic usually consisted of horse-drawn wagons, some larger than trucks. They would have something like a telephone pole support that went from the front all the way to the back past the wagon bed. On our way home from school, we liked to hop on that back pole and get a free ride. But on Sunday afternoons we saw cars, probably on the road for Sunday outings.

The *bahnhof*, or train station across the street provided a major form of transportation. People who had to go to Graz, the big city that had a hospital, or any other place out of town, would take the train but, actually, not many people used trains. Sometimes we saw motorcycles with little passenger bucket seats on the right side. There were probably as many motorcycles as there were cars. Sometimes we'd see a small sports car going up the mountain, where some people had summer homes. Though cabins in the mountains didn't have running water, they were a cool place to go on hot summer days, and usually had a beautiful view. In this part of Austria there were soft rolling hills covered in every shade of green, with golden sunrises and iridescent sunsets. People often grew gardens there; everyone had a garden somewhere, if only a minimal vegetable plot. People who lived in apartments, like we did, usually rented a small space in someone's backyard with several different cubicles separated by chicken wire fencing, and grew their own vegetables there. Flowers were always considered a pure luxury, grown from hoarded seeds that were sometimes shared with others. Anything with a bulb was a real rarity, and you'd be very lucky to find someone who would share bulbs.

On Sunday afternoons as we watched vehicles climb the hill, we'd count them. Six was the most we saw one Sunday. I was much too young to be able to identify the mark of vehicles. I have a tough enough time even today telling one from another! I think I'm a typical woman in terms of thinking that a car isn't quite as important as a house or other domestic item. I view vehicles as a means of transportation, so it's got to be reliable, clean and, of course, the color is important. Horses and carriages still filled the streets. Manure dropped onto the paved roads, but people would rush out and scoop up the poop to use in their gardens as fertilizer. We needed no street cleaners.

In Köflach there was a general store owned by Mrs. Uri. The reason I remember her name is that my mother got a job cleaning Mrs. Uri's house. It was common for someone like my mother and my grandmother to clean other people's houses. Austrians viewed us as ignorant, with only four years of education.   It was typical of a mistress-maid relationship to give us gifts. Mrs. Uri had a daughter a little older than me and, on rare occasions, I would get some form of hand-me-down. But Mrs. Uri gave my mother something very precious that I still have in my kitchen today, a ceramic plate with a metal cover at the bottom and a small opening at the top. For many years, I didn't know what it was until I found out that the bottom metal opening was for hot water to keep children's plates warm while feeding them. It was a luxury item, one of the precious gifts that I saved.

Michael and I went to school in Köflach. The school had a wooden floor with a tarred finish. Some children came to school without shoes. There were times, especially in the summer, when we would go without shoes. I went to first and second grade in Köflach. There were two different classrooms; one for poorer kids and the other for kids who were better off. However, we were not taught differently. My parents couldn't afford to buy books, so we borrowed them to do homework.

I learned embroidery, though I had learned how to crochet before I went to first grade. We learned different embroidery stitches and how to fray the ends and secure them with stitches all the way around. In second grade we used pen and ink with ink wells.

On the small downtown street, there were ten or twelve shops. I remember the ice cream store, the closest thing to a restaurant in the town, and the book store next to it.

In Köflach, like in Yugoslavia, there was no shoe store. Frank Wittman, my cousin, had already established a shoemaker shop, so we went to him when we had to have shoes made. There was also a fabric store where, for the first time in her life, my mother bought fabric to make clothes for all of us. I don't recall ever having ready-made clothing until we came to the United States.

Finally, my father was earning some money. The income was so little, though, that we could only afford to have meat once a week, but we became creative cooks and bakers. I have never met anybody who cooked and baked better than my family, and I'm talking about not only Mami and Oma, but all of my relatives. I didn't realize until after I left home how good the food was. They made all of our noodles. In Krindija, we grew our own wheat and had it ground, but in Köflach we bought flour at the general store. All the bread was made from scratch. Brown bread made of whole wheat or rye, was the most common, because white flour was much more expensive and was actually considered to be cake flour. We seldom used white flour to bake something, unless it was a special occasion. On rare occasions, we made butter. The cream floated to the top and we would skim it off and churn it to make butter that was usually used for pastries. We made croissants with every kind of nut, plum and apricot fillings. Having pastries was part of our richer life now.

My grandmother found a place to rent near us, where she had a little yard with chickens, ducks and geese. Goose liver makes a very fine paté. The fatter the goose liver, the better the paté. Oma would take the goose and hold it between her legs and force feed it corn with the straight end of a wooden spoon, pushing it down the goose's throat while stroking its neck to make it swallow. We'd also have chicken at Easter, on a birthday, or at Christmas, maybe four times a year. Chicken was considered a real delicacy, because chickens laid eggs and produced more chickens, something you could sell.

Lard was used to make all kinds of dishes with potatoes, parsnips, carrots and lots of cabbage. They made a strudel with cabbage in the traditional way, with flour, water, a touch of salt and an egg that they'd mix together, then knead it for half an hour until their elbows were sore. Then they'd let it sit half an hour minimum, or overnight. For strudel dough they'd put a linen cloth over the table, sprinkle flour all over it and rub it in so that the dough wouldn't stick to it. Then they did what looks like the preparation of a pizza. They'd start stretching this little piece of dough and keep stretching it thinner and thinner. A small lump would stretch over the entire table, maybe six by four feet. It was so thin you could read a newspaper through it. Then heavier end pieces that hung all the way around were pulled off and squeezed together to use later, maybe to roll out and cut noodles. Nothing was ever wasted. They'd have to work fast and, for some reason, believed they couldn't make dough in a draft.

In addition to lard, they used *schmaltz* -- pork fat. By the way, all pork fat is not the same. There is a finer pork fat from underneath the neck and belly that was used for pastry that they called *schmar*. It had an extra delicate flavor, and was melted for baking only. They made a brush out of chicken feathers, dunked the brush into the melted fat and sprinkled it all over the sheet of translucent dough. Then they'd sprinkle fresh apples. cinnamon and sugar, or cherries over part of the dough, and cover another section with cottage cheese mixed with egg and sugar, or sautéed cabbage with salt and pepper and perhaps a pinch of sugar. It may sound unusual, but we were accustomed to eating cabbage rolls as a dessert. Years later, in the United States, I'd serve it as an appetizer, like an egg roll. Once they spread filling onto the dough, they'd start rolling it, lifting the end of the tablecloth and, as the dough gained momentum, it would continue to roll right down to the end of the table. Then they'd cut the dough into rows into rows with different fillings, then into squares.   It all baked into beautiful flaky puffs. That's the way a real strudel is supposed to look, like puff pastry. Phyllo looks and tastes almost the same. (I'm concerned, however, about what they make the phyllo out of today, perhaps something artificial, because it doesn't go bad or spoil.) We ate strudel or crepes once or twice a month. Crepes are the European version of a pancake without leavening flour. Other than that, the ingredients are just about the same as for strudel -- milk, eggs, flour, a little bit of sugar, and a touch of salt – beaten until it's nice and smooth, then poured in a thin layer onto a hot skillet.

Because we were Catholic, we were not allowed to eat meat on Friday or during Lent, which was no big deal, because we couldn't afford meat but once a week anyway. Friday was usually bean soup day. We'd brown flour in fat to make a roux, then mix that into the soup to thicken it. (In the States, the first time I ate Marie Callender's soup I thought, "This is the first soup I've tasted that's like my mother's soup.") Without exception there was fresh soup every day. The chicken soup that my mother made was so delicious that the entire family would never eat chicken soup in a restaurant. I was grateful she taught me how to make it. One of my mother's secrets was parsnip root that gave the soup a slightly sweeter flavor. Of course, chicken soup always called for fine cut noodles. Thick noodles were for other vegetable soups of different sorts.

I don't recall ever eating anything like lamb, unless there was a big festival with a rotisserie. Very seldom did we ever have the luxury of roast beef, but we did buy beef ribs and bones that had some meat for a rich broth. As a second course, any meat on the bones was served with boiled potatoes and maybe some horseradish and a salad. Our salads had vinegar and oil with a bit of salt.

We felt that our dreams had come true as we built a life in Köflach for more than four years. Then my father started thinking about the New World and he applied to come to the United States!

Coming to America

In Austria, emigration applications were processed through the post office. Even today, people still get passports through a post office, and it takes as long now as it did then to process a passport. After a long wait, we finally got word that we had been denied, because they wanted us to leave my handicapped brother behind, and then apply to have him come after we got to the United States. We understood that Americans did not want us to be dependent on their government once we got there. They wanted a guarantee that emigrants would be an asset to the country and not a liability. You can imagine that, with all that we had been through, there was no way in the world that we were going to leave Michael behind. I'm not sure how Mike felt about that. He became such a strong child; his handicap made him an over-achiever. He was very handsome, with sculpted cheek bones, a high forehead, fine brown hair, and a smooth complexion. He was on the short side, with broad shoulders and an extremely strong upper body that compensated for his frail leg. He was humble, but very strong.

In any case, we were now rejected by the United States. My father went back to the post office and applied to go to Australia. The answer finally came; we were rejected by Australia, also. They wanted my grandmother to stay behind, because she was too old. My grandmother was close to fifty and they were concerned about her not being able to take care of herself. Needless to say, we were not going to break up the family, so we turned that down, too.

Sometimes to get what we want, unfortunately, we have to go to the very edge of the law. My father had applied for us as Germans before he realized that the German quota might have been already filled so, as proud a German as he was, he thought that if we dropped one letter in our name, changed it from Sippl to Sipl, and reapplied, claiming to be Yugoslavians, we might be accepted. He reapplied to the United States as Yugoslavians. And the letter came that we were accepted. The whole family!

28

We had only five days to decide what to bring with us, to choose things that we had worked so hard for and couldn't sell. Fortunately, they gave us a specific crate size that we could take with us. There was one allowed for my grandmother and one for us that was thirty-six by twenty-three and twenty-three inches high. Of course, we packed our very precious tub that we considered to be one of our finer things, and filled it with feather bedding, and we took a change of clothes for each us. We sold, gave away and got rid of all our things in five days before beginning our journey to the United States.

There was a train station down the street where we boarded a train into an area in Salzburg, Austria that looked like barracks, where the Catholic Relief Fund took us in. We spent eight weeks in transit. We were next transferred to Bremerhaven, Germany, the port where our ship was docked. Here again, we were in barracks for a period of time, undergoing medical examinations and questions, and all kinds of tests to be sure we did not have any disease that we might bring into the country. Fortunately, we were all healthy.

In Bremerhaven, I saw my first American grapes and couldn't believe how large there were. We had grown only small concord and white. For the first time, I saw a banana, and I was not sure I liked it. Such things take getting used to. We had tasted an orange for the first time at Christmas in Köflach. That was our lovely Christmas present and we divided it among four of us. We later tried eating a grapefruit that puckered us up in surprise. We discovered canned peaches. My mother had grown fresh peaches in Köflach, and she would dunk them into hot water and smoothly peel off the skins, but those canned, peeled peaches were so beautiful, so appetizing. If only we could have eaten them! They gave us wonderful food; we couldn't believe how much meat!

Also in Bremerhaven, for the first time I saw an American military Black person. It's amazing how we were taught certain manners that we immediately forgot. In passing this gentleman, we all turned around and stared. Of course, we weren't supposed to do that, but we were astounded!

Before we boarded our ship, my father happened to look into a music store where he saw a Hohner accordion, considered the best German accordion made at the time. He had bought an accordion years ago for Michael, who played it very well. Music was a very important part of our life. My father stood there wondering if he could get a German accordion in the United States. Who knew. He gave in to temptation, went in and, with the last few dollars he had, bought the accordion. That left him with nine dollars for our entire family before we boarded the ship. My mother, who was very conservative and worried, nevertheless felt that my father made the money and he could buy what he wanted. He told her that this Hohner was the finest made and might not exist in the United States, so the matter was settled. I can't help thinking that nine dollars would be quite important, if you had no home, no means of transportation, no certain job, though it was promised, a family of four and a grandmother to take care of. Anyway, we didn't need any money once we boarded the ship. We trusted that we'd be taken care of in the States, because a job had been promised to my father by his step-sister in Pennsylvania, and a job had been offered to my grandmother by a priest for whom she would serve as housekeeper and cook, living at the rectory in Pennsylvania, where we were headed. Promises were as good as gold in those days, especially among my people.

Things certainly were looking up in comparison to the life we had built in Köflach. My mother was in her twenties and my father was seven years older. At sixteen, she had married my father, who was twenty-three. She had my brother at nineteen, and me when she was twenty-two. They had lived a tumultuous life already, and they were very mature.

When we boarded the SS Henry military troop ship, men were separated on one side of the ship and the women on the other side. Our dormitory was a very large room with hammocks strung three high, one on top of another, where we were supposed to sleep. We had no privacy. There were rows and rows of toilets with no dividers. No wonder we were separate from the men. There were also rows of showers in a large room. They were a total shock to me, not only because I'd never seen one, but because I had never seen an adult woman in the nude. At eight years old, I kept my head down a lot.

The food we were given was unbelievable. We had meat at every meal -- and the amounts of food! We could really eat as much as we wanted. So how much do you think we ate? Hardly anything because, once the ship sailed, we were seasick every day. Everybody on the entire ship was constantly seasick. We would be so happy about the food below decks, but we'd immediately race to the deck to vomit, though many people didn't make it up those stairs. We were so disappointed because we longed to enjoy the food, yet we couldn't hold it down.

Ships were built quite differently at that time. The construction of ships nowadays prevents them from pitching so drastically. Sometimes that ship plummeted down until it seemed like it was only a foot from the water, and you had to hold on to something so as not to fall forward, especially children. If the motion was too much, they didn't allow us on deck. When the weather calmed, everybody rushed out for air and sunshine, but the only place we could sit was where the exhaust came up from the kitchen, which made us nauseous. Our crossing was bittersweet, because our spirits were high, but our stomachs were miserable, and the only way we could see my brother and father was to spot them on deck or in the restaurant area.

On the ninth day of our voyage, we woke up to discover that we were no longer nauseous, because the ship had come into port. All the passengers ran to the deck. We were so tightly packed together, there was no room to maneuver through the throng. Everybody was talking excitedly, pointing at the Statue of Liberty. Sadly, nobody thought to lift me up, so I never saw the famous statue. It was October 12th of 1951. How wonderful that we would arrive on Columbus Day! We, too, would be explorers of the new world.

We disembarked with long lines of passengers and waited a long time on the docks for our transport. My brother had been practicing during those nine days at sea on his new accordion and, to our astonishment, he started playing "The Star-Spangled

31

Banner." He played it so well that people all around stared at him in tears, overwhelmed with emotion. My father must have felt very satisfied about money well spent.

When my mother saw the New York high-rise buildings, she cried. She thought that we would have to live in a concrete building with no garden, no greenery. She was already missing the beautiful countryside of Austria, immediately assuming we would have no privacy in such buildings. Fortunately, trains were waiting to take us away, so many trains going to different places.

In applying to come to the United States, my father named a step-sister in Allentown, Pennsylvania, as our sponsor, whose family was the first of our people to emigrate. Later on we, in turn, sponsored people to come to America. I have goose bumps when I tell you that we were the second family to emigrate, and now when we get together there are hundreds of us at our reunions. I remember one reunion where I was walking through the church parking lot, and there were all these Mercedes cars, and I realized that so many of us had become successful. There was no story in our family of anyone not being successful.

So began our life in the United States.

Discovering the New World

We were so elated to be in this wonderful country. My brother and I felt like we'd been let loose in a candy store. As grateful as we were that American people seemed to accept us, however, we still felt like undesirables, displaced persons. When we came to America, people were very kind to us, but we did not understand their ways. They seemed to take their bounty for granted, while we had always feared losing whatever we had. We lived in the concept of 'easy come, easy go.' We did not understand English, and sometimes we thought people were rude when they might simply have been direct but, of course, we never talked back; we were always polite. "Please" and "thank you" were the first words we learned.

Arriving in Farrell near Sharon, Pennsylvania, was like a fairy tale come true. Everything we saw changed from black and white to technicolor: the cars, the modern appliances, the beautiful houses, the abundance of food, the kindness of the people. We had arrived.

My father signed up for Pennsylvania because my step-aunt had sponsored him for a job there. If he hadn't had a job prospect, we would not have been able to emigrate. She also found a job for my grandmother as housekeeper and cook at the rectory of Saint Anthony's Catholic Church in Farrell, near the Ohio border. However, my aunt lived in Allentown. We had no idea how far Farrell was from Allentown, but we got onto a train with my Oma, so we wouldn't be separated.

It was a very long ride. We arrived early in the morning in Farrell, and were picked up by my grandmother's new employer, the priest who had sponsored her. He hadn't planned on receiving five people; he thought there was only going to be one. He showed up in a brand new black Ford. We had never been in a car before. The upholstery was spotless and soft, and the vehicle absolutely wonderful, shiny as a mirror. I couldn't believe it. My childhood secret dream come true. We had arrived in America and we were going to live here. I sensed that we were going to have a wonderful life, and I could hardly contain the excitement bubbling up inside me, as I sat in that back seat smiling, trying not to laugh out loud, bobbing my feet in the air.

The priest drove us to the rectory, a brand new house where he lived with another priest next to a new church called Saint Anthony's. Saint Anthony is the patron saint of the lost. We had prayed to Saint Anthony when we were in the concentration camp, and here we were, by some miracle, at St. Anthony's church. The priest parked in front of the rectory that was built of warm red brick with concrete stairs. We walked into the house on wall-to-wall carpeting, and sat on plush furniture. We had never had running water or sat on upholstered furniture. Then he took us to the kitchen where there was a stove and when he turned a knob there was gas. Unbelievable! He opened the refrigerator, and we felt cool air waft out, and peeked inside to see stacks of all kinds of food. Then he took us upstairs and showed us the bedrooms, where each room had a double bed. We had never seen beds like that, and we had just come from sleeping in hammocks for nine days. He called a parishioner who had a young daughter just one year older and a little bigger than me. Michael and I went to meet that family, who invited us to stay with them until our family got settled. They had another beautiful home, another beautiful kitchen, another private bedroom that my brother and I slept in, and that is where we stayed for a time.

The girl gave me some hand-me-down clothing. I will never forget the plaid cotton dress with ruffles. I was more than delighted; I was in heaven. Later, we went to see our parents at the rectory, showing them our new clothes. My mother was embarrassed because, according to her values, nothing was free. As soon as you received something, it entailed an obligation. She instantly worried about how we would ever repay our hosts for their generosity.

My aunt had lined up a job for my father in Allentown but, obviously, he lost that opportunity, as we never went there. Not long after we arrived, my aunt came and visited us, so we were able to meet her. It was important for us to be together as a family. As newcomers, none of us spoke English. On the ship we probably learned about ten words or so: "Yes" and "no," "barrette," which means "bored" in German, but it sounded like "bread" in English, so that was an important word to remember.

As soon as we arrived in Farrell, my father went to apply for a job at Sharon Steel. Sharon was a town near Farrell where there was a large steel company. He got a job as a common laborer, which he could not understand, as he was a stonemason. One of the jobs in this steel mill was as a bricklayer who actually lined the walls of smelting furnaces with brick, but he was not allowed to start with that job. My father was extremely hard working, and he was happy to have a job, but he did not unions. They didn't like the fact that he worked so hard and so fast; they wanted him to slow down. My father thought that the harder he worked, the more money he would get and the better he would be liked. In reality, his co-workers didn't like him, because he was working harder than any of them and sabotaging their production quotas. He eventually got it, and conformed to the other workers tempo, though it was so against his nature.

A week later, my father received a paycheck and we started looking for an affordable apartment. My parents found an old abandoned butcher store, a building that was more than a mile away from the church, uphill and on the outskirts of town, but the price was right. The butcher store had an apartment on the ground floor and another apartment upstairs. We could afford to rent the whole place, so we moved there.

When Mike and I went to the neighborhood school, the kids called him Mike, and that's when I started calling him Mike, too. More than anything, we longed to fit in. When people asked my name, I no longer replied "Anna," but "Ann." When I was a baby, my ears were pierced and I always wore tiny gold earrings, as was the custom. None of the other girls wore them, and I wanted to get rid of them, so when one fell off and got lost I immediately pulled the other one out, free at last from what I considered an "immigrant look."

We were placed in first grade, because we didn't speak English. I should have gone to third grade and Mike should have gone to sixth, but it was best for us to start there. They brought in different chairs for us, because we were too big to sit in the first-grade chairs. They also evaluated what we knew. Math is the same in any language, and Mike and I were always good in math. Schools in Austria were actually a little more advanced than American schools. They were much stricter there, and they taught common sense skills, like sewing for a woman and learning a craft for a man, in addition to basic reading and writing and arithmetic. In Austria, we had already learned to write with ink and pen and we had little inkwells in each of our desks. There were no ink wells in our first-grade class.

The first day, students treated us kindly, and the teachers were very polite and welcoming, and made us feel at home. When you don't know a language, you quickly learn body language. We could read what people had in their hearts and minds from their gestures. Austrian teachers and people in general, including Germans, were authoritarian, conveying a message: "This is business and we're going to do it like this, right now." Americans had softer, sweeter voices. They had not suffered the hardships we had gone through. In Austria, there was a big class distinction between the rich and the poor and, because we were at the bottom of the barrel, nobody wanted us around. At least there was no hypocrisy about them; they just treated you like dirt, and that is how we were used to being treated there and, of course, even worse in the concentration camp. Now, all of a sudden, we found ourselves in a world where we felt not only welcome, but embraced.

When we walked home the first day, a whole crowd of kids walked with us. They were chitter-chattering. "I don't understand" was one of the phrases that we learned. "I don't understand." We were saying that a whole lot, but we could tell from the kids' body language that they were relaxed and happy to be with us. They were very interested in Mike, especially, who walked with crutches. Though we couldn't explain anything to them, we tried to be very polite. We said "yes" and "no," never "yeah." We never took things for granted, we did not assume, and we never asked for anything. If things were given to us, we could respectfully accept them, in spite of my mother feeling obliged. I'm so grateful today for that kind of a value system, because later, through all my years of business, I understood that nothing was free. If someone is good to me, I automatically feel grateful and try to find a way to return a favor.

In spite of the kindness of people, we still felt quite insecure. Not only were we in a new country, but we couldn't understand what people were saying, and the memories of our life in Europe were so traumatic that we were distrustful and fearful, like when we saw New York and those intimidating high rises, we were dismayed. But once we came to Farrell, we found joy in every single day, from the time the priest picked us up in that beautiful car, to all the days filled with wonderful new experiences. Though we took an apartment in the poorest part of town, no one scorned us, everyone accepted us.

My mother had frustrating, embarrassing experiences sometimes, like shopping and trying to explain an item that she needed. We went to a local grocery store within walking distance. We had no transportation, so we walked everywhere, which was okay. We were just happy to be where we were. The grocery store was a sort of mom-and-pop shop, where she was astonished to see chicken backs all lined up, row by row, then chicken wings, legs and breasts all lined up in rows. For nine cents a pound, she bought chicken backs. We ate so much chicken *paprikash*! I still salivate thinking about my mother's *paprikash* that she served with potatoes or dumplings or homemade noodles. She was accustomed to using lard, but in the grocery store display case there was no lard. She tried to explain to the woman, but didn't know the word. She spied sausages that contained pieces of what appeared to be lard in them. She pointed to them and when the woman took out a sausage my mother borrowed her knife and showed the woman that the bit of lard was what she wanted. The woman didn't understand, naturally, and made my mother feel uncomfortable. We were accustomed to prejudice, and people making us feel dumb. When you don't understand a language, people assume you are dumb. They didn't realize how smart my parents were, even with only four years of education.

The priest insisted that we go to catechism school at the church two nights a week, because we were not going to a Catholic school. Mike and I walked more than a

38

mile to class and back. We loved those walks home in the dark, mostly because we could look into windows and see televisions. We had never seen a television before, and we were mesmerized. We never left the sidewalk to get closer to the houses, perhaps because respect for other people's property was ingrained in us. We would just stretch to look and we'd see people moving on a screen, like "I Love Lucy" and "Howdy Doody," and we were just amazed, wondering when we would actually be able to watch it up close. Our walks home were very slow.

October 31st came and we were already in our new apartment when grown-ups and kids with masks on appeared at our door. We had no idea what was going on, but we figured out that their bags meant they wanted something, so we gave them apples. It was a crazy night with all those kids knocking at the door. What did we know about Halloween!

Imagine what a wonderful Christmas we had! We did not allow ourselves to spend a lot of money, as my father received only minimum wage as a common laborer, but we had the most joyful Christmas of our lives! Mami and Oma baked strudel, Napoleons and croissants and roasted a whole chicken, not just backs. A cornucopia of fruit of all kinds inevitably reminded us of the Christmas when we shared one orange. Mike and I received a Monopoly game, a harbinger of my future career. We had saved our pennies and I proudly presented Mami with an orange juice pitcher with matching glasses, and Mike hand crafted a polished wooden box for them. Giving gifts expressed the spirit of Christmas for us far more than receiving them.

*   *   *

Among all our relatives, we were the second family to come to the United States. We heard about another family named Tremell who had gone to Alabama. The father was married to my father's step -sister. They had arrived in New York in 1951, but they were extremely upset to find themselves transferred to Alabama. They didn't like the heat; they didn't like the terrain; they had never spoken to a Black person before. They moved into a house on stilts that had raccoons under it. Their nearest neighbor lived half a mile away. One day, they told us that a Black man had come to their door and welcomed them, saying, "Please don't tell your master and please don't tell my master, but welcome." Everything was segregated then, even the school buses. My cousin Kathy told me that when her school bus drove past the Black schools, kids would wave at them, and she wanted to wave back, but was told that was not allowed. They were very uncomfortable there. The inside stove did not work, so they used an outside barbecue for all their cooking. Fortunately, they found us in Farrell.

My father invited them to come and live upstairs in the second apartment. Knowing my father, he probably planned to use their rent to pay ours. They were very happy that we helped them to come north, and eventually they moved to Cleveland. They wound up having a total of eight children, though when they came to us they only had four or five. They were all very talented and beautiful. I have a picture of me sitting with one of the teen-age boys on the stairs. He had already found a little sweetheart in Alabama, and he had a picture of her. He drew that photo into an eight-and-a-half by eleven portrait, a perfect image, as if it were the photo itself enlarged. I was very impressed with his artistic talent. I later learned that artistic talent actually ran in our family, though I had assumed that all Germans had such talent. I didn't know if it was something that was developed or in your blood. The most famous artistic people I've spoken to say that it's in your blood and then you have a choice of developing it or not.

We had arrived in October and by the following January Mike and I had learned quite a lot of English. We were able to help our parents, actually for the rest of their lives, read important insurance or legal papers. They learned how to read at an elementary level at night school. My mother read better than my father, but whenever we read a legal paper we found a little trickery, sometimes in the legal language that implied something slightly different than you might understand. We didn't comprehend idioms or legal jargon, but when it came to simple things, common sense, we were okay.

In January my father came home and told us he had found a house in Sharon near the steel company where he worked. The house cost $5,000 and required $500 down. He went to the priest and asked to borrow the $500, which amazed me, because we were taught never to borrow. My parents believed in spending only as much as you earn and avoiding debt. But in America, we learned that most people had debt, that it was normal. The priest lent him the $500. He must have had a lot of faith to lend all that money to somebody he had met only three months before, who barely spoke English.

He took us at face value, although he probably perceived our values through grandmother, who worked meticulously and was competent and honest. She worked for him until she retired. Can you imagine hiring somebody on the basis of a piece of paper from another country, having them come and fit the bill so well that you keep them until they retire? Even after we moved to our house, grandmother continued to live at the rectory.

Oh! My mother's joy when we moved into that house! There were two bedrooms and a bathroom upstairs and, on the first floor, there was a kitchen, dining room and living room. Having just one bathroom and having to run up and down the stairs was nothing, even for Mike. There was a little basement, like a fruit cellar, which was crucial to her. The house was on a narrow lot with an ailing peach tree in the back yard that, when my mother got finished with it, had the biggest, most luscious peaches in town. She made a compost pile and a garden in the back. We were ecstatic about this house.

Mike had no problem with the stairs. He was a super achiever. He never used his handicap as an excuse. He always did better than the average person in everything, always ready to show that he could be as much of a man as anybody, and nothing was going to stop him. He loved to race the other kids; he could run faster with those crutches than almost anybody else. He was a better swimmer with one leg than I was, and he played basketball and shoot hoops. He got a brace later on, so he only needed to use a cane. Throughout his life he was a strong person, a good student and very responsible and smart.

Maybe because of our attitude, the faith we had that we would have a wonderful life in America, made it all come true. It took me many years to realize just how much influence our attitude has over our lives. We certainly didn't have much control when I was growing up, but finding happiness and feeling so privileged to be in this country, where we had real opportunities, filled me with deep gratitude that never left me. On the other hand, I always felt that I wasn't good enough or smart enough. I had an inferiority complex, and perhaps compensating for it led to my eventual success. I always had to fight for my grades, and I never felt that my clothes were as nice as the next girl's. As a matter of fact, when we went to a new school in Sharon, I suddenly felt self-conscious about the hand-me-downs that had so delighted me, so I was thrilled when we sometimes actually bought clothes, though they were always the cheapest, and they looked it. My mother got a pair of matronly shoes that laced up, with a small heel. I was growing and when she noticed that those shoes fit me, she made me wear them to school one day. The other kids laughed at my old-lady shoes, that I never wore them again. I would cry when girls pointed out that I wore the same clothes to school the day before. Because I only had a few things to wear, it appeared that I was wearing them every day. I sometimes felt that I was still the poor girl who went to the farmers' school in Austria.

The people in Sharon were a little higher class than those we knew in Farrell. Our neighborhood was certainly not rich, but everybody owned their own homes. We were no longer in the worst part of town. While people were still very polite, occasionally there would be some hint of prejudice against us being refugees -- the sideways look, or patronizing greeting -- though it was nothing compared to what we had experienced in Austria. We were the politest kids, and we thought that American children were somewhat rude, forgetting to say "please" and "thank you" and being unruly.

Betsy Reed, a girl who lived two doors from us, became my best girlfriend. There were eight in her family, and they'd gather around a big table for supper, and every meal was a feast, which might have accounted for most of the family being overweight. Betsy taught me a lot about the American way. She often invited me to eat with them, a new experience in my life. Unless we were traveling and needed to eat at someone's home, it was not a common practice in our family, and my parents reluctantly permitted me to eat there. Betsy and I washed and dried the supper dishes, like sisters, I thought. It was wonderful to be with a close-knit American family. They were not high-class people. As a matter of fact, my family was more formal and mannerly than they or the average American family was.

Betsy took me to the local grocery store where they sold ice cream and root beer, and she introduced me to my first root beer float that cost seven cents. On rare occasions, I would save up seven cents for that root beer float. I had tasted ice cream one time in my life in Köflach where it was cut into pieces smaller than a deck of cards, and placed onto a piece of waxed cardboard. I was heartbroken when, as soon as I got out the door, mine fell off into the street. The new taste of American ice cream still makes me salivate thinking of it.

In our wonderful home there was joy that we could sense in our parents, in our everyday life, a feeling of well-being. Every day was better than the last, though we wondered how it could become even better all the time.

One morning, my brother and I got up and my parents weren't in the house, which was very unusual. We always listened to the "Milkman" radio show, so we were in the kitchen getting our own breakfast before we went to school, listening to the radio. All of a sudden my father came through the door with a beautiful grin on his face. I'd never seen him look so happy. He said, "We have to listen to the radio." They were broadcasting all the new births and we heard that Magdalena and Joseph Sipl had had a baby boy on January 21st, 1953! My mother had been pregnant all that time and I had no idea. Being pregnant was not something that was not discussed. So my brother, George, was born, yet another fantastic happening. As it turned out, I became his second mother because I was, after all, ten years old.

My mother stayed in the Sharon Hospital for a few days, as was common in those days, where she felt very pampered. She had had a midwife for the birth of her first child, and for my birth the midwife didn't even come in time, so I was already born by the time she showed up. Women would go into the barn with the midwife, so they would not disturb the rest of the family with cries of pain. So imagine my mother, after giving birth twice in the barn on the hay, with no assurance that someone would be there to help, with no anesthesia, fearing she would die, she delivered a child in a modern hospital. It had to be heavenly. Mother was glowing when she came home with baby George.

*   *   *

My father heard about Cleveland, Ohio, from other relatives, as every year new arrivals came to our new country, and we sponsored many of them. He had no problem guaranteeing that the new person would have a job, knowing very well the work ethic of our family. Whether it was scrubbing floors or any other kind of labor, they would take any work they could get.

My father went to the J&L (Jones & Laughlin) Steel Company in Cleveland, and he found a job there for much more money, not as a common laborer, but as a brick layer lining furnaces. That was an extremely high-paying job, because the bricks from the old stone of those furnaces weren't totally cooled down, as my father explained it. He could only stay about twenty minutes at a time inside those ovens to reline the bricks. He stayed in Cleveland five days a week and came home on weekends, driving an old Dodge car he had bought. He waited until he felt secure about keeping the job – about ninety days – before making the decision to move to Cleveland. Mother was very sad to leave the house she loved so much, but she had no say in the matter.

We rented an apartment in Cleveland in a densely populated neighborhood, at 1456 East 93rd Street between Wade Park and Superior. The reason I mention that is because I loved to tell people about where we lived. They'd usually say, "You lived in the ghetto?" In fact, we were in a neighborhood that Black people were moving into. We lived there for several years because, as always, being financially secure was always my parents' utmost priority. The apartment was the same size as the house we had just moved out of, but it was a duplex and there was an equivalent unit upstairs where somebody else lived.

We were thrilled to find an upright piano in our apartment that former tenants had been unable to move out. At the age of two, George started to bang on those keys, and Mike played the piano easily because, if you can play the right hand of an accordion, you can play the piano. I also took piano lessons. Whenever I was practicing, George would whine, "Mommy, she won't let me play!" George learned how to play by ear, so my parents thought of giving him lessons, too, but the piano teacher declined to give him lessons until he could read. By the time he could read, George could already play all kinds of pieces by ear. I thought, this brat is never going to play piano as well as me. As it turned out, he grew up to become not only an adept pianist, but a well-known composer and music arranger.

We were near St. Thomas Aquinas Catholic school, taught by Saint Joseph nuns so we went to Catholic school there. Later, we went to Saints Philip and James Church School. I had always been the biggest girl in my class, because I was behind in grades, but there they gave me a math test and decided that I could skip a grade, though that left me still one grade behind. I never did well in spelling, and don't spell very well even today, but math was much easier for me.

St. Thomas Aquinas school was close to a large public park called Wade Park. When I was eleven years old I had reached my full height and wore the same shoe size as I do now. When I got my period and started to develop breasts, I didn't know how to react. I couldn't discuss my bodily changes with my mother, who was always secretive about such things. Boys flirted with me, and a guy exposed himself to me in Wade Park. I was very frightened, and when I told my parents, they started looking frantically to buy a house in a more secure neighborhood.

We had a cousin named Ava Zimmerman who was on the west side of town on a beautiful street called Fortune Avenue. Every weekend we'd go there with my parents to look at houses. That's probably where I developed my love of real estate. It was like playing live Monopoly.

My parents ended up having four children. There were twenty-three years between the first and the last. I was ten when George was born, and when George was ten, my mother was forty-three and my father fifty when their last child was born. In fact, my mother was pregnant at the same time that I was with my first child. She was ashamed of being pregnant because, in her culture, people aren't supposed to be interested in sex at her age. My father, however, was elated. They named the new baby Rudolf Joseph, but Mike and I were so appalled by that old-fashioned name that they changed it to Joseph Rudolf and we all called him Joey. He became their favorite child. They were able to enjoy him more than their first children, because they had more money, more time, and they had already learned from their mistakes with the first three. Finally, in 1957 we came across a house on Fortune Avenue. It was a big house, but the rooms were small. It also had only one and a half bathrooms, but four bedrooms upstairs, one with a double window facing south. When my parents told me that would be my room, I was so excited to think of having such a beautiful room with light pouring through that big window.

We took in Frank Wittman, the shoe maker cousin, as a boarder who shared Mike's room. Typical Mike, he didn't complain. Here, again, was a way to earn a little extra money, having a boarder. In fact, Mike got a newspaper route and gave all his earnings to our father. At that point my grandmother, Oma, came to live with us, and George shared his bedroom with her. She had retired at that point, and received a pension or Social Security, so she, too, contributed to the family income.

I went to Saints Philip and James school at that time. My experiences at Philip and James were not as positive as some of the earlier schools. There was a Sister Ester who taught seventh and eighth grades, and I was in seventh grade. I was developing very fast and she kept accusing me of wearing uplifts. I didn't even know what uplifts were, but I assumed that she was insinuating that I was wearing some kind of breast enhancers. Finally, one day I opened my blouse and said, "This is the cheapest brassiere that K-Mart sells and I don't know what uplifts are." She left me alone after that. I was rather well endowed, so that's probably why she thought I was doing such a thing, which I wouldn't have dreamed of. Boys used to tease me a lot, embarrassing me totally, because I had developed so noticeably. I used to roll on the carpet, trying to flatten my breasts, because I was so ashamed of them. I was growing up, in spite of myself.

Later on, when I graduated from eighth grade at Saints Philip and James, the same teacher predicted what we were going to do in life. Her prediction for me was that I would be a good clerk. I can still remember her saying that, and how upset I was that she would think I could only be a clerk. I was already smart enough to know that I needed a higher education to make something of myself, something better than a clerk. But I didn't know what I was going to be.

On September 1st, 1957, when I was fourteen years old, there was a carnival at Saints Philip and James where I met a cute boy named Dave Fredmonsky who was thirteen. Even though he was a year younger than me, he was a year ahead of me in school. He flirted without teasing me. Dave was staying with his grandmother, a parishioner he called Nana. He invited me to his grandmother's house, where I tasted my first pumpkin pie. I hated it. Another new experience. Later on, I met Dave's dad, who took us out for lobster and I hated that! I guess I eventually developed a taste for both, because I love them now.

I used to sneak out on Sunday afternoons to meet Dave, though I was petrified that my parents would find out. He would take the bus from Parma to my neighborhood, at least a half-hour bus ride, then we would walk to the movies, then come home. In the fall of that year, Dave asked me to go to his Parma High School homecoming dance. I wondered how in the world I would handle that, because I had not told my parents that I was seeing a young man. He insisted that I get permission, so I finally asked them if I could go to the dance, and they reluctantly agreed. I still remember the picture that Dave's mother took of us. I looked so much older than him! Dave's mother actually questioned my age. His parents and my parents drove us to and from the dance. That was my first date.

At that time my grandmother took me to her dentist named Dr. Bauman, who asked me what I did on Saturdays. I told him that I helped my mother clean house. He said, "How would you like to work here?" I told him I would love to! I think he also thought I was older than I was, and I still had an accent at that time that I couldn't seem to shed.

The second time I went to him with my grandmother, he asked, "Well, why didn't you come in?"

"Oh," I replied, "I apologize. I didn't know when to come in."

Then we arranged to have me work at the dental office on Saturdays. I was fourteen years old. Dr. Bauman took me under his wing. I first learned how to clean instruments and sweep out the bays. He had six different bays, plus a laboratory, three dentists, and several girls working for him in different capacities. I would also reassure the patients. I'd stand on the left side of patients and put my hand on their shoulders to comfort them. That was challenging, because I didn't know if a patient wanted me to touch them. Dr. Bauman, however, encouraged me, especially when he had to drill or do extractions. At that time, we did not have the more modern equipment of today. He used Novocain to extract, or gave patients "mild air" to put them to sleep. When I was allowed to go into the "mild-air room" the first time, I felt strange, weak in the knees. Later on, however, I learned to assist in the mild air.

Dr. Bauman became almost like a second father. On Saturday at lunchtime he would take us girls to a Chinese restaurant around the corner, and he would steer the conversation into the importance of education, and the importance of not getting pregnant. I felt so privileged to be among grown-ups in a restaurant, and I took our conversations very seriously. I don't remember if I ever ate at a restaurant before that time because, of course, our family would never eat out. It was too expensive, not to mention my mother was a wonderful cook. I don't think the restaurant food was as good as hers.

I continued to work for Dr. Bauman all through my high school years. When I went to high school at St. Stephen I had to take one or two buses. I'd always ask myself if I should walk a longer way and take only one bus, to save the fare, or take two buses. I worked from 3:00 until 6:00 o'clock three days a week after school, and all day Saturday. In the summer I worked there full time.

St. Stephen's was the least expensive all girls Catholic high school connected to a German parish, and my parents liked that affiliation. I was interested in going to other schools, but there were none as inexpensive as St. Stephen's. To be admitted, my parents and I had to have an interview with the principal. I was always a bit embarrassed by my parents, because they still spoke broken English and their style of dress was always clean and neat, but old-fashioned. And here I was a modern American teenager! I was accepted, and my grades were mostly B's. I probably had a B average graduating from eighth grade, so I wasn't exactly the smartest girl on the block, and St. Stephen was a secretarial prep school. And of course, what was I going to be? A clerk!

They were very strict at St. Stephen's, and they got into the students' personal business. I felt quite smug about sneaking out to see Dave on Sunday afternoons, which was considered going steady. My parents knew we dated on occasion, but not every week. When one of my jealous student friends told the principal that I was seeing somebody on a regular basis, he called in my parents. By this time I was fifteen. They forbade me to see Dave until I was sixteen years old, which was about six months from then, so we waited and then I started to see him again.

We had some proms and dances at St. Stephen's. Two nuns would stand at the entrance, separate the girls from our dates and take us to the Home Ec room where there was another nun who examined our clothes to make sure our dresses weren't too low cut or too tight. After passing inspection, we were allowed to come out and meet our dates. When we danced, we had to make sure that a paper could fit between us and our partners; in other words, we were not allowed to touch.

In high school I was proud to earn my own money, and I had already learned to sew. I had taught myself when I was eleven. When I asked my mother if she would buy a pattern for a poodle skirt that was the rage at the time, she refused, because the pattern was too expensive. For almost the same price as the pattern, however, you could buy polished cotton for around twenty-two cents a yard, and she allowed me to buy the fabric, and let me use a zipper from discarded clothing. With a pencil and a string I made a circle for the skirt and then I cut a smaller hole in the center for the waist and put a slit on the side, but it was a challenge to put that zipper in. That's how I made my first red skirt when I was eleven years old, using my mother's Singer pedal machine, which she continued to use the rest of her life.

In high school we wore an attractive uniform, a white blouse and blue pleated skirt with a vest. Dresses or skirts that we wore on weekends stayed neat and fresh. I made myself many pleated skirts with wool that was on sale. Sweaters were the only things I actually bought.

Dave had graduated high school a year before me, and had gone away to the U.S. Air Force. I felt free to date other fellows, and was asked to go to a prom at John Carroll Men's Catholic college. It was Wednesday night, the prom was on Friday, and I had no prom dress. I went out and bought blue taffeta. On Thursday I didn't have to work for Dr. Bauman so, without a pattern, I made a strapless full-length gown, adding an ornate necklace that I sewed onto the bodice, and I cut a piece of fabric to make a shawl with fringed ends. I was very proud of my first prom dress. In retrospect, making that dress set a behavior pattern of my entire life. I often had to seize an opportunity, feeling that it was now or never, and I would often do important things on the spur of the moment

For my sixteenth birthday, my parents gave me an electric Singer sewing machine that I still have to this day. It was the best that money could buy at the time. The last time I took it in for a tune-up, I was told that my sewing machine would last the rest of my life. Come to think of it, I made that prom dress on my Singer machine, and my first skirt on the pedal machine.

Even though I was sixteen, every time I asked to go out with a gentleman, my parents would discourage me. They seemed to dread my growing up; they did not want me going out with men. I was only allowed to go out on Friday or Saturday; not both days. Later, I was allowed to go out on Sunday afternoon, but that was it.

At the time I met a gal named Anita Tuma who went to school with me at St. Stephen's. Her parents were German and they belonged to a German folk dancing (*schuhplattler)* group. Anita invited me to come along, so I started to learn folk dancing with the group. We would meet once a week, and occasionally we'd actually perform on stage, like at city hall. We performed at different festivals, like Octoberfest, where I wore a white peasant blouse and black vest that Oma had embroidered so beautifully, and a full skirt with a little apron. Men wore *lederhosen*, short leather pants with high socks and tassels.

I always enjoyed dancing very much. When my parents went out, there was no such thing as hiring a babysitter; we all went along and I danced with whoever asked me. It was considered rude not to accept a dance. At all our family weddings, relatives would ask me to dance. I learned how to follow them, which works well when the gentleman feels he's doing a good job. If you learn to follow, it doesn't matter if his dance steps are right or wrong, whether his style is international or American, following him makes a man happy. Actually, my love of dancing started at a very early age, from being swung around the kitchen in Köflach to attending nine family weddings between the ages of fourteen and nineteen. I was even maid of honor several times. I would be chosen because it was considered proper to have immediate relatives in the wedding party. Choosing a best girlfriend as maid of honor was occasionally done, but more often people felt obliged to choose someone in the immediate family. At fourteen, I wore a beautiful dress with a crinoline skirt to be maid of honor. Oh, it was so wonderful. I had so many gorgeous dresses, but my mother would be very upset that each dress cost so much, but we were all *nouveau riche* in a small way, feeling that we were in America and we could celebrate.

Weddings started around ten o'clock in the morning, followed by lunch for the immediate family that lasted almost an hour. In the afternoon they would take all kinds of pictures. At six o'clock in the evening there would be two hundred people there and a band and fabulous food that my grandmother usually made. She was the only paid person who orchestrated all the food. Everyone else donated pastries and served wedding guests. My godmother, Anna Wittman, was a fantastic baker who served the finest pastries imaginable. A multi-course meal started with homemade soup and then a main course of either chicken or pork, all served family style on platters and in tureens on each table. At least one band would play, but sometimes a second band would play till two in the morning; one even played until four in the morning. That's how I learned how to dance.

*   *   *

I continued to work for Dr. Bauman, and I saved my money. I was, of course, very frugal. My parents would buy me a winter coat, and every Christmas I got flannel pajamas, though I bought all my other clothes. I saved my money because Dr. Bauman encouraged me to do so. He told me I could become a doctor, though I never believed it. He said, "If I could become a doctor, you can become a doctor," and "You get yourself an education," and so on. But when it came time to apply for college, my father said, "What are you going to go to college for? You're going to get married and have children. You don't need to go to college." The only way I could go to college was to pay for it myself. As a matter of fact, I finally packed my bags and moved to Kent State. I paid for the first quarter, and I did exactly what my parents expected. I flunked out.

I think that, in a small way, I was psychologically affected by my parents' low expectations, but I take responsibility for failing my first quarter at college. I took a five-hour zoology course, though I had no biology background, as my high school was a secretarial school, and I really needed biology as a prerequisite to the zoology course. I also took another course on art history. Those two courses spelled my demise. First of

52

all, I guess I never learned good study habits. I wound up going to summer school for chemistry, because I thought of the possibility of going into nursing. I didn't know what I wanted to do, but I wanted a decent education and Dr. Bauman kept encouraging me.

My room mate was Irene Gerves, who became a very dear life-long friend. Sadly, Irene died a few years ago. Irene wanted to become an interior decorator, and I decided to do the same. We wanted to become art majors. I remember saying to Dr. Bauman, "I want to be either an interior decorator or an airline stewardess." He responded, "Oh, you want to be a flying waitress." That was the end of my wanting to be an airline stewardess. I was down to being an interior decorator or a nurse. I was worried about nursing, though, because I always wore a nurse's uniform working for Dr. Bauman for five years, with nurse shoes, but at the end of a Saturday I was so tired that I used to come home and complain about how much my feet hurt, though that never stopped me. I'd soak in a hot tub, get dressed and go out dancing. But I wondered if I had what it took to be a nurse.

I didn't know how I was going to be able to afford school. I only had enough money for that first quarter. The first week at Kent State I got a letter from Dr. Bauman's office with a ten-dollar check enclosed. Ten dollars in 1962 was probably equivalent to about a hundred dollars now. I was so surprised and happy. I was astonished when, the next week, another came, and the third week, and the fourth week. He never told me he was going to send me a weekly allowance. That made a big difference in my life.

I was horribly embarrassed to flunk out the first term. I had to pack up everything and go home again. I sensed my parents thinking "I told you so." Fortunately, I had a job to come back to with Dr. Bauman. After all his encouraging words and sending me money, I could barely face him. I had to stay out of college one or two semesters before before they would let me apply again.

At Christmas, Dave, my teen-age boyfriend, came home from the service for the holidays. I had already decided that Dave was not the man for me, that we had

53

outgrown each other. His mother talked about him becoming a good policeman or fireman. I wanted someone with a higher education who was not going to be satisfied being a policeman or fireman. I was determined to get an education, and I wanted an educated man. It was more than financial ambition. I wanted an academic genius, if possible. Before Dave came home, I decided to break up with him. I was sorry, though, that not only was it Christmas, but it was his nineteenth birthday. When I told him I didn't want to see him anymore, he cried and I cried, and I ended up agreeing that we could have one more chance.

We had been so good as far as being virtuous and not having sex, though we dated on and off for five years. That one more chance led to a lot of petting and fumbling attempts to have intercourse. The month after Dave left, my period didn't come. I asked a doctor if I could be pregnant, even though Dave had not penetrated me. I did not know that sperm could swim. I had a rabbit test — and it died.

Being pregnant was absolutely the worst thing I could tell my parents. My mother, who washed my clothes, noticed that my period hadn't come. I was trying to think of a way to commit suicide. I couldn't get an abortion; that was illegal, as well as immoral. Telling Dr. Bauman was almost as bad as telling my parents. Dr. Bauman was disappointed, very, very disappointed, but he didn't call me names. Telling my parents was worse; my father could not handle it. He said such painful words to me that I could barely stand it, and cannot bear to remember them.

Marriage, Motherhood and the Military

My mother immediately planned a wedding in the house. We tried to contact Dave, but we couldn't find him, as he had gone to Spain and our communication through letters was very slow. Finally, we contacted him to say that as soon as he came back we had to get married. My mother would not allow me to wear a white dress. I had always dreamed, like most girls, of wearing a white wedding gown in a gorgeous church ceremony with celebrations and music. I was not allowed to have any of that because I was pregnant. I borrowed a white suit from my girlfriend, Mary Ann Mowtauk. For several years, I was not able to look into any bridal shop, because it hurt so much that on my wedding day I could not wear a proper wedding dress.

My parents made a wedding party in our home, and invited any relatives they could face with the shadow of shame over us. We spent our wedding night in my bedroom. It would have been much too frivolous to stay in a hotel. Obviously, I was still very much under my mother's thumb.

That was the worst day of my life. I didn't want to marry a man expecting to divorce him. I wanted to be married the rest of my life but, as far as I was concerned, a wife could have a life only as good as that of her husband, and I knew I would not be satisfied with Dave's. It was almost like dancing; you were only as good as the leader. In the 1960s, the man was the leader and whatever he did in his life he shared with his wife. Dave was an airman third class, an MP, a policeman. And I was not able to go back to college now; I was going to have a child.

Separation from my parents, even with all the shame involved, was a relief. With the little money I had saved, we bought an old Rambler car. My parents had offered us a wedding present of $1,000, a very generous gift in 1963, except they didn't give it to us, they were going to hold it for us, because they were concerned that we would spend it in a stupid way. We probably would have spent it on a better car. Dave was stationed in

Salina, Kansas, where his next assignment with the Air Force was as an airman third class, an air policeman. Right after the wedding, we packed that car full of things my mother had salvaged, like extra pots and pans and dishware and anything that might help us start a life of our own. We were only two hours out of Cleveland when the car broke down and cost us all the money that we had to fix it. So did our marriage begin.

Dave was well aware of my unhappiness. He was a sensitive person and he loved me very much and was happy that we were married and going off together. To be loved by someone as he loved me—and I don't think any man ever loved me as much as he did—was a beautiful feeling. I had always felt insecure, and to have a man love me as he did compensated, in part, for all the poverty and negativity that our future life would bring.

As we drove into Kansas, all I saw was flat land and very few developed areas. If it wasn't for the military station, there wouldn't have been anything in Salinas. Ironically, the people in town didn't like the military, even though it probably enriched them quite a bit. We found a small house with three rooms—a living room, kitchen and bedroom, but at least it was a private, and I was able to make a small garden in the back yard that made me happy. It was our first home.

Shortly after I had planted the garden, however, Dave received a new assignment to Great Falls, Montana. Again, we loaded up all our possessions into the same car. I don't know why we saved the tires that we had replaced, but we strapped them onto the top of the car, because there wasn't any room inside. We looked like the Beverly Hillbillies going down the road. We calculated that we could afford to pay for gas and buy food in grocery stores, but we stayed in a motel room only one night. Other than that, we slept in the car. We turned it into a good trip, though. We saw the Grand Tetons and stopped in Yellowstone Park before we finally made it to Great Falls.

Unforgettably, we arrived in Great Falls the day President Kennedy was shot. It was extremely alarming, because they were like a king and queen, a beautiful couple so loved and respected. It was a very depressing time, and we worried about political and social upheavals throughout the country.

Once we got to Great Falls, we looked for the least expensive apartment we could find. We spied a "For Rent" sign outside an old Victorian home that had been converted into several apartments on three different floors. We rented one room on the first floor that was the living room with a kitchen so small that if I opened the oven door it would hit the cabinets it faced. We shared a refrigerator out in the hallway; the left part was our neighbor's and the right part was ours. There was a toilet and sink on the first floor that we shared with three other apartments. We had a choice of sharing a bath upstairs with other tenants or downstairs in the basement with several construction workers. Our bedroom was the size of a closet, with just enough room for a double bed to squeeze into. It cost fifty-five dollars a month.

We lied about when our baby was going to be born, because it would have been shameful to let people know that we had to get married. We said that the baby would be born three months later, though I was huge. On September 28th I went to the hospital and gave birth to Bridgett. (I had tried to deliver naturally, but quickly became hysterical, convinced that I was going to die. I was haunted by the story of my mother's first two births in a barn, without even a midwife when I was born. That's when I was given a little gas and a doctor's help.) The day Bridgett was born was the most wonderful day of my young life. I believe that no one can understand the incredible joy of motherhood unless they give birth.

Oma took the train from Cleveland to Great Falls to stay with us for several weeks, which was grand, though I doubt she was very comfortable sleeping on our sofa. It was the first time we had seen any of my family since we left. We found another apartment at only $60 a month where we had our own refrigerator and bathroom.

Two weeks after Bridgett was born, Dave wanted to go on a hunting trip, and he asked me to go with him, while Oma took care of the baby. We drove into the mountains above a little creek where he lit a blazing fire to make coffee. In the morning, the coffee pot was a cube of ice and the creek had frozen over. I had not slept because, wanting to be the good person I strove to be, I had taken the sleeping bag with the broken zipper and could not get warm. I tried to sleep in the back of the car, but I couldn't.

Next day we went hiking through the hills looking for deer when Dave spotted one. He only had a .22 rifle, but he shot the deer from about three hundred feet right into its ear. The deer dropped, and we went running over to it. I was supposed to gut the deer; that was my job. I had watched my mother gut chickens and fish and rabbits, so how different would it be to gut a deer. I took a knife and when I stabbed into the stomach, gas came pouring out. The smell was bad enough, but with the steam from the body cavity I couldn't see where I was cutting, and I was so cold, but I had to clean out the carcass immediately so as not to contaminate the meat. We needed that extra meat; we were living on $225 a month. I managed to grab inside the cavity of that deer and pull out its intestines and organs. Then we dragged it down the mountain and wrestled it into the back of the Rambler. When we got back to our apartment, we dragged it up the stairs into the kitchen where we skinned and butchered it. Getting it skinned was the most important thing because of ticks that might infect it. We used a handsaw, because our knives were not sharp enough to cut that deer apart. I did most of the carving, though Dave helped me with the most difficult tasks, like cutting bones. Too bad Oma had left the day we returned and wasn't there to help cut it up, because she would have known how. There was a lot of meat; probably 150 pounds. Fortunately, in our new apartment we had a freezer, so we froze some of it. For the next three months we ate nothing but venison. I hate venison! You know how many different ways I learned to cook venison? Stewing it in Lipton onion soup like a pot roast was the best, because some of the gamy taste diminished. We tried to make sausage, mixing it with ground beef in a hand grinder that I still own, and it was pretty good mixed with pork. Money was so tight we just bought necessities and ate that disgusting venison.

At that time, the Missouri River overflowed and wiped out a nearby town in a low area outside Great Falls. It made national news, which prompted a call from my mother and dad. Keep in mind that making a telephone call was very expensive at the time and my parents were extremely frugal. So were we, and we never called them. We had not spoken for about a year. They did not even call when my daughter was born, so their call was a cause for excitement. They were worried about us, but we told them that we were on high ground, and the flood did not affect us. We asked again for some of our wedding present money. The first time I had done a major grocery shopping to buy staples, I had asked them for a little money, but they turned us down. When the baby was born, I asked again and was refused again. During the phone call, we were denied one more time, with a reminder that we needed to be more frugal. We had been keeping in touch with letters, receiving lectures from them for the most part. We were nineteen years old and we were definitely more frugal than our neighbors. There were other airmen who were married and had children, and they got money from their families, but we didn't get any.

Dave applied for a transfer to Germany. I guess we didn't think too far ahead, because the military certainly would not have paid my way, though I would have liked to go to Germany. I could have gone back to Austria and seen my relatives and, of course, I still spoke German. We both thought it was a great idea, but we didn't think about who would pay for me and the baby to go. We counted on living on Dave's money and saving any money I made for emergencies. We were smart enough to realize that you always had to put a little savings away, no matter how tough things were.

Before the baby came, I had put an ad in the paper to do alterations, and I earned a few dollars from ladies coming in have their dresses altered. I was afraid to go and apply for a job anywhere else, because I knew nobody would hire a pregnant woman. After the baby was born, I went to the telephone company and got a job as a service representative, which basically is a sales person who solicits new orders. I thought the job went extremely well; I was very a happy with it. When Dave got his orders to go to Germany, I thought, well, I have a job here, so I'll just stay in Great Falls. When my supervisors heard about my situation, however, all of a sudden they evaluated my work and pointed out different things that I had done wrong -- filing something incorrectly, for example -- and they let me go with no warning. I don't think I was doing anything wrong; I thought their complaints were fabricated. I assumed they felt that, at my age, now twenty, I needed to be with my parents and my baby while Dave was in Germany.

We packed up everything once again to head for Cleveland. By now we had a VW, which only made things more difficult, because it was smaller, so we shipped many things to my parents and set out on the long drive. On the way back, we stopped to see Mount Rushmore. We couldn't afford a motel room, so we slept in the car, me in the front seat, Dave in the back seat, and the baby in a pocket at the back window.

It had been fifteen months since we had left Cleveland, though it seemed a lot longer than that. My mother had given birth to my third brother, Joey, three months earlier than me. Bridgett was about eight months old and Joey was eleven. We had a lovely reunion. I thought I would be staying with my parents until I could find a place for myself when, to our astonishment, one of Dave's relatives announced, "We're going to pay your way to go to Germany, one way." Bridgett would fly for free as a baby. They thought it was critical for us to be together.

The day came of my first airplane flight. We arranged to fly as close to the same time as possible, so that Dave could pick us up at the Frankfurt Airport. My plane took off a few hours earlier than his. I arrived at the Frankfurt Airport and waited and waited, went to the bathroom while Bridgett crawled around under the stalls. I had not brought cloth diapers, so went into my carry-on suitcase and tore up a few items for rags. There was no way I was going to buy disposable diapers that were very expensive. When night came and Dave still hadn't shown up, I was frantic. We were both very tired, but there was no place to sleep. A Black woman with her family spoke to us and, when I told her about our situation, she kindly invited us to sleep on the floor in their motel room. We spent the night with them, and next day came back to the airport and waited again. Finally, later that day Dave arrived. He had misplaced his orders, left them on a bus somewhere and wasn't able to get on the plane without them. I hate to say it, but sometimes he was absent-minded, which created a lot of discomfort for us, to say the least.

Once we were in Germany, we stayed with another air police family who took us in for several days until we were able to find an apartment that we rented for $60 a month. A lot of Germans had small apartments in their houses. Rather like our Victorian house, we shared a bathroom and once a week were allowed to go downstairs and have a bath at a scheduled time. Actually, they had a wonderful big bathtub that we really appreciated. Dave was still earning the same amount of money, $225 a month. We lived in Germany for two years, and he never got more than $300 as an airman third class. However, there were four Deutsch marks to the dollar, so we got along on his pay.

Gas was fairly cheap, so we were able to drive to Köflach. I remembered everything there from my childhood. It was 1964 and we had left in '51, so it was thirteen years later. I still remembered where the schoolhouse was, and the book store, where I met a girl who appeared to be my age. I shared with her that we had lived there from 1948-51, and I was coming back now at twenty-one.

"I went to school over there," I said, waving my hand in the direction of the school.

"Oh, yes," she replied, "what year was that? I went to school there, too." I told her it was the same year that she had attended.

"Yes," she added, "but you were in the lower class with the farmers; I was in the upper class."

I did not respond. But I could not help thinking that most Europeans would have loved to emigrate to America, where I had all the wonderful opportunities that they missed, while she was still stuck in a book store employed by her "upper class" parents.

We went to the apartment that my father had built on the third floor in the attic, where my aunt now lived. She had resided across the hall from us with two adult children, but later moved into our apartment. We visited with them and many of our other relatives. My cousin, Vogel, had lost his leg in the war and was on crutches and, though Austria had socialized medicine, they didn't give him a prosthesis. He wove baskets for a living.

My relatives were unbelievably hospitable. We went to see Dante Moser, a sister of my grandmother, and her children up the street. When we stopped and asked a woman if the Moser family lived nearby, she replied, "Oh, yes, and we're expecting you." Our arrival was the biggest gossip in town. We felt like celebrities. When we went to the church on Sunday, all heads turned to look at us. We were quite uncomfortable with such notoriety.

When we returned to Germany, we found an apartment in a community called Merhenlundt, which means fairy tale land. It was a charming newer community on the edge of a forest. A long road led into the forest to a place called the Rheinblick Golf Course. Rheinblick means a peek at the Rhein. It was a fabulous golf course on the side of a hill that sloped down to the Rhein. I got a job there as a bookkeeper doing reports of slot machines. I had no idea that, later in life, learning to do slot reports would come in handy. Sergeant Pendleton was my boss. He was delighted when, at Christmastime, I painted a large mural of a Christmas scene with snow and mountains. I met Sergeant McAllister, a military man who was a golf pro. He told me he had twelve children in the States whom he missed terribly. My heart ached for him. There was also a handsome young Scottish golf pro who offered to teach me how to play golf. I didn't think that would be proper, being a married woman. To this day, I regret missing that opportunity to learn how to play golf. Of course, I had no idea how difficult or expensive it would be.

We were also able to take trips to Berches Garden in Garmisch, and we tried to ski for the first time, though we couldn't afford to have ski lessons. I took a lift up a mountain side and I asked the person next to me, "Could you give my a few tips on how to get down this hill, because I've never skied before?" She said, "Well, we'd better get off right now." We got off half way, and she told me how to place my feet. I went flying down towards the bottom of the hill where a building loomed, and I didn't know how to stop, so I just let myself fall. I tried it several times. My hips were black and blue the next day. Dave didn't do as well as I did, but he tried the same thing. We obviously couldn't help each other, but we both had fun our first time on skis. He never learned how to ski in later life, though I did. I was twenty-nine before I tried it again.

We also took a trip to Spain's Costa Brava, north of Barcelona, a beautiful beach resort area. We were told that it was inexpensive, otherwise we wouldn't have gone there. It cost a dollar a day per person and that included three meals. Unbelievable! When we went for meals, there were three plates for three different courses. We had a specific place to sit that was assigned to us, almost like a cruise ship. The Spanish people were lovely, very honest. We didn't even lock our door. But, unfortunately, I picked up some kind of bacteria towards the end of our trip that made me very sick with horrible diarrhea. Somebody offered me medicine that made me hallucinate and made me even sicker. Several hours away there was an Air Force military base at Zaragoza, and Dave drove me to a hospital there. Nobody spoke English. They put a tube down my throat to pump my stomach. I couldn't understand if they telling me to swallow or not to swallow. I was dizzy and faint, in a stupor. It took a few days for me to recover, and we would remember that episode as the downside of our trip.

*   *   *

We really wanted to go to Italy, but Dave was finishing his assignment, so we gave up the idea, as we started to prepare to go back home. We could not wait; we had missed our families very much. We bought all kinds of presents—silver goblets and swords and beer steins and cuckoo clocks. That cuckoo clock in my kitchen today. I had bought it for my parents and they had it for many years until they died, when I took it back. I also still have beer steins that we bought when we were there.

We were still living on $300 a month. We had saved all the money that I had earned, which amounted to $4,000. We planned to spend $ 2,000 on a car. Everybody we knew had saved money to bring a car from back from Germany, because they were so much cheaper. We bought a brand new Simca, a French car. We saved the other

64

$2,000 for whatever we needed once we got to the States. I flew back first with the baby, and Dave came a little later. The military did not ship the car for us. I had to pick it up from some kind of a shipping yard in New York, taking a bus there through Harlem with Bridgett. I was really scared, but I managed to find the shipping yard and drove the car back to Cleveland.

Dave was out of the military by now, and we decided to settle in Kent, Ohio, where Dave planned to go to Kent State University. We had $2,000 and we found a used trailer for $4,000, but the bank wouldn't loan us the money, because neither of us had a job. I applied for a job at that bank, was hired as a teller, and then they loaned me the money for the trailer.

Dave had intended to start school right away, but he took a job as a policeman on campus instead, and he didn't take courses. I can't remember what his reason was, but I wasn't happy about that. I wanted him to have a university degree.

That Christmas my parents were preparing like no other Christmas. We had two three-year-olds, my parents felt financially secure, they lived in a brand new, beautiful ranch style house that my father had built in a neighborhood with doctors. It was going to be a special Christmas.

In the meantime, I had been trying to summon the courage to divorce Dave. I had announced my intentions to him more than a month before, and it was time now to tell our parents. Christmas was totally spoiled by our news. Everyone's heart ached.

I had always wanted a well-educated, conscientious, hard-working man. Frankly, I thought Dave was lazy. Actually, compared to me, a lot of people are lazy. I've always been an over achiever. To be fair, I have to say that Dave was a good person; he wasn't a druggie or a cheat; he had good values, but he was just not as ambitious as I was. I didn't think I could ever be a millionaire, but I wanted to be successful, whatever that meant. That's why the worst day of my life was our wedding day, because I knew that he did not have the same goals that I had. I was heartbroken to take our beautiful child from her father. He loved her so much. It was very difficult, but I knew that I could do better without him. Once the divorce went through, I felt like a ball and chain had been lifted from me and I could start a new life.

Love, Lies and Living Rooms

I was still working as a bank teller in Kent and living in the trailer. During my first two weeks at the bank, I had not been able to balance my money drawer, and I was so embarrassed I wanted to quit. Bob Davis, the head teller who had hired me and saw that I was a hard worker, encouraged me to stay. Bob was an astute, mild-mannered man devoted to his family, who would one day become my good friend. Only a few weeks later, when Bob went to manage his own branch, I had improved enough to take over his position as head teller. Shortly after Bob transferred to his own branch, I followed him there.

A lot of students used that branch near Kent State University. One day a student in the queue sneezed and I automatically said, *"Gesundheit,"* and the man responded *"Danke."* His name was Leon Meyers. He was a student professor at Kent State, studying German. We exchanged a few phrases in German and, to my surprise, he asked me to go out with him. Leon was Jewish. My parents had never taught us anti-semitism, but we were certainly aware of the prejudice that existed in general against Jews. Leon was a very intelligent man who had a fantastic photographic memory. I was in awe of his brilliance. He had started his first teaching job that fall, and was finishing his dissertation. As a matter of fact, I had become acquainted with several student professors and dated some of them. I loved having intelligent young men vie for my attention, but Leon wanted to marry me, and I was swept away by the idea.

My little Bridgett was about to enter kindergarten, and I wanted her to have the same name as me. I thought she'd be embarrassed later about having a name different from her mother's. Leon solved my problem by agreeing to adopt Bridgett. As Leon and I began to make arrangements for a wedding, I wanted to include my mother. I was accustomed to having her manage such occasions, baking, cooking and organizing. Friends of our, Irene and Bunny Johnson, offered a condo recreation room for a wedding reception. I assumed we'd have our ethnic food, and so I made preparations for it, but my mother was not very enthusiastic, which worried me. I had always felt that my parents had never liked to see me with a man, though they had accepted Dave and seemed to accept Leon. It was strange; they supported me without encouraging me. They even gave us the $1,000 they had offered when Dave and I married. They always kept their word.

Leon and I got married in a Jewish temple. Leon's relatives let me know how lucky I was – a blonde *shiksa* – to marry into his family. I still had enough of an inferiority complex from my past to be intimidated, suspecting that they were prejudiced against me.

Leon didn't want to move into my trailer; he wanted us to live in his apartment. I insisted that we live in the trailer, though, because it cost less money. I had almost paid for it in full, and felt that it was not financially sensible to pay rent to his landlord.

While I was working at the bank, and Leon was working on his PhD, he would pick up Bridgett every day after school. Her father, Dave, had remarried and left Kent when Bridgett was three-and-a-half years old, and he gave Leon permission to adopt her. Bridgett never saw Dave again until she was sixteen.

A few months later, in the fall, Leon got his degree, and was qualified to look for a teaching position. One of the places he applied to was Frostburg State College in Maryland. Bridgett, Leon and I went to interview with the head of the English department there. Bridgett was an angel of a child and sat quietly through that interview with the department head and his wife in their living room. They hired Leon.

We immediately started to look for a house. We would use the proceeds from selling my trailer and my car, which totaled $6,500. Leon had no money. As a matter of fact, he owed his father about $300, which I paid when he not so subtly reminded Leon of it. I came into the marriage with $6,500, he came with debts, but he did have a car that his father had given him.

We looked at a home in Frostburg that cost $30,000, a modern ranch style with a

68

beautiful backyard that I wanted to buy. We also had a choice of a $20,000 Victorian home built in 1894, with three stories, a turret and a circular library on the third floor. Leon told me that Mark Twain had had a circular library, and all he could think of was that library. On the other hand, all I could see was a lot of rooms that needed painting, a wool carpet infested with moths, old wallpaper and endless repairs. Leon didn't know what end of the hammer to use; not that I knew a lot more, but I was much handier than he was. Leon won. The owners of the Victorian house offered to sell us the furniture for $2,000, so for $22,000 with $6,500 down, we bought the house with a fifteen-year mortgage and high monthly payments.

We very much wanted to have a baby and we were happy when I became pregnant. I was going to school full time, studying art at the school where Leon taught. He brought his students home regularly, until I finally had to ask him to limit the number of students he invited, because I was too busy to entertain them, and we couldn't afford to feed guests, even though I made everything from scratch, including bread. Leon was earning a thousand dollars a month, totally $9,000 a year, because he was not paid for three months in the summer, so it was difficult to make ends meet. Two girl students asked if they could move in with us. Leon was amenable.

"Okay,", I agreed, "but if they're going to pay room and board and I'm going to have to do all the work to earn this extra money, may I have that money to spend as I want?" He agreed.

Frugal as I was, I splurged and spent that money on flying lessons! Yes! I was twenty-eight years old and had found a flying club in Cumberland, Maryland where an old World War II pilot gave lessons. He looked at me incredulously, not understanding why a woman would want to fly. It was very uncommon in those days. After six hours of lessons, I was soloing. It was one of the most exciting things I'd ever done, and I thought, my goodness, what next!

When summer came, Leon had no job. His uncle in Michigan had an ice delivery route, and offered Leon work carrying ice. He had to take it, because he wasn't able to get a job in Frostburg. Our boarders left, and I was pregnant, with no job. On the 24th of July 1970 I gave birth to Leah Marlene Meyers. We were elated about our child.

We lived in the Victorian house for two years before I decided to paint the whole thing, but I dreaded scraping all the old paint off its eighty-one angles. When the house was built, there was gas lighting, so it was constructed to allow light to come in from three angles in each room. Besides the turret, there was a bay in the living room, and in the dining room, and then there were three sides to the kitchen, a back staircase and a front staircase. I looked into aluminum or vinyl siding instead of paint. Aluminum was cheaper, but I knew I would have to cut it, and I feared cutting myself on the sharp edges, so I decided to use vinyl siding. I hired an eighteen-year-old Black boy for minimum wage, who helped me side the entire house. That boy had a voice like a canary and he and I sang while we worked. I didn't like the way he cut the vinyl, so I cut all of it myself, but I needed him to hold the other side of ten-foot-long pieces. The siding just sort of clips in; anybody could figure out how to do it. My thumb turned black and blue and was very sore. While Bridgett was in school, I'd put Leah on a blanket on the ground beneath us, where she'd roll around, watching us work and listening to us sing.

Before the siding was done, Leon and I had some discussions about his career, facing the fact that a professor didn't earn very much money, and that if he worked for his dad selling dry goods, he would be able to earn possibly twice as much. He decided to leave teaching and work for his father. It meant moving to Columbus, so we had to put the house up for sale. I scraped off the wallpaper, painted and installed a new carpet. I saved more than a hundred carpet scraps, and nailed them down onto the wood floor in the bathroom. In our little garden, I had grown blackberries, raspberries, rhubarb and other things that took a long time to mature, but were a great satisfaction to me. Giving up the house was painful for me, because I had put so much into it, it felt like a part of me. However, we sold our house for $30,000, so we realized a profit of $18,500. Leon kept all the money.

When we set out for Columbus, I sensed a distant coolness in Leon. We found an apartment in Columbus, a two-bedroom town house that was too small for our furniture, but I guessed we would figure it out. The night we arrived, we were sitting together on the sofa, and I felt confused and frightened by his aloofness, fearing he didn't love me any more. I felt compelled to ask him outright if he was going to leave me. "Yes," he said. He gave me $50, got up from the sofa and walked out the door. I sat there in shock and disbelief.

I soon learned that Leon had transferred the $18,500 into another bank account. I didn't find out until quite a bit later, however, that he had run off with a childhood sweetheart to whom he had been married when he wanted to marry me! He was a bigamist. Before our divorce was final, they had a baby. Leon eventually married four times, taking on a new wife each time before divorcing his present spouse. When I told my parents, they typically blamed me. "What did you do to him?"

I became unbelievably depressed. Finally, Pat Sipl, my sister-in-law, told me that Ohio State University had an internship for doctors in the psychiatric department, and suggested I go there for help. The intern who interviewed me was close to my age, and I had three interviews with him out of a total of six. He was quite pleasant, and I told him many things about myself. He had not read my psychological test results where I had been asked if I had suicidal tendencies. I lied that I did not but, in truth, I dreamed of leaving the gas on in the apartment. Other psychiatrists asked if I ever thought someone was following me, and I lied about that though, in fact, there was someone following me. Leon had hired a detective to try to find some transgression that would make me look worse than him, realizing that having taken all our money and going off with another woman and having a baby didn't look very good for him. So yes, there was someone following me. I didn't lie about all the questions, but they caught enough lies to conclude that I was severely depressed. When I went for my fourth interview, the doctor suddenly treated me like a mentally ill person, insisting on giving me pills that I assumed were Valium. They didn't take complete effect for twenty-four hours, and then

I became like a zombie, lying on the sofa. Leah would go out the front door and I didn't even care. After a few days I called the doctor and asked if I could stop the pills, explaining that I didn't want to exchange one problem for another. He agreed, so I stopped the pills.

I had to look for a job in Columbus. Fortunately, I found a babysitter, Vicky. She was heaven sent, a wonderful woman who had children of her own, and watched my girls at her house. I applied for many jobs, but couldn't find anything that paid more than $100 a week which, according to my calculations, would leave $12 a week for gas, personal expenses and baby-sitting fees. I applied for food stamps, but could only get enough for six weeks, because of where I was living. I would have had to move into a less expensive place to qualify for food stamps, but I didn't have the money to move any place else.

I had divorce papers and food stamps in my pocket when, incongruously, a neighbor told me about a fortune teller that she was going to who was so great she was on television. She told me I could have my fortune told for five dollars. There was no way I was going to pay five dollars to have my fortune told, but she insisted, and I gave in and went with her. The fortune teller took me aback when she told me, "You have two daughters Don't worry about your girls." She rattled off information that was uncanny, like telling me that I had divorce papers and food stamps in my pocket. I asked her, rather sarcastically, when I was going to meet the man of my dreams.

"Before the end of the year," she replied, to my astonishment. "He's going to be involved in airplane wings." She scrutinized my face before she added, "You're going to be a very wealthy woman. You're going to sit on a throne with a scepter in your hand."

Do you think I believed her? No way!

I had been without a job for nine months, still deeply depressed. Leon sent me $200 a month. Desperate, I went into every single store on Main Street and offered to work for free for two weeks and then they could decide whether they would hire me, because I knew I would be a good employee.

I went into a store called Schottenstein's that was like Leavitt's furniture chain. It had 400 bays, each one like a small room completely decorated and furnished. Jerry Schottenstein decorated 23 Leavitt's stores in the Ohio area with glitz -- chandeliers, bling, beautifully matched furniture with an ashtray that matched the picture behind it that blended with the sofa, pillows and greenery. Ah, it was gorgeous. I had always wanted to be an interior decorator, though I had no experience. I asked to see the manager. When he came down the aisle towards me, I summoned all my courage and approached him.

"I'm an interior decorator. I'd like to work with you."

"Well," he replied, "are you willing to work out of town?"

"Of course!"

"We're building a new store in Covington, and if you're willing to travel to Covington, can you be there tomorrow morning?"

"Sure."

I had no idea where Covington was! I walked out of the store, wondering who I could call to find out. Vicky told me that it was in Kentucky, three hours away. Next morning I took a little train case, packed one pair of underwear and my makeup bag and went off to Covington. Thank goodness I had Vicky to keep the girls.

When I arrived at the store it was hustling and bustling. Many gay guys were there from Chicago and Milwaukee, showing off their decorating flair. A fellow named Jack had been decorating furniture stores in New York, and Jerry Schottenstein had brought him out and made him head decorator at his store. I spent most of the day waiting around and watching; nobody knew what to do with me. Then Jack said, "Well, I think we better find you a motel room." I got a motel room with the rest of them, and hung around for two more days before they decided to try me out in the store. They gave us $12 dollars a day for food and incidentals. I spent the very minimal. I bought food in grocery stores. When everybody went out for dinner or whatever, I was always on a diet and I just had a cup of coffee. I spent my money on clothes, because I didn't have the right clothes with me and I knew I couldn't leave to go home and get some. This was an opportunity I intended to take full advantage of. I stayed for fifteen days. I didn't know what was going to happen after we finished decorating that store. Jack would come to where I was working at nine o'clock at night and ask me if I wanted to do another bay, and I'd say, "Yes, sir." I was wearing the only high heels I had, on a concrete floor covered with linoleum, from eight o'clock in the morning until late at night. And I had worried about nurses' shoes! We worked in a huge area with 400 bays, and then there was the warehouse area behind that where we had to get all of our *chatskies*, accessories, to set up the bays. I was exhausted, but "No" was not in my vocabulary. The job would pay me $12,000 a year -- $1,000 a month -- more than my Ph.D. ex-husband earned. I probably only got minimum wage, but it didn't matter, I worked so many hours. I'd never earned so much money, and the other decorators were obviously earning even more.

Jack lived in Columbus, and when we returned there he put in a good word for me to Jerry Schottenstein, who had three stores there at the time. The south store was in a less desirable area so, as a beginner, I was assigned there. A former priest was the head of that store, and I sensed he did not want me there, but that wasn't going to stop me. Eventually I moved to the best store on the north side and worked there for two years.

Fortune Tellers and Fortune Makers

After working at Leavitt's for about three months, during the Christmas holidays a girl friend who belonged to the Columbus Ski Club told me they were all driving to the ski resort at Boyne Mountain, Michigan for New Year's Eve, and she invited me to drive up with them. My first skiing experiences in Austria made me a "wanna be" skiier, among all the other "wanna be" desires I had. Vicky agreed to take care of my girls for a few days, so I decided to go.

On the drive there we talked about men and the fantasy of meeting "Mr. Right." I told them that a fortune teller had told me I was going to meet the man of my dreams before the end of the year. "And there's two more days left!" Seventy-two hours later I met a fellow named Chuck, who was a structural engineer and his specialty was stress on airplane wings. I flashed back to the fortune teller's reference to my "dream man" being involved with airplane wings. In fact, he had published a book on aircraft wing fractures that is still on amazon.com. Chuck was very handsome, six feet tall with wavy hair, a symmetrical face with sculpted features, the kind of face an artist would want to paint. He walked like an athlete with purposeful strides. He spoke correctly, rather formally, like the gentleman he was.

Initially, I just heard the name Chuck, but a day later he told me his last name, Fedderson. I had socialized with a woman named Annalisa Fedderson, a German girl, through Parents without Partners. She had told me about how horrible her husband was, that they were having major conflicts in their relationship. I wondered if she was talking about the Chuck Fedderson I had just met, so I asked him if he knew Annalisa. He went white. He was her husband! I was strongly swayed by the fortune teller's prediction, however, and paid no attention to Annalisa's complaints. I followed my inclinations, and Chuck and I started a relationship that would last seventeen years and mark the rest of my life.

I had finally earned enough money to look for something to invest in. It had taken me several years to get $8,500 from my divorce settlement. I felt quite bitter that I had gone into that marriage with $6,500 when Leon had nothing. Half the $18,500 we had cleared on the house was allotted to each of us but, as I had taken the car, its value was deducted from my settlement. With the $8,500, plus money I had saved as an interior decorator, I had a total of $15,000. I had the idea that if I bought a fourplex and lived in one unit, in twenty years it would be paid for, at which time, the girls would be gone, I'd have income from the other three units and that would be my security. I found a fourplex in an area called Arlington that was very close to Ohio State University. It was considered a rich Christian area, with brick town houses and garages and beautiful fourplexes. One was occupied by its owners, an older couple who was moving to an assisted living facility, and they were willing to carry the mortgage. I bought their fourplex in 1973 with $15,000 down on $85,000 with a mortgage of eight percent. The arrangement was ideal. The town houses were similar to the one I was living in at the time where I was paying $250 a month. My new house had a garage and was much nicer, in an elegant area with spreading trees everywhere. The fourplex tenants in the other three units were paying only $150 a month. I knew I could rent those apartments for a total of $750, which would pay my mortgage. I raised everybody's rent to $250. To my horror, they all moved out! There I was with my new investment and no income from it. I was glad I still had the decorating job but, as it turned out, I rented the apartments very quickly. I started to decorate one of them in a leopard print, with everything in black and gold, a beaded curtain dividing the dining room from the living room, with gorgeous love seats, and a pool table in the basement, transforming it into a real bachelor pad. A prospective tenant showed up, a burly guy, the kind of person you'd think was associated with the mob. He had everything but a cigar in his mouth. I rented the unit to him for $350, and he peeled off $700 to move into the place. I was so excited that I brought the cash to Chuck, threw it up into the air and let it all came falling down on me like snow. I was so happy. Of course, I had invested some money into it, but to think I was getting $350 a month for a place that had previously brought in $150 elated me.

Initially, Chuck moved into the unit next to mine, because it wasn't proper to live together, as he had kids, two girls named Arlene and Susan, and I had Bridgett and Leah. He paid me rent and was glad to live there, because it was close to his work at Battelle Memorial Institute, a prestigious non-profit connected to the university. Chuck spoke fluent German, as he had learned it from Annalise.

When I had first started to date Chuck, I was still looking for certain qualities in a man, and I happened to read a book on finding a mate to keep. It suggested making a list of the qualities you sought, carry it around on your person, and do not change that list just because somebody comes along who triggers chemistry. Chuck was a very classy man, a gentleman. He had all the qualifications on my list, so I happily kept dating him. He was so personable that even my mother loved him. We had our clashes, though. There were times when I closed the door on him, or he closed the door on me, when I told myself, "I'm never going to see him again!" My main problem with Chuck was that he was often emotionally unavailable. He felt guilty, that he was betraying his daughters who loved him dearly. He felt that he had failed in his previous relationship, and so he feared committing to me. Once, after five months of dating, I told him he didn't love me and I didn't love him; we needed to go our separate ways. He suggested we should try seeing each other again for thirty days. During the following thirty days, he let down his guard. We opened up to each other, confided in each other honestly, enjoyed each other, and grew closer every day. In other words, we fell in love.

I'd recommend to anybody to make that list and stay with whoever has the qualities that you respect and wish for in an individual.

We continued to live next to each other, but we started looking in Upper Arlington, a lovely area with classic houses. The cheapest one in that neighborhood cost $51,000, and we were so excited about it we immediately bought it. As soon as we had signed the contract, we talked about what we were going to do with it.

"Are you going to live in it? Am I going to live in it? Are we going to live in it together?"

We decided we were going to live in it together, but he added, "We can't just live together in a neighborhood like this; we have to get married."

Joyfully, we planned our wedding for the Fourth of July 1974, a Hawaiian theme wedding in the backyard of our new house. We bought a suckling pig for a luau, mother came and made 200 meatballs, and helped cook other dishes. We sent out Hawaiian theme wedding invitations, everything was organized and our excitement was palpable. We had even composed special vows to exchange. I had crocheted a grass skirt in white for myself, and the four girls had green grass skirts crocheted in the same style, and Chuck had a shirt to match the tops I'd made for the girls. But the day before the wedding, Chuck confronted me.

"It's all your fault we can't get married tomorrow."

"What?" I was shocked.

He told me there was a three-day waiting period after you get your license before you can get married, and we had just got ours the day before. I was horrified. Why hadn't he thought of that?

I snapped back, "You know, legality is your bag, not mine. We have a couple hundred people coming. We can't not go through with this."

I called a girlfriend who agreed to pretend to be a minister and unofficially marry us.

The wedding was beautiful, joyful and original, with many people celebrating and wishing us well, but Chuck was in a dark mood. A cousin of mine had smoked pot at the wedding and that really aggravated him. He became really upset when, after everyone left, my cousin went upstairs and fell asleep in our round wedding bed that we had actually made together. So much for a romantic wedding night.

The day after our wedding, I went to work at Schottenstein's, and the manager told me I no longer had a job. "You have someone to take care of you now," he said. I was furious, but there was nothing I could do to change his attitude about working women. I tried to develop my own decorating business, charging by the hour for consulting. I didn't earn a lot of money, but I had income from the properties.

After our wedding, Chuck changed. He became controlling. He wanted to manage our money, but I was the one who handled money better than him, and this became a bone of contention between us. Academically, he was much more educated than me, but I was more sensible, especially with money. Of course, he was earning substantially more than I was. Actually, at the time I was earning $15,000 a year and he was at $22,000, but he had to pay child support and alimony.

In the meantime, I bought another fourplex. I believe Chuck was jealous of what I had done with my properties, so we both maxed out our Visa cards and bought a third fourplex together. I went to a seminar about how to become a millionaire by doubling your money every year, starting with a thousand dollars. The premise is that if you double your money every year for ten years, you will wind up a millionaire. I sat in back, while a free introductory course was being taught, the purpose of which was to sell the $360-dollar course that followed. I sat there listening with ants in my pants! I was so excited I couldn't stand it, because I was already doing that. I was already $15,000 ahead of the game. I couldn't wait until the introduction was over. I went up to the speaker and asked him some questions about making investments. He said, "Oh, I'm just a hired speaker; I don't know anything about this course." I never took the course, but I was already following it before I had ever heard of it. This lesson confirmed to me that I could really do it. I knew I was on my way to becoming a millionaire.

One year after we bought our joint fourplex I wanted to sell it, and I had a buyer, but Chuck refused. It was as though he tried to exercise control over me by resisting my ideas, whatever they might be. Maybe I threatened his masculinity, who knows. I was so determined to convince him, though, that I went down on my hands and knees and begged him. I finally got him to sell it, and we doubled our money. I resolved that would be the last property I'd buy with him.

*　　*　　*

I met a professor from Ohio State University who tried to tempt me to go to Las Vegas and, though I explained that I was solidly committed to Chuck, he must have planted the idea in my mind. Then my attorney, Max Zizkin, talked about going to Las Vegas. There are no coincidences. Soon after, Chuck told me he had an opportunity to give a speech in the Los Angeles area. Immediately excited, I told Chuck I'd never been to L.A., my brother, Mike, lived there, and I'd love to go, and would pay my own way. Oh, and by the way, could we stop in Las Vegas? And so we did. We stopped in Las Vegas for two days that would change the course of my destiny.

Viva Las Vegas

We arrived at the Riviera Hotel in Las Vegas late at night, but I wanted to try the slot machines, where I quickly lost ten dollars. I felt like my right arm had come off. I looked around at everybody else still playing and had a strange thought. "I have got to own those slot machines." I had noticed gamblers on the airplane, however, and when I saw even more at the airport and hotel, I felt totally repulsed by their behavior. They exemplified everything I was morally opposed to. They were vulgar, with an unsophisticated manner of speaking, and they were loose with their money. They were not respectful of property, ignoring trash containers, throwing gum and wrappers onto the floor. They elbowed their way to the front of lines. I did not care for any of this, but I smelled all kinds of money and opportunity. I instinctively felt that Las Vegas at that time was like a sleeping giant, and I wanted to be there when it woke up.

We went upstairs and slept and, in the morning, I told Chuck I wanted to go out and look at real estate.

He responded, "We're in the entertainment capital of the world and you want to go look at real estate?"

"Yes," I insisted, "I think there's lots of opportunity here."

I had a very strong feeling that real estate was going to continue to expand. I looked through the Yellow Pages and called several real estate agents and, to my surprise, they weren't anxious to come and pick me up to show their properties. I finally found somebody who offered to drive me around. He was a Polish fellow named Joe, driving a 1976 Lincoln, emerald green with a white leather top which, ironically, I later wound up buying from him. He took me to see apartments, because that's what I was looking for. The second day I did some searching on my own, using the newspaper. I saw a property where the Tuscany is right now, several apartments on something like ten acres, with a little bar that is still there. I sensed this was pretty close to where the action was. The Flamingo Hilton was still there, and an empty lot where the Barbary Coast is now, and The Caesars was there. That looked to my innocent eyes like a really good location.

*   *   *

We left Las Vegas and visited my brother, Mike, in Los Angeles. Though we had kept in touch, I hadn't seen him in many years and I was overjoyed. At sixteen Mike had announced to my mother that he was going to be a priest. We were a very religious Catholic family but, in spite of that, my mother did not want my brother to become a priest. She was so upset about Mike leaving for the seminary that she couldn't eat and lost a lot of weight. Mike wound up in the seminary for nine years. We visited him only a couple times a year, when we were allowed by the church. Seminarians were sometimes not even allowed to write letters. He would tell us about the public confessions they had to make in front of all the other boys, perhaps to inculcate humility and, obviously, shame. Because of Mike's paralyzed leg, he could not genuflect and, if you can believe it, for that stupid reason he was not allowed to become a priest. Things are different in the Catholic church now. They're having a hard time finding priests. He was allowed, however, to become a Marianist brother. They were teachers. With a master's degree in theology, and a bachelor's and master's in biology, Mike became an understanding, gentle, disciplined young man.

He was transferred from the seminary in Utica, New York to one in Dayton, Ohio. My parents were still in Cleveland, but they could not see him often. During the time that my husband, Dave, and I were in Germany for two years, we got a letter from him saying that he was leaving the seminary. We were all delighted.

Within a year he found himself a pretty girl named Pat Rase who was going to school at Ohio State. He bought a trailer in Columbus, and got a teaching position there. Being "Mr. Frugal"—even more than my parents -- he was driving a used Honda that cost him very little and was just a little larger than a VW. If motor oil was on sale, he would buy an entire case.   He looked for a teaching position in California and got one.

He bought a trailer for $40 to hook onto his little car, packed all his things into that little trailer, including the remainder of a case of oil, and went west.

My brother George and his wife, Pat, had also packed up and made the long haul to Anaheim where Mike got a teaching position.

Mike bought another trailer to live in, and started to invest in real estate while he was still teaching biology. To make a long story short, he finally bought 220 apartments before he decided he could move out of the trailer and into a house.

Mike had an employee who one day was jackhammering up a parking lot on his property. That man wound up working for me at a later time, and he told me that while he was running the jackhammer, Mike came over to him and asked him if he'd had lunch.

"Well, no."

Mike said, "Well, you go have lunch and I'll take over here."

Even with his disabled leg he operated the jackhammer. There was nothing he wouldn't try. He was always determined to do anything anybody else could do. I could not help remembering our bitter childhood in Europe during the war, and I marveled at how far we both had come.

*   *   *

Chuck gave his speech in Los Angeles and we went back to Columbus. I was obsessed with the thought of buying that property I'd seen in Las Vegas. I wrote an offer contract and mailed it to Leo Frey who, I found out, owned a lot of real estate there, but I didn't get a response from him. He owned the Moulin Rouge. About two weeks later I called him and he told me we'd have to talk in person. I spent $369 the following day to take another flight to Vegas. I could not get in to see him and, to this day, I have never seen Leo Frey! After spending so much money on the air fare, I decided I could not leave until I found a place to buy. Frey had one of his salesmen pick me up and drive me around, looking at inferior apartments. I met a guy named Schufee who had a lien on the property I wanted, so it couldn't be sold, but he showed me smaller apartments. I was a bit aggressive, saying I wanted to buy a million-dollar property with $100,000 down. I wound up looking at every apartment that was available in the entire city. In 1976 there were only 250,000 people in Las Vegas, and the salesman ran out of apartments, so he started to show me hotels and motels. I looked at an area right behind Bally's, between the Aladdin and the MGM, which is now Bally's and Planet Hollywood. There were motels there, as well as across the street, and some between Tropicana and Flamingo, behind the Dunes and across the street from the Tam O'Shanter. They were all a bit on the expensive side and they didn't have slot machines. There are different regulations about getting gaming licenses and having slot machines. I learned that if a place is not zoned and grandfathered in, you may have a problem getting slot machines, and also you had to have a hundred rooms, and later on it went to 300 rooms.

I went back home to Columbus a couple of times before August of 1976. My poor girls shuttled between Leon and my parents, and Chuck had them for a short time. I had to get them into school in September and, once they started school, I had to keep them in the same school. I wanted to move them to Las Vegas, but if I didn't buy a place quickly, then I'd have stay home and try again next year. I know how that goes; it may never happen. I had to seize the moment, to return to Las Vegas immediately.

I dreaded leaving Chuck behind while I pursued my dream. The night before I was going to drive my VW from Columbus to Las Vegas I told him, with tears in my eyes, "Tell me not to go, tell me and I won't go." He said, "I can't do that." He knew how important it was for me to go. I loved him more than ever for that.

The Casbah

When I was initially shopping for properties in 1976, I came across the Blue Angel Motel where Eastern and Charleston Streets came together at Fremont. There was a big for-sale sign in front, so I went to the manager's desk and a man came out who claimed to be the owner. When I told him that I was looking for a property to buy, he gave me a price of less than half a million. I thought the price was extremely reasonable. It had a decent amount of land, and my goal was to get any property just so that I would have some form of income to be able to justify moving my girls to Las Vegas and to establish myself. Ideally, I wanted something with a non-restricted license.

I wrote a contract, because there was no realtor involved in this particular property and I went back to him a day later and presented it to him. His response was the first of many I would receive several times afterwards.

"Who are you fronting?"

I said, "I'm not fronting. This is for me. I'm the one that's looking to buy this."

Finally, he said, "Well, I'll give you the name of the person you need to go see about this; his name is Louis Wiener. He's an attorney and he's only in his office at six o'clock in the morning." I wondered if that was because we were in the heat of the summer, but I later heard that Louis Wiener usually kept such ridiculous hours.

The following day I went to Wiener's office at the First Interstate Building downtown. He was a personable guy, like a typical attorney, and he told me that the fellow I had spoken to only pretended he owned the motel. No big deal. Then he gave me the real price, which was approximately twice the amount that was quoted to me. Obviously, I wound up not buying the place, which was fortunate because it was in an extremely undesirable area even in 1976.

Kenny Gragson, a Nevada real estate agent showed me around. His father, Oran Gragson was Mayor for sixteen years, and he eventually became a good friend. Kenny would pick me up at 9:00 in the morning and drop me off at 4:30 or so and say, "Okay, I have to go home and do my pledge duties." I had no idea what that meant, or who he was, really, but he was very nice and accommodating, taking me around to look at properties.

The Casbah Hotel and Casino had opened downtown at First and Lewis in 1963. Within forty-eight hours of visiting the Casbah I bought it. Here's how it happened.

I got a phone call from David Atwell, the founder of Resort Properties, who said, "I have the place for you. Meet me there at ten o'clock tomorrow morning." I had met him once before and I'll never forget walking into his office. While I was standing, he was sitting down, shaking my hand. He impressed me as being a rude, arrogant man. Anyway, I met him next morning at a place called the Casbah, a hundred-room hotel. It was a newer building, three stories high, with a rectangular swimming pool in the center courtyard lobby, and a small bar and a cafe. It was grandfathered in for a non-restricted license. The Jackson family owned it, and they were selling it for $893,000. David showed me five of the hundred rooms that looked decent, clean and quite well appointed. I immediately signed the contract and made it contingent on forty-eight-hour closing, because I either needed to get back home or buy something now. Fifty-three hours later I was behind the front desk!

Most people would say that's impossible, but here's how it worked. If you buy under a contract of sale, which is like a glorified lease, with the seller carrying the mortgage, you wind up owning the property at the end of your contract. Mortgages are similar. The difference between a contract of sale and a regular mortgage is that the bank can try to evict you if you don't make payments. With a contract of sale, three months is the maximum time you can malinger before they throw you out. It takes just a bit longer than a lease would. It can be a risky proposition and it's not for the faint hearted.

The first time I met Danny Jackson to purchase the hotel, Chuck had come to visit for a week-end, and he was standing next to me. Shirley Jackson, Danny's wife, told me years later that Danny would not have sold that hotel to me if Chuck had not been standing at my side, as he assumed he was selling it to Chuck. In a sense, he was selling it to Chuck as well, because I got a power of attorney to put Chuck's name on the property. I felt that we were life partners and we needed to share this adventure jointly. Danny's attitude towards women was typical at that time. It didn't make any difference to me, because I knew I was going to become a success.

Danny Jackson's father had built the hotel in 1963. There were thirteen years left on the mortgage, so it had probably been a twenty-five year mortgage. The Casbah was Danny Jackson Senior's dream but, sadly, the day of the opening he died. There seemed to be health problems among the Jacksons. They were all very slender and they all smoked. Three sons, all younger than thirty, worked the property, Terry, Michael, and Danny. Shirley, <u>Danny's beautiful wife,</u> was at the front desk. I had just turned thirty-three. I didn't consider myself young. When you get married at nineteen, you mature fast. I was proud that three and a half years before, I'd been on food stamps, and now I felt as if I were a millionaire already, buying property for $893,000. By the way, they had to lower the down payment by $7,000 because I didn't have enough money. I had said I would put $100,000 down and I could only come up with $93,000, because I had spent almost six months living on that money while trying to find the right property.

*   *   *

I sat behind the front desk of my newly acquired hotel for fifty-three hours straight, gripped with extreme emotions of fear and doubt, not knowing what was going on and how I was supposed to run the place. Fortunately, the Jacksons stayed on for the next thirty days, so they helped me.

I inherited a hotel bellman named Bucky. I couldn't understand why, in such a small hotel, a bellman was needed. I would have thought that if you're trying to save money, and clients are only paying between $12 and $29 for a room, they wouldn't be likely to tip a bellman. There was an elevator, but the place was only three stories high, so clients could certainly take their luggage up to the third floor. What I did not realize was that there were other activities that occupied the bellman. Prostitutes.

I personally had never seen a prostitute before. I thought maybe they were purple or green, that somehow they would stand out. There was a very sweet girl named Cindy in Room 103 and she was paying ten dollars a day which, to me, meant steady income. Then somebody told me she was a prostitute. I was scared to death to talk to her! First of all, I didn't want her there. My girls were still in Columbus, and when they joined me I planned on sending them to Catholic school. We would have to live in the hotel for a while, because I didn't have any extra money to buy a house. I thought that if the hotel did not have moral standards good enough for me and my girls, then it wasn't good enough for my customers either. I decided I would make it my business to turn it into a decent place.

Then I heard that there was another prostitute in Room 115. I asked the Jacksons if they would ask them to leave. They thought I was crazy, because they generated great income. Their attitude was "We hear no evil, see no evil, speak no evil." At that time Sheriff Ralph Lamb was still in office and, even though prostitution wasn't legal in Las Vegas, it was tolerated. I was embarrassed to think that other people might know that I was running a place with prostitutes and drug pushers. They might even think I was like Miss Kitty, the notorious Madame on Gunsmoke.

Bucky was there to guide tricks to prostitutes, getting a few bucks for it, and I think he was also selling drugs. People had used him as sort of a gofer, maybe to check a room, see if it was clean and vacant, before he sent clients there. Bucky had to go. I got rid of him immediately.

One day while I was at the front desk, the elevator door popped open and a man ran out into the lobby stark naked, yelling "Where is she? Where is she? Where's your exit?" The front door was right there, so we pointed that way, and I shouted to Deon, the front desk manager, "Go see if you can find a coat or something for this man." But before he could, the guy went running out the front door. A prostitute had robbed him and taken his clothing so he wouldn't be able to run after her, but that didn't stop the guy.

88

He ran after her, naked as he was. What could we do about it? Nothing.

Then there was the day that I was at the front desk when I saw a young man coming from the hallway wearing a mask! And it wasn't Halloween. He pointed a gun at me and said, "Give me all the money from the drawer." He was one of our tenants. I recognized the guy from his body posture, in the same way that you can recognize someone you know from behind. I called him by name, and he took off out the bar door. I found such experiences total shocking. I had never before met anybody who had been in jail or was a criminal. I had to conclude, naive as it sounds, that such people were motivated by poverty, not a real wish to commit crimes.

*   *   *

When I bought the Casbah, I asked Chuck for power of attorney. Although we weren't legally married, he was the man I wanted to spend the rest of my life with. He came out to visit, but warned me he wouldn't be staying long. I was afraid to even ask him what was happening, but I sensed pressure building up until the Sunday he was leaving. That's when he broke the news to me that he did not want any part of my new life. He was a civil structural engineer, well educated and he had a job back in Columbus. He had a very hard time dealing with our low-class clientele.

I went into the back room with tears streaming down my face and started to write an agreement to quit claim him off the deed. He actually had $40,000 of his money invested, that he had earned when I had showed him what to invest in. I drafted the quit claim for $60,000, and asked him what interest rate he wanted. He replied, "I don't want any." But I insisted. "Eight percent." I typed those words with an old-fashion typewriter where you had to push down hard on the keys and the "O" would cut a hole in the paper. I drew up an agreement to pay him monthly payments for $60,000 with eight percent interest. He signed it and I took him to the airport.

I was heart broken. I felt like I was living in a castle, in a dream world, but without my prince. He didn't call me for two weeks. When he finally called, however, he talked about coming back.

I met five guys who were gamblers, big, cigar-smoking guys who belonged to the Las Vegas Country Club and knew Moe Dalitz, a gangster casino owner and a philanthropist who was often referred to as "Mr. Las Vegas." Andrew Vacilla was one of the cigar smokers. He owned a small motel on First Street and introduced himself as one of the neighbors. A few months after I took over the Casbah, when we were chatting and I told him I was thirty-three, he said, "You are not." I pulled my driver's license out and showed it to Andrew. The incredulous look he gave me said it all. I guess I looked older because I worked so hard and I wasn't getting enough sleep. I lived in the hotel by myself and had nobody. Chuck and my kids were still back in Columbus. Those first six weeks of running the hotel alone were very stressful.

My daughters were staying with Leon, and I spoke to them once a week.

"Oh, Mommy, we want to see you," they'd say, breaking my heart.

"Oh, honey, I want to see you, too," I'd tell them. I missed them so much and wanted to be with them. I actually had custody of them, though Leon had adopted Bridgett. I decided I had to go get them.

"Do you want to come out and be with Mommy?"

"Oh, yes, yes, we want to!"

"Okay, now, if I come and get you, you're going to come with me, no questions asked, right?"

"Yes, Mommy, we will."

They had told me they were having horseback riding lessons on Saturdays. I flew to Columbus at seven o'clock on a Saturday morning, rented a car, and arrived at the ranch where they were riding. Chuck was there to help me. As soon as they saw me, Bridgett and Leah came running to me, and I pushed them into the back seat of the car. Then I saw a two-year-old child in the corral, a child named Tobi whom Leon had fathered with the wife he left me for. That baby was standing there, staring, in an open arena with horses. I could not leave her there alone. I piled her into the car with the girls, and took her back to Leon. When he realized I was taking my girls, he started pulling at the car doors, the kids were crying, and it was a frightful scene. I finally drove away directly to the airport. I hid in the bathroom with my two little girls, scared to death that someone would accuse me of kidnapping. We finally got on that plane. We made it back to Las Vegas at eleven o'clock that night. I could breathe again, because once I had them in my possession I was okay. I had legal custody.

Leah was six years old, and the first thing she saw was the pool in the courtyard. She loved that pool. She would dive into the shallow end and pull herself around, holding on to the sides with her little fingers as if she were playing piano on the tile edges. Bridgett was thirteen and she was at that miserable teen age, but I had them with me at last, and they seemed happy about it. I was overjoyed.

I had taken Room 320, the largest room in the hotel with a king-size bed and a little sofa. There was also an entry hall that I divided into two little areas for the girls. I felt somewhat secure, but still I was worried, because there were some really crazy people around. As a matter of fact, our very finest, most polite customer who came into the cafe worked for Jerry Herbst, who was the owner of "Terrible Herbst," which ran gasoline stations, retail operations and casinos. The ARCO station, which is still there at the northeast corner of Lewis and Main Street right next to City Hall, was owned by Jerry Herbst. Occasionally, he brought his workers into the bar at five o'clock. The customer we thought was so nice would come in and show us pictures of his nieces and nephews, and he was very friendly to my girls, but one day I found out that he was in jail, and that Jerry Herbst was bailing him out. I asked what he was in jail for, and was told it was for child molestation. I was horrified! Thank God he never came back into our cafe again.

Then one day I couldn't find Leah. I was working the front desk, three different people were talking to me while I was still trying to keep an eye on her, and suddenly she wasn't there. I started running through the hotel, asking everybody if they'd seen her. I walked up and down the street, beside myself, especially after hearing about that child molester. I finally found her with a bookkeeper couple who lived in the apartments next door. I couldn't stop hugging her, I was so scared and so relieved to find her.

Another time I had worked twenty-four hours straight with no sleep, so went upstairs in the afternoon for a nap but, soon after, people came knocking on the door and shouting, "Leah had an accident." They carried her up to me, and her arm was like a Z. I immediately got dressed and drove her to the emergency room. The doctor straightened her arm and put it in a cast, making sure she could move her fingers. Leah thought that might be fun, but she soon found out that having a cast wasn't all that great.

During the first year of owning the Casbah Hotel, the Knights Inn was across the street. A young couple who had two little girls, one of whom was the same age as Leah, managed the place. On occasion the two girls got together. One day I noticed that Leah's new friend had black and blue marks on her face and arm. She gave me excuses, saying she had run into a door. She confided to Leah, though, that her father beat her, but she was forbidden to tell anyone for fear of worse beatings. On the other hand, the mother seemed to be a kind, caring woman. We didn't know how to handle this, and we avoided them until one afternoon I saw the man having an altercation with another man in the middle of the street. They were fighting so violently that I thought that the girl's father was going to kill the other man. He wound up beating him badly, and left him lying in the middle of the street. I called the police and the ambulance, but the father was nowhere to be found. We didn't see the family after that, and presumed they had moved away. I was learning that Las Vegas would have many hard lessons.

*　　*　　*

I couldn't bear being separated from Chuck. A little time passed and we were talking once a week, and he promised he'd come out again for a week-end. Halloween, his birthday, was approaching. A week before, he told me he was flying out. When I left the desk to go to the airport, I wondered if he was going to be on that plane, because he had promised before and didn't come. I had not seen him since August and now it was October 31. When I saw him walk off that plane, I was filled with joy.

*　　*　　*

There were many surprises in store for me as the new owner of a hotel/casino. Maybe the most important surprise that first year unfolded as the year progressed into December and business dropped off sharply. I hadn't realize that after Thanksgiving business falls off until Valentine's Day. I mean things just dried up, especially my cash. Then I got a notice that my power was going to be turned off, because I hadn't paid the electric bill. I asked Chuck, "What about the people you sold our house to in Columbus? How come we're not getting money from them?" He admitted that he had never sold that house; he had only leased it for a year. I was outraged. I forced the issue to the point when I said, "Either get them to give us more money or you get out." I should have known better than to give an ultimatum. He left. He didn't pack anything; he just left. His parting shot was "I will never come back to this hotel again." The next day I drove the downtown streets looking for him. I was very worried about him. Taking my daughter to school, I drove down Bonneville, and on Seventh Street I saw a house with a for-sale sign. I took the number and on my way back to the hotel I stopped and called. At ten o'clock that morning I went and looked at the house, 4,000 square feet with a large front lawn, a fireplace and a large open area in back. I made an offer with a contract of sale for $60,000. We had to close at five o'clock that afternoon when I gave them $5,000. All the while, I was thinking that I had to buy a house to get Chuck back, whatever it took – for love or money. In this case, for love *and* money.

I kept searching for him all over town. It took almost a week before I spotted him. He obviously had been on the streets, because his face was tan and his lips were blistered with sunburn. I had never seen him in such condition, and he never told me what happened during that week. I approached him, hopefully. "I found a house. You can come back to the house and you don't have to worry about coming to the hotel." He agreed, relieved, I think, but withdrawn, licking wounds I'd inflicted upon him, for which it was hard to forgive myself.

Chuck eventually took a year leave of absence from the Battelle Institute to follow me to Las Vegas. That was a daring, grand sacrifice for him. He immediately looked for a job as an engineer at the Nevada Nuclear Devices Test Site, which was certainly not up to the caliber of work that he had been doing with the Battelle Institute, but he got the job, and now we had a home.

We moved out of the hotel, though I worried about how I was going to manage -- there was always so much going on there -- but the house was less than a mile from the hotel, and I tried to reassure myself that it would work.

What was nice about the house is that it had a separate entrance with a maid's quarters. I hired a maid who took the girls to school and met them afterwards. She lived there with her son, who was about Leah's age, and her husband. One Sunday afternoon, family day, we all went out to a park and had a picnic and a lovely time. When we came back home, the boy later came to us and said to Chuck, "My dad said he's going to whip you." At first, I ignored it, but the boy went back to his house again and he came back again and said, "My dad said he wants you to come over there; he's going to whip you."

Chuck was the most peaceable guy. He's a typical academic type, prim and proper, and he would walk away from trouble, but when the boy came back the third time, Chuck went over there. I begged him not to go. They wound up on the front lawn fighting, and the neighbors called the police. I had no idea that in a domestic violence situation, one person usually goes to jail. The policeman asked whether Chuck and I were married and he admitted that we were not. I'd always been very worried about that issue. The maid's husband was obviously more familiar with the law than we were, because as soon as the police showed up he pretended to be an innocent victim. Chuck yelled, "You hypocrite, you. Now you're going to act like an angel? Now you're not going to attack me?" The police didn't like Chuck's behavior, and one of them hit him on his legs, and took him to jail, while the other guy quietly watched. I was mortified, and fearful for Chuck, but the worst part was when I looked up and saw Leah in the window, watching it all. We were not that kind of people. All I can say is, when you deal with garbage, sometimes you pick up the smell.

94

* * *

One day I came home and found Leah with her friend, Laura Shaffer, Charlie Shaffer's daughter. Charlie was a well-known a piano player in town. The girls were best friends, and often they would be in the pool with four other kids and I'd find smeared spaghetti plates on the table. She had figured out how to boil spaghetti and heat up a jar of Ragu, which delighted me. One day, Leah said, "We've been getting calls from a man who's leaving us dirty messages and we recorded it." I was impressed. "Wow, are you guys smart! How wonderful you recorded his message. Let me hear it." The voice was that of my maintenance man, Frank. My heart started to pump. I was so angry I didn't know what to do and could hardly control myself. Chuck came home and he listened to it and recognized Frank's voice, too. At that moment the phone rang. I picked it up and Frank was on the line asking for Leah. I yelled, "Frank, how dare you. I don't want to see your face again, you rotten so-and-so." Frank had worked for me for a couple of years and I would never have thought him capable of such a thing. It really shook me up. Frank never returned to the hotel, but he was still walking around the streets and I was told later that he used the Huntridge Theater to molest children. Presumably, he'd been arrested.

We occasionally found guns in the hotel, left between mattresses or elsewhere. and we'd report them to the police. If the police didn't find an owner, they'd give the guns back to us, so we owned a few. I think that if you're in a situation where you might have to defend yourself, it's a smart idea to own a gun, but only when you're thinking straight. In the situation with Frank, however, I could not control my fury, so I stayed away from the guns.

* * *

I worried about money constantly. In the morning, after I took the girls to school, I would head for the hotel. Sometimes I got up earlier than school time, like five o'clock, went to the hotel and then came back for them. My work day started with a call into the bank in the morning to make sure checks cleared. I would write checks based on the

95

income of the previous day that was deposited the next morning. We had to get the cash in before ten o'clock, so the checks wouldn't bounce. That rarely happened, but I'd be charged the same as on a bounced check if we didn't have enough cash in at nine a.m. when the bank opened. At ten a.m. they would make a decision of whether they were going to return checks or pay them.

Before 1980, it was legal to have a microphone provided by AT&T hidden under the front desk, so that wherever I was, even at home, I could listen to what was going on in the hotel. That sort of wire tapping became illegal later, but it was a great advantage for me, as I could overhear how a new employee handled a customer, which enabled me to evaluate that person. I think the older employees became suspicious of being overheard, and they always conducted themselves in a professional way. I appreciated it not only for screening new employees, but as a tool for detecting potential robberies, as happened once when I'd already been at the hotel for ten hours and was home preparing dinner. I heard a new Australian front desk clerk talking nervously to a girlfriend and some other guy in the lobby. I listened very closely to what they were saying.

"Well, now, if we leave the door open, then they'll think that somebody came in and robbed the front desk. We'll take the money and head for the airport."

As soon as I heard that, I called the police and told them to meet me at the hotel, and I took off. The policeman met me there and he very casually picked up his report sheet and started writing, asking my name, etc. Obviously, the situation was uneventful for him, while I was frantic.

"Sir, they went to the airport; we've got to get them before they get on a plane. I heard them; they went to the airport."

He calmly stated, "Well, we've got to fill out this information here first."

I left him at the front desk. "I'm sorry, I have to go."

I took off and sped to the airport, looking for the thieves. I couldn't find them until I asked a policeman to look into the men's room and that's where we found them, and they were arrested. That would have never happened if I hadn't pursued them myself.

*   *   *

Many dramas surrounded the hiring and firing of employees that constantly challenged my old-fashioned notions of working people. The Casbah was much too small to be unionized. The Culinary Union and others usually went to bigger properties. I only had fifteen employees at the beginning, because the bar was leased, and so was the coffee shop. Bobby Lee, who was a chef at one of the other hotels, wanted to have his own restaurant, and I was looking for someone to run our small restaurant that was in the bar itself. Since the bar was open twenty-four hours, we needed to serve some sort of food beyond the typical bar snacks. I offered free rent and utilities to Bobby Lee, in order to provide decent food to our customers. He wore crisp white chef jackets and a toque, and even had his name embroidered on his shirt. He ran our restaurant very well. One night he and some other customers and employees went up to the Golden Nugget for a good steak, which was something he did not serve. Next day I was shocked to hear that Bobby Lee had choked on his steak and died! I felt so sorry about such a strange accident, and I doubted I'd ever find such a great chef again.

We had a lovely bartender called Miss Kim, a Chinese widow, who actually didn't need to work. She drove a Cadillac. She was like a mother to a lot of our customers. As a matter of fact, when some of them got their monthly retirement or Social Security check and they knew they weren't disciplined enough to make that money last through the end of the month, they'd ask Kim to hold the money for them, and dole out a certain amount once a week. Of course, some of them might ask three times a day, because they were totally uncontrolled about spending money, but Miss Kim was strict.

I told her Kim that I was looking for a cook to run the restaurant twenty-four hours a day on a one-year lease, and she told me she thought she knew someone, but he was a Chinese man who did not speak English. I said, "Well, people can point to the menu. Bring him on in." That's how much I trusted Kim. The man she brought to me was sixty-five or older and he kept that restaurant open for 365 days twenty-four hours a day all by himself. To the best of my knowledge, he hardly ever left it. I think he slept

97

on a mat on the floor. When his lease expired, along with his commitment to me, he disappeared, and I never saw him again.

*   *   *

The first Thanksgiving that I owned the hotel, I had my immediate family with me, but I missed my parents and siblings. I looked around and realized that all my employees who were working that day were going to be without their families and, in many cases, they lived alone, so I decided to make Thanksgiving dinner.

I hadn't taken over the bar restaurant yet, but I had one stove in the back manager's office and I roasted a big turkey. I invited all my employees, plus our regular customers to Thanksgiving dinner. I was surprised that many people asked if they could bring something, but I said they didn't need to. We had a wonderful celebration. When the second Thanksgiving rolled around, employees asked if I was going to bake another turkey, so I did. It wound up as a tradition every Thanksgiving. Even when my own parents invited me to join them for Thanksgiving, I didn't want to fly that distance, and I didn't want to disappoint my employees.

Two years after I took over the hotel, I bought the lease for the bar. Now I had the bar and a restaurant and I was able to have our Thanksgiving dinner buffet in there. I had to add one more turkey every year, because now bar customers came. What was amazing was that word got out and we had people I'd never met before coming in off the street. I roasted turkeys at home and at the hotel and in every oven I could find, and I personally carved all of them. It was very rewarding to see their happy faces. They could have gone to the Salvation Army or other soup kitchens, but they came to us. I was roasting seven turkeys before I was forced to limit the number of my guests.

*   *   *

I inherited some characters who had been living in the hotel. Herb Lambeck was in Room 108. He was an odds maker, a single Jewish man who would go downtown and set the odds for different sports betting casinos. Herb was well known in the casino business. He lived alone, but my employees told me that Herb had a lady visitor once a week and she only stayed for about fifteen minutes. You learn a lot about people living under your roof.

Two aunts of Danny Jackson Senior, who later died, lived in larger rooms, 235 and 335. When I took over the hotel, they had to pay me. They required daily room service, so initially we established a figure, probably about ten dollars a day. They were accustomed to being treated well, because I think they had given some investment money to purchase the property, so I suppose they had a right to feel like the place was partly theirs.

We also had certain regular guests. There was a guy named Sid, a small meek Jewish guy who came once a year. He was so sweet, cute and polite, almost effeminate. His best friend was Cindy, who had formerly occupied 103. We couldn't lose Sid and we couldn't tell him who to bring into his room.

There was a lovely customer named Don from North Dakota. Don had never been married. On occasion, when his mother was alive, he brought her to stay at my hotel. But his mother passed away, and afterwards he came by himself every year and would spend several months with us. He was a wonderful bar customer who tipped generously, and was always in that happy retirement, vacation mood. A girl named Deedee frequented the bar, and some people hinted she might be selling her services, but she denied it. The truth came out one day when she came to me and said, "Oh, I've got to tell you about Don. He took me into his room and I thought he expected me to please him but, in fact, he pleased me and then paid me!" Well, I thought that was their business, and I was still always glad to see Don, as well as Deedee.

Sometimes I felt almost manic depressive, high and happy about my purchase, but terrified, because there was so much I didn't know, and I realized that I was naive about people's honesty. I never thought of the possibility of someone breaking into a room. It took me years to discover that one of my workers would take a screwdriver and unscrew the clip that held a door chain, go into a room where people were sleeping and steal from them.

All our personal things were shipped from Columbus while we were still living at the hotel, and I put them into the room closest to the front desk. I finally realized that things weren't secure when I discovered that someone had gone into that room and rummaged through our things. I couldn't believe it, as I was at the front desk twelve hours a day, and couldn't imagine someone sneaking past me. I was saddest about the loss of a black velvet peasant vest that my grandmother had embroidered with mountain flowers. I had worn that vest for Bavarian dancing. Everything else could have been replaced, but not that beautiful vest that had such sentimental value. I couldn't understand how people could be so low.

My head was spinning, trying to learn the different tricks of the trade. I felt protective of hotel customers, and dismayed if anything bad happened to them. The lobby was my living room and I would invite them into it, try to make them comfortable and give them all the service I could, with a smile, hoping they'd want to come back.

One time I had a customer on the week-end who was paying $29.95 for his room. He came to the desk and said, "I want my money back; my toilet doesn't flush." Well, do you think I wanted to give back the $29.95? No way. I had never looked inside a toilet before, but I went to that bathroom and took off the cover, saw a chain and a little loop and it looked to me like they might belong together, but there was no hook to do it. I figured out that a paperclip would probably work. I went to the office, got a paperclip, hooked the parts together and said, "There it is for you, sir. Thank you very much for staying with us."

I learned how to do almost everything. If there was a problem with the air-conditioning, I was up there with the repair man trying to learn how to fix it. So many times it was just common sense. Sometimes you could hit a reset button and it would be okay. Knowing how to fix things was gratifying.

When the elevator repairman came, I followed him, and rode on top of the elevator with him. He showed me what the security stops were, which I found reassuring, because what I didn't know is what I feared. What if the elevator dropped and killed somebody. Because I was always short of cash, things like the elevator breaking down would be a major concern, as it cost $120 an hour to fix it. I used to joke that in my next life I was going to come back as an elevator repairman, because they make such a ridiculous amount of money. Fortunately, I learned quite a lot about repairing elevators. Every elevator door has a small keyhole about the size of a dime. Initially, I had an instrument like a key to open that door. It had a red tape that said "Do not remove, elevator door opener." But it somehow disappeared, and could never be found. We sometimes had the fire department come and open the doors with a crowbar. I'd seethe about how expensive it was to repair those doors that could have been opened so easily with that little key. I finally figured out how to take a clothes hanger and twist it into a little Z that I'd finagle around in the lock, and it worked! Sometimes when I couldn't afford to get the elevator going, or didn't have time to fool with it, I'd put an "out of order" sign on it and hope and pray that a good weekend would come along and we'd make more money and get it fixed. Sometimes the elevator would be down for months, because I couldn't afford to fix it. We weren't required to have a working elevator in a three-story building, so we put people couldn't walk the stairs on the first floor.

One time I got on top of the elevator and played with different buttons, but I touched a wire that sparked and it blew out something. That scared me, but it wasn't any worse than it was before, so it waited to repair it until months later.

One of the pleasures of moving to Nevada was the prospect that it was desert country, and I presumed it never rained there. I thought that would be wonderful, because it rained fifty percent of the time back in Ohio. And then the rains came! It poured in all the way through three floors from the roof to the lobby. I stared at it from the front desk, frantically wondering what to do. I was wearing turquoise high heels with a matching outfit, because of course I always wanted to look my best at the front desk. Somebody told me that there was a roofing material called Wet Patch that could be applied even while it was raining. I dashed out to Von Tobel's, the only hardware store in town, and bought five gallons of Wet Patch. I climbed up onto the flat roof in my high heels and dumped the whole five gallons into the lowest part where I thought it was leaking through to the lobby. That took care of about ninety percent of the leak. Completely drenched, I came back into the lobby looking like something the cat dragged in, but I solved the problem!

I believe in the old saying "a stitch in time saves nine," and I knew that the leak in the roof was only going to get bigger and I could imagine mold and repairs down the road. I learned thirteen ways to not to fix a roof, because I tried that many. I hired professionals, thinking they'd know how to do it. That was not the case. The other thing is that a flat roof turns from a puddle into a pond. We even put drains in to divert water to run off. I bought two-by-six beams, put them up and tried to create a pitch, then I used an asphalt roofing material that came in a roll, and I went up onto the roof and torched that material on, dressed, of course, for the front desk. It finally worked.

The first time a slot machine broke, I called IGT (International Game Technology), and they charged me $50. A repairman came in, had no tools on him at all, looked inside the machine, and the only thing I could see was that when his hand came out of the machine he had a little pocket screwdriver. I gave him the $50 and he left. I wondered if I could do that. When he came in next time I asked him to show me what he was doing. Guys are much more receptive to showing a woman, probably showing off, thinking I wouldn't understand. But I did.

Basically, I would say that 90% of all slot problems were coin jams, or somebody tried using a Canadian coin or a slug. I slowly started to take care of all the coin jams, then learned more intricate things, like how to replace some of the machine parts. Sometimes it worked and sometimes it didn't, in which case I'd have to call the repair men. All the time they were working I'd be watching, so that I could save that money next time.

A lot of people tried to cheat the slot machines. The mechanism of the machines was coin operated; it did not take dollar bills. The slot machines cheats would drill a little hole in a quarter, then they would tie the quarter onto a piece of nylon wire, something like a crochet hook. They'd put this string around their index finger and bob the quarter until it triggered a little mechanism inside the machine. They'd pretend to be playing as they hovered over the slot machine, and they'd hit jackpots until the machine was emptied. The hoppers inside the machines were filled with $200 to $500 each, so they were able to get away with that much money. If the machine was empty, it would freeze, so the cheat would immediately take his money and run. If the machine didn't pay the person enough money, he'd go to the bartender and complain that the machine had shorted him. Then we would write a detailed ticket and pay them. Usually somebody who's cheating a slot machine doesn't draw attention to himself, he just disappears.

One afternoon I observed a girl who appeared to be cheating. I grabbed her fingers, because I had to have that nylon string for evidence. I tried to hold onto her until the police came, but I wasn't strong enough, and she got away. At least I figured that one wasn't going to come back again.

I learned from IGT how to deal with slot machine cheats. I'd find coins with a hole in them, and I'd slowly investigate until I found out who was using them. I picked up information wherever I could, because though there were schools for dealers, there weren't any for casino owners. Whenever I found quarters with holes in them, it was my responsibility to destroy them. I'd wrap them up and throw them into the trash because, in reality, not even banks wanted mutilated money.

*   *   *

There was no parking lot at the Casbah, so people had to park on the street, which was allowed at that time, but they didn't feel secure there. An empty lot on the northeast side was a parking lot owned by the Von Tobels, so I rented their space for parking. Then I met a fellow named Jack Keiser, who was a loan officer for Valley Bank, which had been the Bank of Las Vegas previously, and was acquired by Bank of America in 1992. The Valley Bank had been owned by Jerry Mack and E. Parry Thomas, who built the

Thomas and Mack Center. By the way, Jerry Mack custom built my own house in 1957. I still live in that house. Jack talked to me about their need for extra parking space for the bank, so I made a deal with him to allow parking for their employees in the space I was renting.

I finally negotiated a car repair shop at the southeast corner of Lewis and Main Street owned by an attorney. We went back and forth about the price. As usual, I never had enough money down, but we finally agreed on a figure and I bought that property and made payments to him.

As part of my deal of eight percent interest on $800,000 in thirteen years, there was a balloon payment of $50,000 after one year. I told Jack about it, and he offered to lend me that sum on a signature loan. Not only did he sit across from me at his desk and tell me that, but he added, "I'm going to type it up right now, the promise of this loan, so that if something happens to me when I leave this building, you can feel secure that you've got that deposit." I wondered what was behind that ominous comment. Words cannot describe the relief of having that burden lifted from my shoulders. I wanted to do something for Jack, reflecting, I suppose, my mother's sense of obligation to repay a favor, but giving gifts to bankers was not allowed. I found out where he lived with his wife, and at Christmas time I sent things to them anonymously, like a case of wine. Every year I sent some gift. He's not with the bank anymore and I haven't seen him since 1993 or '94. I would love to ask him if he ever wondered who those gifts came from, though he certainly had bigger fish to fry than me, and he must have done a lot of favors for a lot of people. To me, anonymous giving is really the highest form of giving.

I was fortunate that Jack had offered me a loan to avoid defaulting on my balloon payment. Such contracts can make a borrower very vulnerable. Balloon payments are stipulated for many different reasons, sometimes just to throw a banana peel in front of you, or because there's not enough money down, or because the lenders themselves have a balloon payment or other obligations.

Vacation Village used to be farther down on Las Vegas Boulevard, in the median between I-15 going north and south. It was quite an expansive property owned by a family that included an attorney and an accountant. I had met one of the sisters – four family members owned the property -- who was very active in the Village's management. They took out a one million dollar loan for one year. When that loan became due and they could not pay it, the mortgage holder called the note, and auctioned off the property to get that million. That property was worth 23 million dollars and they lost it, because the one million dollar loan was called instead of being renewed. I was at the auction of that property. Bob Stupak was there and so was Kenny Gragson and Al Levy. I had the pleasure of meeting the woman manager, who became a friend of mine. My heart ached for her. Here was another sad situation where the father had put so much work into his project, built it up, passed it onto the kids and then lost it all.

In 1976 downtown Las Vegas was frequented by all the locals. Bob Bigelow owned the El Toro Motel, which he later named The Daisy, behind me on Main Street. The Apache was owned by Barbara and Moshe Ram. Barbara was a gynecologist from Israel and they had come to this country for a new life in 1976. They were in the bedspread business and I wound up meeting them as a result of buying several bedspreads from them and we became very dear friends. I grieved when Moshe passed away a year or so ago.

Binion's was very popular. The doors were wide open, so you could just walk in. The old Golden Nugget was popular, too. That year they hired Kenny Rogers to perform there. I think Steve Wynn took it over. His father was a major investor who started to build and build, doing all of us downtown owners a wonderful favor. There were approximately twelve hotel/casinos, as there are right now. They'd tear an old one down and build a new one. Actually, Binion's only had a hundred hotel rooms on the Casino Center/Second Street and Fremont corner on the northwest side. The Mint high rise was right next to it. When they bought The Mint —I was so jealous of this— they simply knocked a hole in between the two buildings and connected them, so they didn't need to apply for licensing. If you make a presentation to the Gaming Control Board that formally requests adding tables or additional floor space, presenting a floor plan and specifying the number of slot machines, the formal request is never denied. They had a non-restricted license already, so they didn't have to go through any investigations by the Gaming Control Board. Whenever you go in front of the Gaming Control Board, enormous amounts of money are involved; payments to attorneys, and a huge sum to an accountant for a financial Proforma as well, along with a floor plan and documented history of the place. Even though they're constantly monitoring you, it's like there's an extra investigation, and there is never a guarantee that it's going to go the way that you want it to.

The main reason I was so elated to find the Casbah Hotel was because it had a hundred rooms and was grandfathered in for a non-restricted license. Grandfathered in does not mean zoning, but it's similar, and affects whether or not the property can have a non-restricted casino license. A restricted license allows fifteen machines or less. The rules and regulations on a restricted license, as well as taxes, are totally different. If you have fifteen machines or more, you need a different license with different regulations and totally different internal controls. Requirements are similar to a publicly held company where details have to be precise. Navigating rules and regulations is complicated, and investigation is intense.

The first investigation into my life dated back twenty years before, when I was in eighth grade, which struck me as absurd. The Gaming Control Board would look for records of criminal activity or other legal problems. These days, if you challenge a speeding ticket, they have on computer all the tickets you've had for the last twenty years. But that was not the computer age and Gaming Control would seek information from, for example, the FBI, but it also conducts its own investigation and does not share information with other entities like the IRS. Normally, the IRS doesn't even bother you if you have a non-restricted license, because Gaming Control is so strict. Today I am amazed by the fact that companies like Station Casinos and The M went into bankruptcy, and then a family member wound up owning the property. As far as I'm concerned, that would be using the court system for personal gain and to avoid paying debts you should be responsible for. I am looking at that situation from a distance and don't know the specifics, but I know that bankruptcy is not the way to dump debts that you created and be absolved of paying them. I can't imagine them allowing me to do anything like that, because they gave me such a hard time over insignificant debt payments.

You actually have to get permission from Gaming Control to buy property, because you have more than a five percent interest where gaming is going to take place. At the Casbah there were slot machines already in the bar, but the slot machines were owned by a route company that has its own license to go into different places -- 7-Elevens, different bars and so on. My bar was actually leased by a man named Woodie, who owned Carlson Electric, a motor repair shop on Main Street, so Woodie became my tenant.

Because the non-restricted license was grandfathered in, I would be able to pursue my dream of having a casino, a grand dream that years ago might have seemed unattainable, but that never stopped me. I reminded myself that three and a half years before, I had been on food stamps and here I was with a debt of $800,000 at eight percent interest for thirteen years. My thinking about real estate is that today it takes keen intelligence to make the correct real estate decision, but it's still a wonderful investment. Before Las Vegas, $15,000 a year was the most I ever earned during the only two years of my young life that I earned more than minimum wage. Now I looked at my thirteen-year mortgage knowing that it would be worth at least $1.3 million, because real estate was booming. Now I earned $100,000 a year that I could put money into savings and future investments that I could pyramid.

In any commercial property, if your tenants pay your mortgage, you're all set. How much property do you want to own? Well, I'd want to own the whole city. Why not? The only thing I had to worry about was that monthly mortgage payment, even before utilities and employee salaries. If I were starving, I'd still make those payments first.

I also looked into the Klondike Inn, south of Russell on the east side of the street, the last property before Howard Hughes' airplane runway. He owned many hotels in Las Vegas and spent his later years there as a recluse. John and Ellen Woodrum had purchased the property for only $15,000 that they had borrowed from the owner of the Big Boy restaurant in Baker, California. The Klondike Inn was across the street on the Strip where the Mandalay Bay is now, which made it desirable. It had almost five acres and something like 150 - 180 rooms. It cost more than a million or more. I offered my measly $100,000, and John Woodrum was open to accepting my offer. He had bought it for only $15,000 down, because the owner who ran junkets between Hawaii and Las Vegas gave it to a relative to run and they weren't making the payments, so he gave this great deal to John. John was a salesman who had worked for the Boyd group. He could sell snow to Eskimos. He had his whole family with him, including a little boy, about whom he said, "My biggest problem in life is going to be to keep this boy out of jail." That comment filled me with a sense of foreboding; I couldn't understand a parent feeling that way about his child.

I put my offer in writing, and he contacted the carrier of the mortgage because, in reality, he was not able to sell it on his own. The mortgage holder becomes almost a partner, so I assumed that the next time that man came to town he would take a look at my offer. When he arrived, he stayed in the top suite of the MGM, which is now Bally's, and I went to see him there with the real estate man who was representing the property. We walked into the suite and saw a big round tub in the center of the room. An Asian man came in, looked at me silently, then said, "I'll get back to you later." In fact, he brushed me off, without allowing me to speak, probably because I was a woman.

I always faced challenges as a woman. People often looked at me in disbelief, as if wondering what I was doing there. When I first bought the hotel in 1976 we had a Downtown Progress Association meeting in the early fall. All the owners of downtown properties were there. I saw a cocky guy leaning up against the wall, lauding the benefits of prostitution. I spoke against prostitution, while he encouraged it. I thought he was low-class and I wondered how we'd ever get rid of prostitution if everybody thought like him. That was my first encounter with Ted Binion. He was a wealthy U.S. gambling executive and one of the sons of famed Las Vegas casino magnate, Lester "Benny" Binion, owner of Binion's Horseshoe.

The only connection I had for promoting my hotel was the Chamber of Commerce and the Convention Visitors Authority. In 1980 I went with the Las Vegas Convention and Visitors Authority to South America with Bill Briare, who was mayor at the time, and his wife, and Bill Trent, who owned the Maxim at the time, and Bill Boyd. He had just taken over for his father who was still alive. We went to Caracas, Venezuela; Bogotá, Colombia; and Rio de Janeiro. We had parties at each of those places, promoting Las Vegas. I offered a week free stay at the Casbah. People we had met actually came and stayed with me within a matter of a month or two. That was exciting!

Other than the Convention Visitors Authority, the Downtown Progress Association was like a tight-knit family, including the Binions. By the way, Jack Binion lived across the street from my house for twenty-two years. When I heard Ted had died, the first thing I guessed was that he had drug overdosed, but who knows. His death has been a subject of controversy. His girlfriend, Sandra Murphy, and her lover, Rick Tabish, were initially charged and convicted in Binion's death, but were later granted a new trial and acquitted of murder charges.

And then there was Benny Binion's daughter, Barbara. I came into my hotel early one morning and was told there had been an incident the previous night. Apparently, Barbara went up to Room 208 and took a man with her. An hour or so later she called security thugs from The Horseshoe and they went up to the room and beat up the man badly, dragged him out into the hallway, and Barbara left with her body guards. That room looked like they had painted the walls with blood, and we called an ambulance for the guy in the hallway. This happened many times. She would bring different guys in, and I'm sure they were doing drugs, but I wish she hadn't chosen to do this in my hotel.

The response I got from many people that I approached to conduct business with was "What experience do you have? Have you ever done this before?"

One guy asked me, "What's the most money you've ever earned? What makes you think you can do this?"

Even Jackie Gaughan said to me in front of Linda, his secretary, "Don't buy it. You're not going to make it. Do you know how many times I've taken this property back? Nobody else could make it; what makes you think you can?" In the end, I was the only one who didn't give it back to him. I eventually had the pleasure of giving Jackie a check in full payment when I sold my hotels twelve years later.

*   *   *

Though I spent much of my life stressed about money, afraid that maybe I was too ambitious, I always had some kind of faith in myself, a conviction that I would succeed. What would we do and what would we dream if we thought we couldn't fail?

In spite of my seeming self-confidence, though, I always had an inferiority complex. I was always afraid to share my dreams. I listened to many motivational speakers. Brian Tracy advised people not to share their dreams with others, because they're might laugh at them. I couldn't tell my parents; I couldn't tell my brothers and some of my friends, because I was afraid they might laugh. They had no idea how expensive my small budget hotel was or how valuable.

In 1985 I joined the Toastmasters Club through a friend, Dawn Lundquist. She had great artistic talent, but she was working with computers and doing telemarketing, which she hated to admit. She came in on a New Year's weekend all excited. She said she had gone to a seminar in San Diego and had done a fire walk.

"You did what?"

"I walked with bare feet on a bed of hot coals."

I couldn't believe it. She told me about Anthony Robbins, a young man who taught people to walk on fire. I thought the idea was absolutely fascinating. She pushed me to go try it myself, so I made plans to go. I mentioned it to Chuck, but he was always much more skeptical of such things. I was a freer spirit, interested in spiritual and psychological issues. I wanted to try the fire walk. I paid the $300 for the weekend, and Dawn shared a room with me.

On a Friday night we got there at about seven o'clock. The first that happened was that Robbins led us to the second floor of the hotel where there was a concrete deck, and built a fire on it before we went back inside. He gave a really inspiring self-help speech, talking about the possibility that our parents or teachers had put us down, and how all those negative thoughts had stayed in our minds and affected our lives to the point that we lost confidence in ourselves, and the courage to move on and to dream. He would give examples like asking your boss for a raise, asking for things that you want, but are afraid to ask for.

Around eleven o'clock, we went out to that fire and he tamped it down with a shovel and flattened it out. Earlier he had told us to imagine taking a lemon, cutting it in half, then picking it up, putting it up to your nose, and taking a big bite. Your saliva glands would secrete, he explained, but the mind wouldn't know the difference between reality and imagination, so what we had to do was trick our minds to overcome the physical reaction of our tongues by imagining biting into something bland. Looking at the fire he suggested that, just like the lemon, imagine that it was cool moss, not hot fire. He had us hold up our hands, look up to the sky, think cool moss and walk over ten feet of red-hot coals in our bare feet. At the end of the coals we wiped our feet on some wet grass, because we could get some cinders in between our toes. I did it. The whole class did it. The whole lesson of that fire walk was, if I can do this, what else can I do? Anything.

Another exercise was to take a clean sheet of paper and started writing our dreams, no small plans, but big dreams that some might ridicule. Dawn always wanted to be an artist in Hawaii, so that is what she wrote. I wanted to own a high-rise hotel/casino, so I wrote that down. It's not something that I would have shared with anybody else, but Dawn and I shared this because we went through the class together. Eventually, the Nevada Hotel would become my high-rise casino, my dream come true.

Not only did I follow Anthony Robbins, but I listened to Zig Ziglar and Brian Tracy, all the popular motivational speakers. I'd listen to cassette tapes in my car, sometimes on my way to the bank, only two blocks away, but those tapes would inspire me. It was like being in the middle of the desert with no water and taking a long refreshing drink that picked me up. I deprived myself of listening to music so that I could listen to those cassettes. I love music as much as my whole family did, and I had listened to music in the car whenever I had even a few minutes. But motivational speakers were my friends, the only people I felt I could relate to, and I believed in what they had to say, so I listened to them instead of my beloved music.

When I came back from that course, Chuck asked me what had happened, because I was so high, so hyped up after fourteen hours of inspiring seminars. He was incredulous about what I had done.

"Come,", I offered. " I'll pay for your weekend and let's go and do this together because it is so wonderful."

We went together to share the experience, which was again transcendent for me, but Chuck didn't get the same effect at all. I was crushed that he didn't experience the same thrill or see the same positive potential that I did. I discovered that we couldn't share something that personal any more than we could share the same dream. I was very disappointed, because he was my synergistic partner in many ways and I wanted so much for him to be part of my dreams. For example, I couldn't imagine him not wanting that hotel. What I couldn't fathom was that he did not see the potential in my dream. To me, I saw an open door to becoming a millionaire, but it wasn't as important to him as fulfilling his own dream of being a civil engineer or getting all those wonderful degrees. He was a mathematical genius, but he couldn't see that my venture was going to make a hundred thousand dollars a year guaranteed. It just wasn't part of his vision.

On the other hand, Dawn and I both had high goals and dreams, and we got over being afraid of people ridiculing us. We never laughed at each other, that's for sure. We believed in each other. We felt that we had learned how to achieve our dreams.

112

At that time, in the 1980s, Dawn was forty-five years old and, in order to follow her dream, she sold everything she owned – her condo and all the furniture in it – to move to Hawaii. Whatever she couldn't sell in a garage sale she brought to my house and I stored it for her. Since I never throw anything out, it was there for quite a while. Before she left for Hawaii, we had a farewell party for her with the Toastmasters and the Ski Club. About seventy people came. It was important to support Dawn in her big decision, in pursuit of her dream.

I collected Dawn's art, from large paintings to refrigerator magnets. She eventually got commissions for large paintings for thousands of dollars. When she first got to Hawaii, she didn't tell me that she was sleeping on the beach, and having a hard time, but she was always optimistic and self-confident. We've always remained bonded. She puts me to shame whenever I go to Hawaii, because she rolls out the red carpet for me like I was royalty. If she had not shared the Anthony Robbins course with me, would I have learned to take more responsibility for controlling my destiny? Maybe that never would have never happened.

OCTOBER 4th 1937

My Parents Wedding 1937

Horse-drawn transportation in Yugoslavia

My father, Joseph Sipl, in German uniform, 1944.

Koflach, Austria, home for five years before coming to the USA

1948 Kofflach, Austria: Left to right: Resi Seiber (cousin), Father, Mother, Michael, Oma, Ann.

Michael, Ann, Mother and Father in our two-room apartment in Austria,1950.

1952, First house in Sharon, Pa.; brother Mike on Bike.

1952 First family car

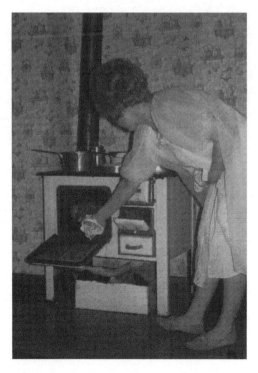

1966 Wiesbaden, Germany, Cooking on a Cole Stove; Turkey in the oven

Oma and daughter Bridgett

Chuck Fedderson and Ann at a luau party

Christmas 1982 Bridgett, Ann & Leah

Ann, Bridgett and her father, Dave Fredmonsky

Ann's plane that she piloted herself

Daughter, Leah, receives B.A from Bradley University in Social Services and Psychology with Ann. Leah later earned an MSW from University of Chicago in social services administration.

Ann with Jackie Gaughn

One-month mortgage payment to Jackie Gaughn: $22,000 in cash

Las Vegas Swing Club met weekly at the Nevada Hotel

Jimmy Guy, entertainer at the Nevada Hotel

1976 The Casbah Hotel before remodel

Queen of Hearts -- 1990 remodel

Brother Joe's 37th Birthday July 12, 2000 with George and Ann

Grand-daughter Aspen Gaines

Hotel Nevada Grand Opening . Rudi Wittmann and Annie Scrow Vilches

June 2004, Alaska Cruise. From left to right; Michael Smith, Ann, Ed Gaines (son-in-law), Bridgett Meyers Gaines (daughter), Jan Sipl (sister-in-law), and George Sipl (brother)

April 22, 2013, Ann in "The Boneyard," taken by Bob Davis, my first boss from CitiBank, Kent Ohio.

April 2, 2013 Nevada Hotel and Casino, Neon Museum Tour.

My house at Lake Tahoe - Before

My house at Lake Tahoe - After.

Chamber Of Of Achievement' The Riviera Hotel

Saluting Nevada Women in Business

August 1993

BUSINESS TO BUSINESS
"Capturing the Entrepreneurial Spirit of Las Vegas Valley"

Ann Meyers
Perseverance, sweat, and hard work brought success

Judi Woodyard
President - Lee & Associates

Joyce Dawson
President - Sonitrol of
Southern Nevada

Ann Meyers

Perseverance, Sweat, & Hard Work Brought Success
by JACK WARD

Ann Myers, owner of Queen of Hearts Hotel and Nevada Hotel & Casino, resident of Las Vegas for seventeen years, didn't arrive in style to earn her success. She had to persevere, sweat, and work hard. Driving into Las Vegas seventeen years ago in a 1971 VW, she set out to accomplish her goals. With her goals pre-set, her story goes back to Yugoslavia.

There Ann lived with no running water as a child. She never saw running water until she arrived in the United States with her parents at the age of eight. In Yugoslavia, she never saw a flushed toilet, nor sat on an upholstered piece of furniture, stood on carpet, and never had been a passenger in a car. At a very young age, she suffered in a concentration camp run by Tito of Yugoslavia for being a German.

Ann explains the day she came to America "as the most wonderful day of her life!" Through the assistance made possible by the Catholic Relief Fund, the trip to freedom was made possible. She integrated into the American way of life, got married at the age of nineteen. Later she experienced divorce because her husband left for his high school sweetheart. Ann was left with two children, $50.00 to function in a strange city that she was not familiar with and had no qualified job skills. Her exhusband took off with all the hard earned savings that they made together in their marriage. Fear, despair, and uncertainty challenged the best of her wits. "I didn't know what to do and didn't know how to secure a future for the kids and myself," explains Ann.

At this point in time Ann's only conceivable desire was to somehow provide a moderate home for her family. As Ann said, "I never thought I was capable of more than that, and I thought that would be the ultimate."

After nine months of not being able to find a job, on food stamps part of the time, the future didn't look so bright. Ann was quite honest about her being suicidal at this time. "I couldn't support the children, my exhusband was willing to take the kids, and I had a low self esteem like I had no purpose," explains Ann.

One day she met fate face to face and decided she must find a job. Determined to turn it around, keep her kids, and meet the challenge of change, she went downtown and went to every business offering to work for free to just prove her skills. After she found someone to take her two weeks of free labor she had enough confidence to go across to their competitors and sell herself as an interior decorator. And she was asking for three times the minimum wage! Ann was not a qualified interior decorator, but had confidence in her natural artistic talents, and she decided it was just time to get it done.

Ann achieved employment and ended up working eighty to ninety hours per week. She never said no and had a money strategy in place. It was a simple one . . . SAVE! She brown bagged allot and never paid for a meal out. Persevering in hard work, and patience in saving, she eventually had enough for a downpayment on a house. She discovered that for the same down payment she could buy a four-plex. She decided that the four-plex would be her long term retirement plan, an investment for the future. She figured in twenty years the property would be paid off, the children raised, and income from the other three units would be retirement. However, within six months Ann bought two and a half four plexes and one house. She did this by purchasing the worst property in the best neighborhoods. Plus, she was her own gardener, wall paper hanger, carpet layer, plumber and you name it. She never hired anything out. She made a silk purse out of a cow's ear due to necessity.

So, how did Ann Myers end up in Las Vegas? She came a for a two day visit in 1976 on her way to visit her brother in California. She fell in love with the business opportunity. Ann said it could "be felt and seen. Thick in the air!" "There was more business opportunity in Las Vegas than I have ever experienced," states Ann. She decided that she had to be here and immediately started to call Realtors while on her visit.

She immediately sold out in Ohio, and was able to double her profit on every piece of property just like the seminars had taught. Ann's first property in Las Vegas was The Casbah Hotel, now the Queen of Hearts in downtown Las Vegas. Again working eighty to ninety hours a week, she was back to everything on the line. With her future retirement goals at total risk . . . it had to work! Four months after buying the property a shut off notice from the electric company arrived with no money to pay the bill in dead of winter. It looked like checking out of this hotel wasn't going to be easy. Barely hanging on to the first good holiday came the blossoms of spring and the no vacancy sign.

Her first move was to buy a house. Again putting her future in real estate. With time the thirteen year mortgage on the hotel was paid for and the decision to refinance came when Ann set her heart on the purchase of Nevada Hotel & Casino. This process took three years from the first offer until the time she took over. It took one and a half years to convince Jackie Gaughn to take her earnest money to make a commitment to buy.

When asked what it takes to be successful in business, Ann responded, "In every business, you have to show up, take care of your customer, control your spending and monitor your business. Teach, motivate and be an example to your employees. Just like a parent would." (Continued on page 26)

> "I couldn't support the children, . . . and I had a low self esteem like I had no purpose," explains Ann.

(Continued on page 26)

131

Queen of Hearts

Ann Meyers owns two downtown casinos and isn't afraid to roll up her sleeves to get a job done

By Pauline Bell

LAS VEGAS SUN

EVEN though Ann Meyers owns two downtown hotel-casinos, she hasn't forgotten how to push a mop or plunge a toilet.

Being willing to work alongside her employees, no matter how dirty or distasteful the job, along with plenty of confidence, determination and a positive attitude, got Meyers where she is today.

The owner of the 100-room Queen of Hearts Hotel, 19 Lewis Ave., and the 160-room Nevada Hotel & Casino, 235 S. Main St., is one of a few women in the state to earn a casino license entirely on her own.

The native of Yugoslavia attributes her success, in part, to treating employees well and nurturing them as if they were members of her own family.

"Employees are no different than your family," she says. "They're just children of different ages. ... They need to know you're there.

"You've got to observe what they're doing and help them with what they're doing. You've got to praise them and show them by example how you want them to be leading their lives and doing their jobs."

Meyers also enjoys energizing her staff with regular sessions that include yoga and listening to motivational and inspirational tapes.

Many in the gaming industry thought Meyers was crazy in 1991 when she bought the financially troubled Nevada Hotel from veteran gaming executive Jackie Gaughan.

During her licensing hearing, State Gaming Control Board members were skeptical that Meyers would be able to turn a profit when Gaughan, a casino operator in Las Vegas since 1946, had failed to do so.

But Meyers insisted she could succeed, and she's still singing the same tune today — 18 months and a lot of hard work later. In her first full year of ownership, the Nevada Hotel showed a $500,000 profit.

She says the purchase was a "sure bet" because the property was appraised at $6.5 million and she bought it from Gaughan for what she describes as "substantially less."

Meyers is betting on herself and her staff to make the investment pay off, and she has made many sacrifices to reach that goal. Though she owns a house about a mile from her two hotels, she goes home only once a week to water the plants.

The rest of her time is spent at the Nevada Hotel, where she lives in a room, "not a suite because I don't want to sacrifice the money I can make on the adjoining rooms." She applies a hands-on touch to running the property full time.

She calls it "minding the store" and says it's another ingredient of her success formula — being there to show employees she cares about her endeavor.

Some might consider living away from their house a huge sacrifice. Because of Meyers' background, though, living at the hotel isn't much of a hardship. It's a far cry from the Yugoslavian concentration camp

where she, her brother, mother and grandparents were imprisoned when she was 4, after the Communist regime of Marshal Tito confiscated her family's property.

Her father later helped the family escape to Austria, where they recovered from malnutrition and other illnesses in a Red Cross hospital.

They lived five years in an unfurnished attic that was converted to a two-room apartment in Kolfach, Austria. They finally achieved their dream of immigrating to the United States under sponsorship of a priest through the Catholic Relief Fund.

"The day we made it to the U.S. was probably one of the happiest days of my life ... It was the first time I had walked on carpet, seen a refrigerator, seen a gas stove or ridden in an automobile," Meyers recalls.

They were taken in by parishioners in Pennsylvania and later moved to Cleveland, where her mother worked as a maid and her father became a bricklayer. She was educated in Catholic schools and enrolled at Kent

SEE QUEEN, 2E

BY STEVE MARCUS / STAFF

DOWNTOWN hotel owner Ann Meyers swabs floors and oversees gaming in the casino and, above, consults with accountant Frank Mazza.

132

Ann S. Meyers, PHC

I had not fully realized how much work would be involved in owning a hotel, especially a budget hotel, but I quickly learned that I had to work relentlessly to make it a success. I gave myself a title on my business card, like other people who have all those letters after their names. I added PHC and that stood for Professional Hotel Cleaner.

There was never a day that I didn't get out of my car and walk from the parking lot into the lobby without trash in my hands. To me, picking up trash was virtuous. I would never refuse to clean something, even if I were wearing a white suit or meeting with the media. When I trained maids I used to say, "Okay now, we all want a nice, trim, sexy figure, so what we need to do is stand up, pull our shoulders back, our stomach in, and reach -- don't bend your knees -- and stretch all the way down to the floor and, when you pick up that piece of trash, think about what a lovely body you are creating." Training became a game but, beyond that, I was demonstrating a virtue to others. People who have the right attitude in life pick up trash, and anyone who is not willing to do that will never be successful. I also believe that anyone who thinks that they're only going to work forty hours a week is not going to be successful either. Kids should learn that in school. I knew I had to do whatever it took. It was difficult, though, to find employees with that attitude.

I bought wholesale or secondhand furniture, draperies, bedspreads, and I bought linens in bulk to get the best bargain. I sometimes would take a single flat bed sheet and have my seamstress sew the corners to fit a double bed, or I would take a double flat sheet and sew the corners to make queen or maybe even a king size. Since we didn't iron our sheets, we took them out of the dryer and quickly folded them to create a pressed effect. We had a full-time laundry person on week-ends or when we were really busy.

I could buy a hundred feet of the least expensive carpeting for something like $500, but installation was extremely expensive. The rooms were typical of most hotel rooms; when you walk in there's a space for the closet and the bathroom in an L shape. The typical carpet layer would want to cut and patch that area. I would roll twelve feet of carpet out on the sidewalk, measure for whatever rooms needed it, and cut it, then I'd mark the end with a room number, roll it up and stash it in the hallway. Even a so-called carpet layer couldn't understand what I was doing, and they usually got the measurements wrong. I got the most out of every carpet.

I would do my office work until about two o'clock in the afternoon. At that point, I'd tell everybody that I needed some peace and quiet, and I'd go up to the room that needed carpeting, go inside with a radio and close the door. Except for the front desk, nobody was supposed to know where I was. I'd go into that room and lay that carpet by myself. Did I do a good job? Not really. Did it look a lot better? Well, even if you don't have the edges perfect, a fresh new carpet creates a nice appearance. That way the carpet actually cost me half the normal price. I never paid more than a $100 a room; in the earlier days, $50 a room. When I went into a room to lay a carpet, that was my time to stop thinking, to avoid streams of questions or conversations that drained my energy, trivial things like customers asking me for toilet paper, instead of going to a maid. For a little while I'd focus on using my hands instead of worrying about money.

Before buying the Casbah, I had looked at only five rooms. Of course, I was shown the most attractive ones. All the other rooms had black fuzzy dust around the edges of a blue carpet. The hotel was really in bad shape. The Jackson boys had been smoking pot in some of the rooms and they still reeked of it. At that time, we had Mission Linen Service, but most of the bedspreads had cigarette holes in them and the pillows were flat. There were no matching draperies, but the carpets could be cleaned.

Initially, I cleaned all the rooms myself with a brush, on my hands and knees. I discovered that the maids did a better job if they knew I would check after them. I understood the psychological effect of having somebody like me care about what kind of job they did.

Finding maids who understood my standards was extremely difficult. What I

135

discovered is that if a woman or a man had never learned cleanliness at home, there was no way you could teach them to see the dirt, which is key.   If they don't see it, they don't clean it. I also learned that in interviewing maids I needed to ask them how many servants they had been raised with at home. A lot of Filipino and Indian people who applied for jobs came from wealthy backgrounds. They may even have had an education and a degree but, in many cases, they couldn't find jobs in their fields, and they were willing to do anything. When people say they're willing to do anything, you assume they can clean up after themselves, but if they had grown up with servants, they had no clue.   I avoided hiring them, as I was not willing to teach them as if they were my children.

I would check at least five rooms a day. I'd always wear a jacket that had pockets in which I carried a short-handled toothbrush, a straight-edge razor blade, and a paper towel or washcloth. If I didn't check those rooms, I was always sorry, because even though the front desk or the head housekeeper was supposed to check rooms, there was always something they would miss, such as nail polish on the vanity that I would clean right away with my razor blade.

I also carried a pad of work orders in duplicate, so I could write notes to let the maid responsible know what was wrong. If I waited for her to come back and clean something, then I'd have to return once again to see if she did it. It was way more efficient to do the task myself, and leave a note for the maid.

Whenever I was on the floor with the laundry room, I would peek in. On an extremely busy weekend, I'd walk around and see how the maids were doing. When I saw a maid's cart, I'd ask if she was out of towels, to which I often got the response, "Yeah, they're not ready in the laundry room." Often they were ready, and I would take them out of the dryer, fold them and bring them to the maids.

I might notice that a room that looked like it hadn't been vacuumed, and I'd ask the maid about it. Sometimes she told me that the belt on the vacuum was broken. I'd go find a belt and change it, then teach her how to change the belts. So many times, the maids didn't do a good job because they didn't know how, or just weren't thinking.

Motel 6 paid three dollars a room to clean each one in twenty-two minutes. My maids were also paid by the room, not by the hour. To go and fetch extra things took extra time, so I often did it for them to show them my support. If there was a spot on the floor, I'd take that toothbrush out of my pocket and demonstrate how to clean it up in a minute.

We had staff meetings where I'd try to encourage people to meet my standards. They knew that I was tight with money and they were obviously much tighter than I was, earning minimum wage. I'd tell them about my food stamp days, about being broke with no job, so that they could relate to me and so they would understand that I knew where they were facing. We'd go from there to "This front desk and this lobby is your living room and you are the host or hostess." We'd talk about the importance of eye contact when a customer walked through the door. If you're on the phone, you still look at a person, nod and smile. Answer the phone with a smile, because people can hear the smile in your voice over the phone. That kind of pep talk made every person feel important, and I think they appreciated my efforts at mentoring them. We increased business by fifty percent the first year and I think it was due to the attitude of my staff that kept bringing customers back.

The Casbah Gets a Face Lift

I steadily cleaned up the hotel, got rid of much of the riff-raff, and increased business. Initially, I didn't even take credit for it. I thought the Jacksons had been making as much income as I did, but they hadn't. I realized in later years that people can sense how hard you're trying and will support you. I always let clients know that if there was anything wrong, I'd be there to fix it.

When I started thinking about remodeling the Casbah, I befriended a young Filipino called Rudy Crisostomo (a name I tied my tongue around), who worked for Young Signs. Rudy was an artistic fellow who made gorgeous facades. At that time, at Stateline they had just opened a casino and they paid half million dollars just for the façade, which was all made by Young Signs Company. It looked like a castle that could be seen from a distance. Rudy and I met each other at some kind of business function and I told him I'd always considered myself to be a bit artistic, too. I tried to get Rudy to help me do something with the exterior of my building, but I didn't want to pay $500,000 for it, because I'd have been lucky to have $5,000!

Rudy came over and we stood back and scrutinized the building, wondering what we could do with it. It was after five o-clock, and poor Rudy was tired. He was coming to me more as a favor than anything else, because he figured he couldn't make a commission on me, he knew I was too cheap. As Rudy looked at the building he got ideas. He had shown me a picture of a remodeling job that featured a turret about a hundred feet high. I thought that was a beautiful architectural concept, but unrealistic. I finally said, "Hey, Rudy, let me just share my thoughts with you. Planter boxes around the building, because we definitely need some greenery to cover up concrete blocks that look so cold." We started talking about planter boxes that we could build. At that time, I hadn't learned how to lay brick yet or cinder blocks or anything like that, so I suggested using a wet saw to cut into the concrete and put plants into it, and he agreed that would be cheaper. I added that I really liked the elegance of fabric canopies over the windows. He agreed that would be nice, too. He took his sketch pad and drew canopies resembling Roman arches.

"No, no," I objected. "Casbah is Moorish; we want a Moorish arch."

"Okay," he said, "but I want to tell you it's going to cost you a lot more to do that Moorish arch."

I insisted. "It's the theme."

There were some things I was willing to pay extra for, and I absolutely wanted the Moorish design. Once again, he agreed with me, but I could not afford to hire Young Signs to do it, so I had to let it go. Less than a year later, the Golden Nugget installed yellow and white canopies with a Roman arch.

Next time I saw Rudy, I said, "Rudy, you know that was my design."

He replied, "Well, if you don't use it, you lose it."

I said, "I'm complimented that you used my design on the Golden Nugget, but only you and I know." Whenever I look at the Golden Nugget, I think of that long-ago inspiration, but I only feel good about it.

Rudy's daughter, Kim, married Tim Bavington, a famous artist who lives next door to my house. Tim is English, but he earned his Master's Degree in Fine Arts at the University of Nevada. He's especially known for using chromatic colors that correspond to the twelve musical tones. Kim teaches children's art next door. I discovered that they were my neighbors when Rudy visited them and their twins, and came over to say hello, after not seeing each other for many years.

It took me about two years after I bought the Casbah to start remodeling it. I wanted wrought iron, but the crafts people I showed my drawing to didn't like it. They wanted a professional drawing with specific dimensions. My sweet, dear Chuck did the engineering drawings for me. I never pressed him to help me with things at the hotel. Though I'd tell him about daily problems at the hotel, he was often shocked and had difficulty handling sordid dramas. He became a prestigious civil engineer. When we went to his professional conventions, he was often pulled from the crowd to sit at the head table. However, he was kind enough to do the drawings for me, so the craftsmen could see the exact curves I had in mind. I hired a separate canvas company to make beautiful yellow, tight-fitting canvas awnings. I carried that golden color throughout, used it on a sofa in the lobby, and on arches painted on the side of the building. At the time, shimmering dangles the size of a coin were in fashion. They hung from metal sheets, so when the wind or sun hit them, they would gleam. I found a place where I could buy them in Los Angeles and had them shipped and I glued them onto the wall all the way around to create a glisten effect.

An eighteen-year-old Asian boy barely five feet tall came to work for me. He was a Superman. There wasn't anything he couldn't do. I wanted to install the gold dangles from the roof. The metal sheets were ten-feet long, and I needed two of them. I could install one of them from a twenty-two-foot ladder, but some had to be installed from the roof top. I trimmed the metal sheets into an arch. The young man and I were tarring one side of it, hanging it over the building, using an elongated mop to make it adhere to the cinder block on the side of the building. We went up onto the roof, but our pole wasn't long enough. "Here, you hold my feet," he said, and leaned over from his thighs, pole in his hands, straight out from the building as I sat on his legs. I was touched that he trusted me, and that he was so determined to get the job done. He was a proud person, and when he saw me putting all my energy into the project, I think he felt that he had to show more. I was impressed!

Another challenge was trying to get better exposure of the hotel. We were 140 feet off Main Street, and the building was three stories high. We really needed a sign facing Main Street. I designed a big sign with our logo, phone number and "pool," measuring the building's cement blocks to draw it to scale. A sign company wanted a fortune to make it. I rented a cherry picker for $153 and had it delivered. It was just a big hook with a motorized mechanism that moved up, down and sideways, left and right. I decided I was going up there to paint the sign on the wall. After I sent the delivery men away, there I was in the alley, all alone, painting the sign on the building in big red and black letters.

Another young man who proved to be an inspiration was Adam McGaugie, whom I met when he was sixteen years old. He worked for the company that had installed our yellow canopies. He was unbelievable! He crawled around the wrought iron canopy frames like a monkey. When he finished at four o'clock or whenever his eight hours of work ended, he would come into the hotel and ask if I had any other work for him. I was always looking for good maintenance men with a positive attitude and energy, so I was interested in hiring him, but he told me he couldn't work on Saturday or Sunday, because he went to the swap meet to sell things. Normally I would never hire a maintenance man who couldn't work on Saturday, because Friday and Saturday were our busiest days, when we needed a maintenance man on hand for unexpected problems and emergency repairs. I hired Adam anyway.

My daughter used to say that he repaired things with chewing gum and spit. But at least he repaired them, if only temporarily. Adam was looking for a place for his family and him to live. It so happened that Chuck had invested in a duplex and one side was empty, so Adam rented that apartment. When I had occasion to go over there, I found the entire back yard filled with twenty or thirty lawnmowers. He had started a lawnmower business, repairing and reselling them, while his brother cut grass to make money. Adam never threw anything away; he'd save parts and pieces. He would buy used trucks for $600 or $800 and repair them for profitable resale. He'd load a truck up to the maximum with stuff, everything strapped down, and off he'd go to the swap meet. He had junk cars in the driveway and even in the street. One time I even saw his mother with her nose under the hood of a vehicle doing some kind of a repair.

He stayed with me through 1993. When I bought the Nevada Hotel he was overjoyed, because he would be next door to the maintenance shop of the Golden Nugget. He applied for a job there and got it. He went with my blessing.

I told him, "Adam, you're going to be a millionaire before you're thirty."

As a matter of fact, I happened to go by the Golden Nugget one day years later, and stuck my nose into that maintenance shop, and asked if Adam was still there.

"Oh, yes."

"Please tell him that Ann Meyers said hello."

"Oh, you're the lady that owned the hotel next door," and so on. I knew the message would get through.

The last time I saw Adam he had a disc jockey business called the Knight Kings, and he had a different cell phone in every pocket for his different businesses, still selling cars and real estate, still working and getting all the benefits at the Golden Nugget. He was not yet thirty, and he did, in fact, become a millionaire.

*   *   *

One of my favorite people in Las Vegas at the time was former Mayor Oran Gragson, who was in office when I bought the Casbah, and he served for fifteen years. In later years he would ask me to lunch. I guarantee you I wasn't calling the mayor for lunch; the mayor was calling me! I was so flattered. He would pick me up at the hotel. We all knew him as the mayor who stuttered, but he had a sincere smile and a warmth about him that was charismatic. I can understand why he made it as mayor, in spite of his speech impediment. When he was comfortable with you, he talked without stuttering. I was very fond of him and his wife. I went to their fiftieth wedding anniversary celebration that was held at the DI, now the Wynn, in a beautiful facility in the back. Everybody was there. It was a wonderful anniversary celebration, and I was honored to be invited.

The Queen of Hearts

In addition to remodeling the hotel, I thought a better name might improve the hotel's image. In 1990 I staged a contest among the employees to rename the hotel, with a prize of a hundred dollars to the person who won. David, our bartender, came up with "The Queen of Hearts." He won, and the Casbah became The Queen of Hearts. That resonated with me and actually gave me the chills when I instantly recalled the fortune-teller of my past who told me, "You will become very wealthy. I see you with a scepter in your hand on a throne." I was glad someone else had thought of the name. I didn't want people to think that that was how I regarded myself. I was still struggling to win respect, but it didn't come easily.

We went to the Joan of Arc Church downtown. The priest treated me as if I were a low-class citizen. The reputation of the Casbah stuck to me. People thought that I was a bad person, because it had a bad name, and was still seen as a hooker haven. I wondered if I'd ever be free of that reputation.

I wound up joining the Las Vegas Country Club. Andrew Vacilla made it possible. One evening a person whom Chuck and I were socializing with had the audacity to say to me, "Well, how many times a night do you turn your rooms around?" I was so angry that it was very difficult for me to be polite.

"We only rent a room once a night," I replied. "We have no control over who is renting that room. If we know it's someone undesirable, we don't rent to them, but we often don't have a way of knowing."

People still assumed that I condoned the seedy things that sometimes happened at the hotel. That hurt so much, because I did my best to enhance its reputation. Even with the name change and a remodeling, the hotel still didn't have a good reputation, but our business prospered.

As well as being the best place for business networking, the Country Club scheduled entertaining events, like our first Halloween party. I went to the nearby costume shop where I saw a line of at least fifty people waiting. I thought that by the time I got through that shop I could make something by hand. I bought fabric in purple and orange with balloon-size polka dots on it, and I made clown costumes for Chuck and me. Needless to say, we were way outdone by other elaborate costumes there. We saw a coffin in the entryway with a person lying inside, made up to look dead. I leaned over and whispered, "You sexy thing," and the guy jumped out!

Elaine Wynn made a grand entrance as Lady Godiva on a horse, seemingly naked, though she actually wore a body stocking and a wig that draped around her. There were so many incredible costumes, I could only think that a lot of people were living out their fantasies. Wonderful food and drink, music and dancing kept us going for hours, though both of us had arrived so tired we wondered if we'd make it through the evening.

*   *   *

Business flourished at the Queen of Hearts. It was 1990 and Las Vegas, that sleeping giant, was fully awake. We had a wonderful unsolicited return business from Europeans. Somebody wrote a review about us in a travel magazine, which was like a free ad, recommending us as the ideal economy place to stay in Vegas. Then we were written up in a guide book that did not accept payment for reviews, so that was really wonderful. We could tell right away when those people came in carrying a guide book that they were probably from out of the country. I knew this might be the only time they ever saw Las Vegas, so I would get out maps and show them which places on the Strip they should see and recommend good buffets and tours. That kind of personal approach earned us return business. I couldn't believe it. I figured if they came back to Las Vegas they'd stay on the Strip or someplace else, but they would actually come back to us.

In the meantime, I found horse riding lessons for my daughter Bridgett, who had always loved horses. A Hungarian named George taught Bridgett *dressage* and to ride an English saddle. Since I had learned to beg in Hungarian, we had a tie there. He and his wife, Lydia, were a lovely couple. He was also in charge of the liquor supply room at Caesars.

One day, George, who was probably my father's age, said to me "You know, you're going to have to let employees steal a little bit."

Appalled, I replied, "What? I'll fire them. They're not going to steal from me." I found out that his advice was right, however. You have to control theft, but you can't eliminate it. Unfortunately, we did have theft of cash from the drawer as well. If you have a "graveyard" person -- someone who works through the night -- there's a problem of control. I would have no idea how many times that person might re-rent a room or rent it for ten minutes for ten dollars, for example. I couldn't be there all the time; I had to have a little time, at least, to sleep

*   *   *

I was always good to street people. Whenever I saw a man standing on the corner with a sign that said "Will work for food," I'd give him an opportunity to come and work for me. I'd take the time to show him where things belonged, what to do, how to clean and take care of the pool and this and that. Sometimes I'd still be teaching him and an hour later he'd say, "Okay, I've had enough now; you can pay me." I knew I was legally responsible for paying him for that hour, but then I'd let him go. I went through nine people like that. Nine!

One day, I went up to a guy who was begging with a little basket near the Nevada Hotel. I walked up to him.

"What is a good-looking, healthy man like you doing begging on the street?"

His response was, "You must be Ann Meyers."

I got a reputation among the beggars who knew I would give them a job. Once I saw a family begging. I said, "I need to have the carpet shampooed and I'll give you $500 to shampoo every room, 100 rooms, five dollars a room." The mistake I made is that I gave them a little money up front, because they said they hadn't eaten in a while. I knew there were many soup kitchens where they could get free food, but I'd often give them food and write it off. Do you know what this particular family did? They sold the offer to somebody else, so they got money from other people to do that job. The cons you come across, even from people on the skids who seem hopeless!

Across the street in the alley I'd see a fellow named Ray pushing his grocery cart with his stuff in it. Only a few years ago Ray had been paying a weekly rate at the Queen of Hearts as a long-term tenant. He had been working at the hospital. I don't know what happened, but he ended up pushing a cart, and maybe he felt comfortable near the place where he used to live. "Oh, hi, Miss. Ann," he'd say. Most of the street people knew me by name and I knew them. I never ignored them, but always said hello to them. My smile might have been the only one they got that day.

I had hopes for many street people. I'd think that as soon as they learned how to do things, I might put them at the desk or at the bar. I saw some of them as diamonds in the rough, and I was ambitious for them to advance before they even started.

I had hired so many people off the street near the Salvation Army shelter that one of the men working there came to me and said, "You've hired so many of our clients, I want to give you a tour of our place." I really didn't have time for a tour, but I walked through the soup kitchen and even had some soup that they served there which, by the way, was good. Strolling around, I was surprised that so many people called out, "Hello, Miss. Ann; Hi, Miss. Ann." I laughed and told my tour guide, "I'm known in the finest circles."

Several homeless people were actually my customers. They came in whether they had money or not. It was a cool place in the summer and a warm place in the winter. I never discriminated against them because of how they were dressed. If they did not behave correctly, say, if they threw a piece of trash down on the floor, either from a cigarette pack or gum or whatever, I wouldn't throw them out, but I'd pick it up, and hope that they saw me picking it up. I believed in teaching by example.

*   *   *

One morning when I came in, the front desk clerk told me, "The man in Room 228 can't get up."

"Why can't he get up?"

"Well, he weighs 600 pounds; he fell off the bed and he called emergency and they're up there trying to get him up."

I looked at the folio and saw that they had given him the cheapest rate.

"Do you know that I can't fix the bed for this price? Besides, why didn't you put him on the first floor? Why did you put him on the second floor?"

"Well, he could use the elevator." He didn't think about the possibility that the elevator could break. No common sense.

Sometimes people would come in reeking of alcohol or urine. I'd tell the staff that, if they smelled something, to give them a room with a rubber-sheeted bed. But sometimes employees who earned maybe a couple dollars more than minimum wage would not feel invested in doing a good job. They weren't paid to think.

*   *   *

And then there were the con artists. On the wall in my office I hung notes and pictures of people who had conned me or tried to. I called it the Con Artist Wall of Fame.

One guy gave me two drafts, copies of papers that indicated their worth might be $224,000 and $720,000 in the future. They were worthless at the time, but he was making fuel out of corn in Kansas, and believed they eventually might be of value. I suspected he was showing off, trying to impress me. He was one of those characters who wanted to con me for love or money, or maybe both. I eventually threw them into the trash.

Then there was a very handsome young man who approached me about leasing the cafe. Incidentally, when I took over that cafe I had Mission Linen deliver a beautiful starched white chef's smock and toque, because he could be seen cooking in the open kitchen. Waitresses wore white aprons. We did very well, with wonderful breakfast and lunch menus, but I tried to lease out the place, because it was labor intensive and too much for me to monitor food costs. The handsome young man told me about a place called Brannigan's, a restaurant/bar kind of place that I had never been to, but the way

147

he described it, it sounded very appealing. I told him he was certainly welcome to lease the restaurant from me, but he could not have the bar. I also wanted the restaurant to offer free hors d'oeuvres at the bar from 4:00 till 6:00, five or six days a week. I estimated that would cost $20 to $50, but would stimulate bar business.

He put a little toolbox inside the restaurant, which was closed at the time. The toolbox stayed there for two months, and I never saw its owner again. In most cases, when I entered an agreement, I'd ask for a security deposit, but in this case I don't remember if we signed a written contract or not. After two months he took me to court, because I didn't decorate the place like Brannigan's. If I had known I was supposed to decorate like Brannigan's, I could have asked some pretty big money for it, but what did I know. That was one of many crazy lawsuits.

Sometimes a customer would not pay his rent and would leave his belongings in the room. I'd have to pack up his things, label it and leave it with a bill of how much money he owed. It might happen that the person was in jail and that's why they disappeared. Sometimes they'd lost all their money gambling. One man eventually came back for his belongings and claimed that his $2,000-dollar suits were missing. In a hotel that charges ten to thirty dollars a day, you'd have lots of customers with $2,000-dollar suits, right? I brought an appeal to the small claims court and had to put up $5,000 in cash, in other words, the amount that I was being sued for. I was mailed the date of the appeal, and when I went there on that day I was informed, "Oh no, that date was yesterday. We've already given the man the $ 5,000." I was horrified, of course, and frustrated, but had to admit that, because I was preoccupied with so many other things, I could only blame myself for missing the date.

Since I didn't have much education, I signed up for a course on hotel law, real estate law, and contract law at the community college. I was working sixty hours a week, but I attended those classes in the evening two nights a week, and then went home to my family, exhausted. Nick Mastrangelo, who was a former Gaming Control agent before he became an attorney, taught the law course. It was very hard, because the last thing I wanted to do was leave work and go sit in that classroom. What made it even more grueling was that there was little information I didn't already know or couldn't figure out.

Then one day we had a fire in the hotel. The news media was there in a flash. I hopped over the front desk to get to my office, because I was scared to death that important things in my desk might get burned. As I ran toward my office, firemen were blocking the doorways, so I opened a window and started to crawl out, and the news media outside turned their cameras on me while I was backing out of the window butt first. Reporters were trying to get me to say something dramatic, but I said, "Everything's okay; everything's fine."

The fire taught me another important lesson. It's very commonplace for a fire to start from lint in the clothes dryer. All it takes is a spark. Lint is everywhere in the back of a dryer, and also in the cavity where the electrical box is. We had a guy working in that area at the time and he left some exposed wires, so he might have actually started the fire.

That evening I had a class and, though I only lived a mile away, I didn't have time to go home and change my clothes. Nick could smell smoke on me. I apologized and sat through the class. After a few months, in the last class he said, "Now for the most important and only hotel law you really need to know... " and he held up a piece of paper maybe four by eight entitled "Hotel Law" that listed what the guests' rights were, and instructions in case of fire. We had one of those on the back of every single door in the entire hotel, and one posted at the front desk. "This is all the hotel law that anyone needs to know." In other words, I had wasted all that time, because all I really needed to know was on that paper that anybody who's ever stayed in a hotel has read. It would have been nice if he had said that in the first class, not months later. I never told Nick what I thought, because he represented me as an attorney later

*   *   *

Three-day holiday week-ends were always very important in the hotel business, because lots of people would come to Las Vegas. We'd charge $50 a night for a room. Sometimes people would take a room for three days for $100 or $150, and I needed that money. For $100 I could buy five bedspreads or pillows or a TV. At such times I always made sure the rooms with two double beds or a king-size bed had matching bedspreads. I couldn't always get the maids to do that. Maybe a spread needed to be washed and they didn't want to wait until it was finished, so they'd put on any kind of spread. That might seem trivial, but not to me, and I would check all the rooms I could to make sure they looked proper and that everything matched.

In the 1970s African-Americans began to move into professional jobs downtown and on the Strip as dealers, cocktail waitresses, and maids. I had one such maid named Vicky. I couldn't help but remember the maid I had in Columbus, who watched over my kids when they were small, and helped me get a start in the interior design business, so I was disposed to like the second Vicky. She was a very good maid, in spite of the fact that she had only one eye. One day I asked someone about her eye and was told that she had had a boyfriend who knocked out her eye. When she had a false eye implanted, the boyfriend came back and knocked that one out. Obviously, she needed another false eye, and I assumed that must cost thousands of dollars. When I asked Vicky, she told me, "Oh, it would cost $500, but I can't afford it." That sounded affordable to me, so I asked her, "Vicky, would you be willing to maybe pay me just a little bit every month if I buy you that eye?" "Oh, Miss Ann, Miss Ann." She was so happy, and I was so happy to do it for her. Vicky got a new eye and, oh, my goodness, she looked so good and she did so well as a result of having some self-esteem again. It looked so natural, I couldn't believe it. It was just perfect, and it was only $500.

*   *   *

To a certain extent, the Gaming Control Board controlled my life. I always thought that a hotel owner should be included on that Board. Naturally, there were attorneys on the Board and there was a member of the police department named Steve DuCharme, who gave the Board a broader perspective. Going in front of the Board was terrifying; I never knew what to expect. At one hearing, I was astonished to hear, "You had 365 phone calls to the police department." Those phone calls were not made by me or my staff, but mainly by hotel guests who called 911. I would say we made less than five calls a year when we felt that someone in danger, as we had some domestic violence issues. When we couldn't fill our rooms with transient guests, we took weekly renters, a lower income type of person, some of whom drank too much and became unruly. Then there were people on prescription drugs who had MediCare and, if they ran out, they would call an ambulance that would take them to the hospital with no question. They'd get their prescribed drugs and then come waltzing back into the lobby. Another problem was that, if there was an incident in our parking lot across the street, the police often reported it as happening at The Queen of Hearts.

I paid a few thousand dollars to an attorney to look into some of those calls, and we found out that many came from transient guests. We had a rule at the front desk that no one could call the police unless someone's life was threatened. If the police were called, it was written in our daily journal, along with the purpose of the call. Because of all the calls from tenants, a lot of annoyed policemen would come into the hotel. Sometimes policemen assumed that I was as low-class as some of my customers, even though I always very polite to them, and there was never alcohol on my breath. The first few years that I had a liquor license, I used to have cocktails at five o'clock with my customers, but I quickly discovered that I couldn't keep that up, because my brain and my body would feel the effects immediately. I didn't like feeling fuzzy-headed and sick, so in 1980 I quit and have had almost no social drinks since then. In fact, when I smell alcohol on someone, I immediately feel that his or her thinking is impaired.

One personally regrettable incident happened on the graveyard shift when a policewoman came in. On the wall behind the desk she saw my lovely painting by Pierre Auguste Cot, called "Springtime" in a Rococo gold frame. It depicts beautiful young lovers on a swing in a bucolic setting. I thought it was a nice image that might inspire people, as it did me. The policewoman looked at it and said to the night auditor,

"I want to buy that painting." He replied, "Well, I'll have to ask the owner if she wants to sell it." Next day I was given that message, and I told the auditor it was not for sale. When she came in next time, the night auditor told her that. He told me that her comment was, "What a beautiful painting for an ugly place like this." I was offended, of course, but when I think of what policewomen go through and how difficult their jobs are, it reminds me of how much more a woman has to try. I could relate to that woman, in a sense, because she was probably often viewed as taking over a man's job and she would have to work harder to prove herself. Tough as she was, maybe she was also an art lover. She would not have thought about the fact that the hotel was worth a million dollars, and she might have been surprised to find out who the woman was who ran that "ugly" place.

I never let friends know about the problems I had, certainly not my ski club or Toastmaster friends, and certainly not people in my church, because they already thought, just like the policewoman, that my hotel was a dump. I kept trying hard to lift the class of clientele by keeping the hotel as clean and proper as I possibly could, but it was never easy.

*   *   *

Then, in 2000, we had another fire. I was a little late getting ready for work that morning, and didn't even have my makeup on when they called me from the hotel to tell me about the fire. I threw my clothes on and sped down there without makeup. The whole hotel had been evacuated. It appeared that the fire was coming from the third floor, filling the hallways and the whole building with smoke. The fire department was there, police and the media, with reporters scurrying around interviewing people. I noticed a Black gentleman on the corner of the street outside the lobby laughing like a hyena. To me, this was not a laughing matter, but he was laughing like maybe he was high on drugs. I had never seen him before and didn't know who he was.

Initially, they didn't let me into the hotel. Once I was allowed in, I headed for the bar to check the money drawers and slot machines. We had to lock the bar. It took some time for the investigation, and I was very worried about opening that bar again, because there are different laws about how long you can close a gaming establishment. We managed to open, finally, but only the front desk and the bar, not the hotel rooms, because there had been so much smoke damage and we had to relocate hotel guests as well. Thank God no one had been hurt! Within a few days we finally got the first and second floors opened, but we could not open the third floor for many months, until it was renovated.

As if all that weren't bad enough, my manager, J.J. Gardner told me, "They're saying that you started the fire." I just brushed that off, because I was used to a lot of ridiculous gossip. The day after he told me that, we did a drop, took the money out of the bottom of the slot machines, which is a very specific procedure with three people witnessing and all kinds of locks and signing of keys and so on.

When J.J. repeated, "They said that you set the fire and they're going to arrest you for it," I snapped back, "Why don't they arrest me now?"

"Oh, they're going to do it on Monday."

How did he know that? Many people around me gossiped, though I was quiet about my personal life or opinions. I didn't laugh at dirty jokes; I didn't let them know if I was going out of town; I didn't even let them know if I was going to the other side of town.

The following day, J.J. again repeated, "They're going to convict you for this fire."

I finally looked at J.J. and said, "You're serious."

He replied, "I'm telling you they said that Wiley, the maintenance man, had like a screw loose, that Wiley would do anything for you, so the police think that you had Wiley set the fire."

I decided to call my son-in-law, Ed, an attorney, and tell him what had happened. He advised me, "When they finally decide to talk to you, don't talk to them unless you're in front of your own attorney." In the meantime, the insurance adjuster came. His response to the investigators was, "Well, she must not be as smart as I thought she was, if she would set this fire with her skimpy coverage."

A time and date was set to go to the attorney's office with two investigators. As soon as they found out that I had something like a $250,000 deductible, and damages were estimated at $175,000 they lost interest. I was under covered and it would cost much more money to repair the hotel than what I would get from the insurance company, though they agreed to pay me $60,000. They dropped the case and that was it. That experience taught me an extremely important lesson. Do not assume that over-insuring will be to your benefit. There is no doubt in my mind that, if I had over-insured, they would have had grounds for suspecting me of creating the fire.

I finally was able to go up and look at room 308 on the third floor. A weekly tenant had stayed there, and it turned out that he was the man who had been hysterically laughing in the street. The room was packed with all kinds of different things, like what you might see in a garage -- gasoline cans, bicycles, televisions. Whether he intentionally or accidentally caused the fire doesn't matter, because he was obviously out of his mind. In any case, I was way too busy to pursue him, and I never saw him again.

It took months to repair the rooms. We had to do the work ourselves, and then I paid a contractor to approve and sign off for us. Thirty-three rooms had been damaged. We had to totally redo a dozen rooms, gutting the bathrooms and rebuilding the walls and ceilings and so on. As usual, I was short of money, so I bought building materials and found a handyman named Charlie Connor who turned out to be a blessing. Charlie had had polio when he was a young kid and he had limited use of his left hand, so he could only hold light things in it, like a pad of paper. His right hand, on the other hand, was like that of a wrestler. He helped me rebuild the rooms and allowed me to delay paying him. He was also an air-conditioning licensed specialist and there were times that the AC would break down and he would come over after he finished his normal eighty-hour-a-week job to help me with it.

An outside independent insurance adjuster showed up, and offered to help get the money owed to me for a percentage of whatever had been promised. They made it possible to obtain $60,000 more than the insurance company had offered. I got about $120,000 from which they took their commission and I got the rest. It took six months to get that money. Their intervention took more time, but it also gave me a few more dollars, which was nice.

*   *   *

Among all the transient people who booked the hotel, we also had some interesting personalities who became permanent residents. A good-looking young couple, Mary and John, moved into 329, one of the biggest rooms, which became their home. They paid the rent, we didn't have to run after them, they didn't disturb the peace. They stayed with us for quite a while, then all the sudden they had a baby. We didn't have any other babies in the hotel, and while it didn't seem appropriate, I didn't have the heart to throw them out. A year or two later they had another baby. With two babies in 329, sometimes the night auditor would complain that late at night they were noisy, disturbing other tenants. I wanted to tell him that's what happens when you have children. As long as we allowed them to stay, we had to put up with it. One morning he told me, "The couple made a lot of noise last night, so I called the police and they came and they took the babies away."

I was appalled. "What, you called the police and they no longer have their children?"

"Yes."

I still have chills remembering this, I was so shocked. I called the couple upstairs and asked them to come down.

"I want to help you with this," I said. "When are you going to court? what's happening?" They told me they had to go to court the following Tuesday. They didn't have a car, so I offered to drive them there and be a character witness. I also offered to write a letter, testifying that they didn't do drugs or drink, and that they were reliable tenants.

Having had some experience in court rooms, the day of the hearing I gave John an ironed shirt and gave Mary a dress of mine. I drove them to the court where I spoke to the social worker and gave him my letter. He said, "Well, they're not going to allow you inside the court room, but I can present this letter to the judge." He pulled me to the side. "These children have been abused, and there's a possibility that the boy's leg is broken. We have them in child protective care and this couple will probably be asked to go for six weeks of counseling before they consider giving the children back."

That was horrible news that broke my heart. I waited until they finished in the court room, and, sure enough, that's what was decided. They had to go to six weeks of counselling before the court would consider giving the children back. I took them to a buffet afterwards. I never saw anyone eat as much as they did at that buffet, so I assumed they had money problems. She didn't work, but he did, while she took care of the children.

A social worker came to the hotel to inspect their room, and told me that it smelled terrible, and they would require more sanitary conditions for the children. We went back to their room, and when they opened the door the odor was overwhelming, like dirty diapers or rotten socks. I told the couple, "I'm going to give you a freshly painted room two doors away from yours, and I'm only going to charge you for one room, okay? Before you take anything into that room – clothes, linen, whatever -- I want you to wash it. I'm not going to charge you to use the washer and dryer. Here is an iron and ironing board. We'll take care of that other room as soon as you move out. We'll have to repaint it and put a new carpet in and so on."

I had not realized that they were just teenagers, maybe early twenties. I reflected that I was a teenager when I first got married. My first husband was eighteen and I was nineteen, but we had been taught quite different values.

One morning the night auditor said, "Well, they moved out last night."

I was surprised. "What's the story? What happened?"

"I have no idea," he said, "I guess she went down to Florida where her mother is and who knows where he went."

Some time passed before the father came in again. I was working the desk. He was very pleasant and said, "Oh, I've got the kids back and we're all living in a little apartment over on 14th Street and I've got a job at McDonald's and things are going just fine." "That's great," I said. "Bring the kids by sometime so I can say hello." I was delighted to hear that this family was reunited. I thought that was the end of the story. A few more weeks passed, and I got a call from a policeman in San Diego who asked me if I knew Mary and John?"

"Oh, yes, they lived in 329."

"When was the last time you saw him?"

"I think it was about a month ago," and I told him what John had told me.

"We found his wife murdered. They didn't have those kids. The kids are still in custody and we're looking for him."

I was as sad and disappointed as if they were my own.

Eventually, John wrote me from jail. He wrote as if Mary were still alive, and he was going to get out, and the kids were okay and so on. He sounded delusional. I've had to make many difficult decisions in my life, but this was one of the hardest, thinking about John in jail, knowing he'd want me to visit him, and he might even ask me to visit his children. As all those scenarios went through my mind, I knew I had to cut off contact with him. I remembered the Corporal Works of Mercy from my Catholic upbringing, especially one of them, to visit the imprisoned. I couldn't. For some reason, though, I kept his letter in the vault for a long time. It was one of the most difficult decisions I had to make in my life.

Any situation that involved children always touched my heart. One morning I came out of my office and there in the atrium area sat a little girl about eight or nine years old, just sitting there with her hands together.

"Oh, and where do you belong?" I asked.

"I'm running away."

"What are you running away from?"

"Well, I live with my big sister and her boyfriend and I don't want to be with them. Don't call them, please don't call them. I want to go find my mother in California."

My heart went out to her. "Honey, come on into the office. Here, would you like a candy bar? Here's an orange. Now, why don't you tell me some more? Do you have the phone number of your sister?"

"No, please don't call them; I want to go to California and find my mother."

I felt so sorry for her that I even wondered if there was a way I could adopt her. She begged me not to call the authorities, but after I had her there for an hour or so, I decided I had no choice. I called child protective services, explained the situation and asked if there was any way I could adopt her. The man on the phone told me I didn't know what I was talking about. I didn't know if she had been abused and had no idea what kind of psychological problems she might have, or anything about her past. He added that if I wanted to adopt a child, I needed to apply and look a little deeper into the matter. "Unfortunately, we have to come and pick up this child." They came in and I felt awful to hand her over into child custody. I had even spoken to my daughters and my mother about adopting her, I was that serious about it. I couldn't bear to see any child mistreated. They thought I was over-reacting. I never saw the girl again, but I think about her to this day, and can only pray that she found a good path.

On the other hand, one of the most joyful parts of my life came from my daughter, Leah. She worked the front desk sometimes during summer vacation. She had a fantastic memory. I'd tell her to make a note to collect from 317, or that Herb's room was supposed to be done, and she'd say, "It's taken care of, Mom." She'd remember everything without writing it down. She had a photographic memory like her father. She was a delight to have at the front desk.

*   *   *

It was difficult to get good bartenders. We had a customer named Mickey, who was a cute fellow in his twenties, with red curly hair. Mickey was always a good listener, an important characteristic of a good bartender, and he was certainly a good drinker, an alcoholic, in fact, but I gave Mickey a chance as a bartender. He needed someplace to live. Many times I'd let employees live at the hotel. The tax laws were such that I could pay a lower wage to people living there. That was a win-win for them and for me. Besides a financial benefit, I could observe people who lived in the hotel, and pretty much guess their values by the kind of life style they led. When somebody lives under your roof, there's not much they can hide.

Before Mickey, we had a bartender named Cindy who looked like Elizabeth Taylor. She didn't have her figure, but she had the beautiful black hair and milky complexion. I loved to have someone like her behind the bar, because the guys would flock there just to look at her. Every once in a while, Cindy wouldn't show up for work, because her boyfriend beat her. I couldn't understand why such a beautiful girl would put up with somebody like that. Then one day Cindy got drunk at the bar. She became so belligerent and used such nasty loud language that customers cleared out. I tried to talk to her. "Cindy, please go home. Cindy, let me give you a ride home. Please leave the bar. Nobody is here. Please leave." She continued swearing, even at me, screaming as loud as she could. Then I realized that this was how she probably provoked men into hitting her. Like a spoiled brat, she stubbornly refused to be anything but miserable when she was drunk, and she made everybody else's life miserable. At least, that's how I understood it. I finally had to let her go.

I can see why there are television shows centered around hotels and bars, because that's where you see so many different personalities and dramas. I constantly perceived the personalities of my own employees, as well as those of our customers, and found them fascinating. My hotel would have provided a fantastic TV series, no doubt about it.

*   *   *

When autumn came and the weather grew chilly, people complained about the lack of heat. The temperature could drop to below 68 degrees at night. Our boiler was down again. I tried to put off fixing it as long as I could to save the money, but it was seriously leaking. In previous years I had re-tubed the boiler, but there was no guarantee, after paying $15,000, that it was going to work. I might get a one-year guarantee, but if it leaked again after thirteen months, I'd be against the wall again. In any case, I tried to figure it out, closing off some of the tubes so it would be less expensive, but it was still leaking. I came up with the idea of buying a hundred portable heaters for each room. I found the best price at K-Mart, marked each one with a room number and put one in each room. Seventy-two hours later the Health Department came in and told me they were illegal and ordered me to remove them.

I was in trouble, trying to figure out what to do, because a new boiler was so expensive. There was no way I could come up with $25,000. We had replaced several hundred-gallon fast recovery hot water tanks that cost $2,400, and I wondered if those tanks would work as a boiler. I didn't tell anybody, but went ahead and ordered the hot water tank, which was delivered the next day, and I found a maintenance man to connect it. Replacing a hot water tank is not a daunting job, but it is awkward to handle, and takes two people to carry it. I crossed my fingers, not knowing if my idea would work or not. We finally turned it on and it worked! We replaced a boiler with a $2,400 recovery tank. I was personally very happy!

*   *   *

Since I had bought the Casbah in 1976, that evolved into the Queen of Hearts Hotel, I'd been overly preoccupied with all the problems and challenges involved with running a hotel, but I never forgot my family.

I was in touch intermittently with my older brother, Mike. I knew about his leaving the seminary and we had visited him in Los Angeles where he was teaching biology. I had told Mike that I'd learned to fly. Maybe he felt compelled to do it, too, as he would take on any challenge. Before I knew it, Mike went to a Cessna dealer who promised to get him a license if he bought a plane, so Mike bought a brand new Cessna and learned to fly it. There was nothing that Mike couldn't do. Except genuflect!

160

In 1980, he was involved in a program to learn Spanish by going to live with a family in Mexico. He was going to leave the first week in June and he had invited different people to go with him in his Cessna. Mike and I had learned the English language together, so he knew I'd be interested, and he invited me. I was in the middle of closing a contract on a house, and I really needed to be there when the closing happened, so I had to decline his offer. He wanted to take his son, Brent, but his wife, Pat, wouldn't let him, so Mike headed for Mexico by himself. At the time they didn't have visual radio transponders in Mexico that stay in touch with various radio signals. VHF Omni-directional Range (VOR) is a type of radio navigation system for aircraft. Usually a pilot zigzags from radio signal to radio signal, not necessarily flying a direct route. Because they didn't have VORs, Mike became disoriented and had to make an emergency landing near the home of a Mexican couple where he spent the night. Next morning he had to do what is called a short-field soft-field take off. He didn't have a runway, only sand. To do that sort of take off you need to have two legs to hold down the brakes and still be able to operate the rudder. With the use of only one leg, he would have had to turn that leg sideways and hold both of those pedals down with one foot. Once he let go, then he could move the plane up. But it takes almost four maneuvers to do that. Tragically, Mike's handicap finally spelt his demise. He flew into a tree and was killed. He was forty years old.

I was devastated when I received that grievous phone call that Mike had died. I wanted to go down and investigate the accident, but my family was scared to death to do that, because my cousin Leo, who had played in a band with Mike, convinced us that the Mexican family Mike had stayed with had killed him. He figured that they would think that anyone who owned a plane had to be rich. We never learned the truth about such a possibility, but simply accepted the fact that he had died in the crash. The Mexican government wanted $4,500 to release his body, so we came up with it. They returned Mike in a four-foot long casket with a small window, a square foot of glass, where we could see his head. It was a rickety plywood box and they must have bent his legs to fit him into it. Mike had wished to be cremated and have his ashes spread over the ocean.

All our family came to Mike's funeral. Bridgett and my little brother, Joe, were sixteen at the time. I promised to hire Joe as a maintenance man at the Queen of Hearts for the summer. My brother, George, was twenty-seven; Leah was ten. Even Dave, Bridgett's father, came to Mike's funeral. Bridgett had kept in touch with him through the years, though she had a close relationship with Leon, too. When Bridgett was nineteen, she went to the University of Arizona in Tucson, where Dave lived.

Mike had a VW camper bus that Pat permitted us to use, so some of my family came back to Las Vegas for a short time. We decided to take a mid-week camping trip, because the hotel was not so busy then. We went someplace nearby, within twenty miles or so of Las Vegas, for a picnic. Because of Mike's death we were all re-evaluating our lives, thinking we should live for the day, because who knew if there would be a tomorrow. Maybe I did most of that kind of thinking, as the sister who had known him longest, who had lost her life-long friend and brother.

We had just unpacked all of our food and put it on the picnic table as I was telling the kids about how wonderful Glacier National Park is, and how Dave and I had seen it and Yellowstone National Park and the Grand Tetons and how beautiful it all was and we had wondered if Mike had ever seen it. Impulsively, I said, "You know what? There's nothing like the present. We will never be together again like this, because Bridgett and Joe are both about to turn seventeen, and next year they'll graduate from high school, and who knows where we will all be in the future. Let's pack everything up right now and drive up to Glacier National Park."

The only obstacle was Joe, who didn't want to go. "I need the money," he said. "This summer I need to save up for a car. And I need money for school and personal things. You promised you were going to give me a job." To settle the matter, I offered to pay him to go on vacation with us.

We all packed into that little camper and the four of us drove up the coast and stopped at Hearst Castle, drove through Monterey and gawked at Big Sur, visited San

162

Francisco and continued north to Glacier National Park. We stayed at the Prince of Wales Hotel, a most beautiful site, with the lake behind it and the mountains on both sides. It was an awesome trip that we will never forget. When we returned to Las Vegas, Joe worked for me as a maintenance man. He inherited all our family traits -- workaholic penny pincher and saver.

My brother, George, had become a recording engineer. He played with Eric Carmen. He had gold and platinum records like "All by Myself," "I'll Never Fall In Love Again" for writing the arrangements. He scored the arrangement for "Dirty Dancing," and was commissioned to compose the Cleveland Browns theme. In Cleveland, where he and his wife, who was a school teacher, built their home from scratch, he turned the basement into his recording studio. He has a brand-new black full-size grand piano in his living room. He has had a great career in music and is quite well known. He never tried anything else, though my parents never stopped hounding him to get "a real job." George has a wonderful sense of humor. He makes most of his money writing jingles and advertisements for companies like Ohio Bell and Citibank, and he's done television and radio commercials.

My brother Joe also played many instruments, but he studied Information Technology in college and became a computer geek. However, he has a brand new grand piano in his living room as well. He married and had two children and could be described as "Mr. Perfect."

*   *   *

My daughter Bridgett was married in 1987 in Columbus, Ohio. Her husband, Barry, had a PhD in astronomy. He actually impressed me as being an impractical star gazer. He was like a playful child who I rarely saw in a serious mood. Predictably, their life together was fraught with financial problems, but we had a big family wedding for Bridgett and Barry. She wore the white dress of my lost dream, and our celebration was joyful and loving.

Just before Bridgett's wedding, my father, tragically, had been diagnosed with pancreatic cancer. It runs in our family. A cousin, Siggy Sippl, died of it when he was barely forty, and I believe my aunt Grastonoff in Pennsylvania died of it, too. The last time I saw my father was at Bridgett's wedding. Within nine months he passed away. At least I'm glad we had an opportunity to have pictures taken with him and our complete family on such a happy occasion.

When my parents celebrated their fiftieth wedding anniversary, shortly before Bridgett's wedding, we had a wonderful party for them. They'd been together since she was sixteen and he was twenty-three. What a long, eventful life! We organized the party in a hall, and all the girls wore bridesmaids' clothes, Mom and Dad dressed to the hilt, and we had it catered, unlike our tradition of doing all the cooking ourselves. There were a hundred or more people, as we had sent invitations to everyone they knew, including extended family members. My parents were always understated and humble, and maybe they thought they we were extravagant, staging such a big affair, but I thought it was just grand to have such a party, before my father died shortly thereafter.

If his funeral had been any more impressive, it would have been on national television. As we drove to the top of a hill in a limousine, and I turned to look out the back window, I could not see the end of the procession of cars. The wake at the funeral home, as well as at my parents' home, was filled with sorrow, but also the joy of a reunion of family and friends.

My mother seemed to enjoy her new sense of freedom, and the independence to make some of her own decisions. The first thing she did was redecorate her bedroom, hanging the wallpaper by herself, but she soon tired of that and became lonely. She was diagnosed with cancer and died three years later. Her funeral was as grand as my father's, attended by so many loving people whose presence was very comforting.

The day after her funeral, a large truck with a thrift store logo pulled into the driveway. My brother, George, and his wife, Janet, had been taking care of family affairs. They didn't tell me what was about to happen. I started grabbing my parents' things and packing them as fast as I could, to take with me. Over the years I remembered my mother collecting the crystal and accessories that were so dear to her, and seeing her things again brought back very emotional memories. My mother still had her old Singer pedal sewing machine. One year we bought her an electric machine for Mother's Day, but she still preferred the old Singer. Since Bridgett was a better seamstress than all of us put together, and collected sewing machines, I packed it and paid $300 to have it shipped from Cleveland to Tucson where she was living. I watched, as forty years of my mother's life, embodied in her precious possessions, were hauled away. I felt like a part of my heart was torn away with them.

My mother died shortly before I took over the Nevada Hotel. I had told her about it with great excitement. She thought I was biting off more than I could chew, which was typical of her. She never understood, really, how much courage and ambition I had. I wonder if she ever thought about where I got it from.

*   *   *

Among the greatest losses of my life was that of my long-time partner and mate, Chuck. Sometimes I blame myself, sometimes I consign it to fate, but I'll always love and miss him. Perhaps emotional strain had been building up between us for some time before catalytic events occurred. I don't think that one incident would have broken our relationship. It happened one Friday evening when we were invited by the famous Bob Stupak and his wife at the time, Sandy, for dinner at his hotel, the Stratosphere Tower, whose signal attraction is that it's the tallest standing observation tower in the United States. A few months before, Chuck and I had spent five very pleasant days in Melbourne, Australia at Sandy's home. After dinner we wandered over to The Mirage Hotel's Polynesian Bar. Around two a.m. I was tired and, knowing that the next day, Saturday, would be very busy at the hotel, I wanted to go home, but I could not convince Chuck to leave. I made the mistake of going home alone and leaving him with Sandy, who was staying in an executive suite at the Stratosphere. When I got home, I discovered I didn't have the keys to the house. I went back to the Mirage, but they were not there. By the time I got back to the house, I found Chuck inside, but I couldn't wake him and I couldn't get in. I went to my hotel, very upset, and tried to sleep, but couldn't. I tortured myself thinking that I was always too busy for him, maybe I'd driven him into someone else's arms. He'd started doing his own thing on Saturdays and I often wondered if he was seeing someone else, though I said nothing. Now I could only think that Chuck was having an affair with Sandy, though he had never been unfaithful to me. I wondered if it might have started in Melbourne. I went back home around six a.m., riled up, and accused him of sleeping with Sandy. When he denied it, I tried to call her, but she did not take my calls for the next three days, which I interpreted as an admission of guilt. I felt betrayed, and told Chuck he had to move out. Within a week he was gone. I was 47 years old and Chuck was 58.

I never found out if he'd had an affair with Sandy. Years later she said I was wrong, but I suspected her, because she had never returned my phone calls. Somehow I never believed her, nor did Chuck convince me. We had a few long phone conversations after he left, and I offered to try again, but he refused. The last time I called him, he cruelly said, "You're just an ex wife." He married somebody else a year or so later, a woman much younger than me, who worked in the school system.

There were budget cuts on defense programs and Chuck lost his job at the Nevada Test Site when he was about sixty. He lost his health benefits, but was able to participate in his new wife's insurance.

I love him still, and I always wonder how he is, especially on Halloween, his birthday, now that he's into his eighties.

Little Annie's Nevada Hotel & Casino

After thirteen years, I paid off my mortgage on the Queen of Hearts. We had a wonderful mortgage-burning party to celebrate. What a terrific feeling to have finally paid it off! My next dream was to have a real casino.

I was constantly looking at my neighbors' properties, as I wanted to expand. There were some shacks across the street that the railroad had built to house some of their people. I bought them and rented them out, so that property was paying for itself.

I wanted a bigger casino, so I had a choice of either expanding the one I had into spaces that were already available or buying something else. I heard that the Western on Fremont Street, which Jackie Gaughan owned, was available. David Atwell had mentioned that to me and offered to go into partnership with me, but we never followed through.

I also heard that Jackie was willing to sell the Nevada Hotel, a complete hotel/casino just a block down the street from me. I had my eye on it. I knew that I'd have to come up with some extra money if I wanted to make an offer, so I decided to get a mortgage on the Queen of Hearts.

No bank would give me a half a million dollars on a property that was now worth one-and-a-half million. They wouldn't even talk to me, especially Wells Fargo. Even though I had been with Valley Bank, which became Bank of America, there was no way. I even put front money up for different loaning institutions that claimed they could get a loan for me, and lost that money.

Then I found a private investor who was willing to lend me half a million dollars at eight percent, the going rate. When I signed the papers for that amount, hoping to use it to pyramid into a larger hotel/casino, at the closing, the seller had me sign a deed that would transfer the hotel back to him after two years if I didn't make the payment. I went ahead and signed it, because he was the only person who was willing to lend me the money, after I had tried many different places. After I signed the papers, I realized that he planned on owning The Queen of Hearts. I could tell by our conversation and his attitude, but it was the only way that I could get the money and hopefully expand, so I did it.

When I found out that the Nevada Hotel that Jackie Gaughan owned was available, I tried to see Jackie early in the morning, when he was known to take a walk and visit all his properties. He owned the El Cortez, the Western, most of the Las Vegas Club, the Union Plaza and the Nevada Hotel. In 2000, Jackie and his son, Michael, owned more casinos — nine — than any other father-son duo in Las Vegas history. Jackie was a nice-looking man, even into his nineties. He had a receding hairline from a young age that turned from brown to white. He wore glasses and had a wide smile that lit up his face. The Nevada was on Main Street across the street from the Greyhound Bus depot, the Plaza, next to the Golden Gate, which was on the corner and was later bought by the Golden Nugget. Years later, I heard that the city would not allow it to be demolished, because they wanted to make it an historic site.

I tried to calculate what it would cost to run a place like that, but nobody would give me any paperwork. Jackie didn't even want to talk to me. I was told that he usually showed up at the Nevada Hotel for breakfast around seven o'clock, so I decided to be there. I took paperwork that I had calculated, even down to trying to figure out how much a washcloth cost and multiply it. I sat in the restaurant and, as Jackie got up to leave, I walked after him, right behind him like a little dog, trying to get his attention.

"Mr. Gaughan, I'm interested in buying the Nevada. Could you give me some bookkeeping documents or reports on it?"

He turned to look at me over his shoulder. "It's losing money; you don't want it." And he walked away.

Next time I showed up at his office. That took guts to go to his office with no appointment, but I knew he wouldn't have given me an appointment, so I didn't even try. I went to his office on the second floor, and his secretary, Linda, was there and so was he.

He said, "Linda, tell her she's going to lose the place. She can't buy this place. I've taken it back three times. She can't make it. Tell her not to buy it."

How would I ever be able to get him to even talk to me? But finally he said, "Our Board is meeting next Tuesday. Why don't you come in and ask the Board?"

I wasn't even aware that he had any partners. Kenny Epstein was one of them. At the Board meeting, I can't remember all the people who were at that table, but I rattled on and on about what I would do with the Nevada. I had triangular pieces of cloth that I had fringed and brought as a sample to show them my idea of having the cocktail waitresses wear a black sort of a bathing suit top to put a little sex appeal into the place. It had no color coordination, no pizzazz. I described what I would do to make it more lively, like having New Year's Eve celebrations. I could have won an Academy Award for my performance in that meeting room, because my heart was fluttering, I was so scared my knees were knocking, but there I was, smiling and pretending that everything was great and I was glad to be there. After my enthusiastic presentation they gave me a negative kind of a response, noncommittal, and sent me away. A little man who was sitting right next to me shook my hand and said, "Now, you have a good day." He was very sweet. I was grateful that at least one person was nice to me. I walked away with no more than that little bit of encouragement, but a couple of days later I was informed that the Board had voted to let me buy it. I was ecstatic!

After chasing Jackie Gaughan for three years, I then went through at least ten months of investigation by the Gaming Control Board. Talk about financials! Imagine when you apply for a loan that you might have a quarter inch of paperwork that would include previous tax returns and all kinds of things to submit to get that loan. Gaming Control requires that much, the financial portion, plus a proforma that can only be done by a formal CPA, indicating the amount you might earn at the property. I ended up with paperwork twelve inches high that included my complete history.

Because my property was relatively small, the Gaming Control Board used new agents-in-training. They were trained to be oppositional. They would befriend you, ask questions, but when their report actually came out, it would be somehow twisted. I was very open in my responses, but wasn't legally smart enough to realize that what I said could be interpreted differently. Even stupid things, like the agent who phoned me at a moment when I was particularly busy, and when he paused in his questioning and I thought he was finished, I said, "Okay, well, thank you very much," and hung up. At the public hearing they said I had hung up on the agent. My goodness, I would never hang up on him. I thought he was finished, but maybe he was just checking his notes. In my life, seconds have always counted. You'd be amazed what I could get done in thirty or sixty seconds.

The Nevada cost two and a half million dollars. I was supposed to put something like $700,000 down, with a mortgage of $1.8 million at ten percent. I thought that was high but, thinking about the fact that they hadn't even wanted to talk to me about selling, I didn't have the courage to ask if they would charge eight percent instead of ten. Eight percent would have made a big difference -- $2,000 a month difference -- but I didn't have the *chutzpah* to ask. Anyway, two and a half million dollars was a good price. The hotel had 160 rooms with a 10,000 square foot casino, seven stories high. It had three elevators that were horrible! We couldn't afford to keep them up. For a short time, the maintenance man from the El Cortez actually helped me with the elevator, but that was my biggest expense. Even when I was in contract the last nine months that I owned the place, when the new buyers were getting their application done for the Gaming Board, I paid $110,000 during that nine months to keep the elevators working. I heard that even after that they still had problems with it. That's why in my next life I'm returning as an elevator repairman.

There were times, however, when I realized that all my grueling labors paid off. It's wonderful to receive accolades that shine some light into your tunnel. One of the first articles written about me was "Under the Big Top," in the Variety Club of Southern Nevada in 1989. I was thrilled when, in April of 1990 Today's Nevada Women gave me a Woman of Achievement Award in the entrepreneurial category. Then I got the Las Vegas Chamber of Commerce Women's Council's Women of Achievement Award in 1991 for hotel/resort category and again in 1992. I kept every article, even multiple copies.

I received the Distinguished Women of Southern Nevada Award in 1991 and 1992 and, of course, I was in Who's Who in America. I was in with a lot of other wonderful women, like Caroline Velardo, who became a leader in politics. While I knew her, we were, unfortunately, so busy we didn't see much of each other.

The Las Vegas Sun, April 2 and also April 22nd, 1991 printed articles about me. Also in August 1993, in the "Business Gaming Section" they ran a piece called "Queen of Hearts Owns Two Hotel/Casinos and Isn't Afraid to Roll Up Her Sleeves to Get the Job Done." There was a picture of me with a mop in front of a roulette wheel. I still have that great photo that most women would not have allowed. That's why I chose the title of Professional Hotel Cleaner, PHC, because I think that if your nose is too high, you're never going to make it.

In Las Vegas People's Press in 1992, Ellen B. Levine wrote an article entitled "Ann Meyers: Just Do It." The subtitle was "Meet Ann Meyers, the Cinderella who didn't wait for a fairy godmother."

A year after I bought the Nevada Hotel, I happened to walk into a convenience store, and saw a stack of magazines with my picture on the front. It was in August of 1993, and I wound up on the cover of Business to Business Magazine. Because I hardly ever left the hotel, I wasn't aware that every convenience store had a stack of them for free. I took a bundle and ran back to the hotel, I was so thrilled!

I was cited as the only woman with a non-restricted gaming license as a sole proprietor in Las Vegas at that time. There were other women like Jeanne Hood, but their husbands earned that license before they died, and then their wives took over their businesses. But there was no woman who earned it a hundred percent herself and was a sole proprietor with that non-restricted license. I wound up having two of them the following year. When I went to the Gaming Board later on, I asked if there was any other woman who had one. They said they were not privileged to give that information, but I knew there was no nobody. I was it!

However, I had a very bad experience in the world of publicity once. An advertising agent named Bruce, who was expert in image enhancing, such as politicians, even Presidents employ to make them more appealing to the public, approached me with an offer to promote my public image. I didn't understand the service really, and never thought I really needed it, but I figured it couldn't hurt and might even be a good investment in myself and my business. I unwittingly bought the package for $2,000 a month. Flattering articles about me soon appeared in newspapers across the country. Leah, at the University of Chicago, was surprised to read about me there. Unfortunately, she didn't save any copies, presuming I would do so, but I didn't see them. The positive publicity continued for about a year, when I came again upon hard times and had to trim my budget. Bruce was furious when I terminated my contract and began to write vicious, threatening letters to me. I kept a file of his dark correspondence and showed my manager where it was, in case anything violent happened to me. Eventually his bombardment stopped and I never saw him again until, years later, when I happened to be flying from the Hawaiian island of Kuai, I saw him on board that flight. Needless to say, I was not interested in speaking to him.

*   *   *

I was given my license in February 1992. I was on top of the world! Looking back on my life, I felt privileged to be in the United States, to have found Las Vegas, and to be prospering. Not too many people are that lucky.

In those early days of opening the Nevada, I didn't get around to the accounting office until maybe four o'clock, and the accounting clerk left around 3:30. I went in to her office a couple of times to ask why she hadn't written a certain number of checks, because we had the money to cover them. One day I went in there and wrote some checks myself. The next morning I was a bit late coming in and I wanted to speak to her about those checks. It was ten o'clock and there was no one in the office. I found out that she had erased all of our data on the computer up to that point, which was six weeks to eight weeks into owning the Nevada Hotel. She had deleted all the data and left. I wasn't that computer literate, so wondered if there was any possibility that the data had been erased by accident. No way, of course. It took a long time to reconstruct that data.

She had told me that she had a son in a prison in Chillicothe, Ohio. I happened to be somewhat familiar with the place, because I had lived in Cleveland and Columbus, and I had heard about that detention center. When she told me, I felt sorry for her, having a child in prison. You have to wonder what you did wrong as a parent if something doesn't go right with your child, but when she pulled that swindle on me, I couldn't help but think that probably had something to do with why she had a child in prison.

My accountant, George Zakilyanis, actually noticed a couple of checks that had been forged at a different time, before this particular woman took the job. I was so busy all the time that I never caught many thefts. It was impossible to cover everything. I pretty much had to take one day at a time, otherwise I could not have survived, so many of those incidents were heavy burdens.

I hired a young man fresh out of college to work in the accounting office. After a few weeks he told me he was quitting. When I asked him why, he said "You're not watching your money and they're stealing you blind in the casino cage." I pulled him into a room and told him, "Please, you know I can't be everywhere. I cannot always see what's going on. You have to be my eyes and ears. Please tell me more specifically what's happening."

"Well, you should know. I'm not staying and working for somebody who doesn't take care of their business."

I suspect that he might have been an undercover agent, and his job was done. Now I had to worry that someone was stealing from the cage. I needed someone I could trust to oversee transactions. As luck would have it, a customer came in from Kent,

173

Ohio, and I told him about my history as a bank teller at what is now CitiBank, and he knew my boss there, Bob Davis. I gave him my card and asked him to tell Bob I'd be so happy to hear from him. Bob actually called me soon afterwards and we had a great chat about where life had taken us both. I told him about my problem with the cage, and asked him to come and oversee that activity. I offered him a full-time job in the casino, if just for a year. "Are you crazy, Ann?" he replied. I was not surprised that he declined, as he had a lovely family and lucrative enterprises in Kent, but he was interested in a temporary Las Vegas adventure and came down for a few weeks. I was very happy to see him again. He was amazed that I had come so far in the world of hotel/casino operations. He'd always known that I was a hard worker, he told me, but I had surpassed his expectations. I described the job to him. He would be there whenever I opened the cage, and I felt confident about him monitoring transactions. Bob may not have known all the Gaming Control regulations but, as a banker, he was comfortable counting money and filling out reports. Most important, I needed somebody I could trust in the cage. He stayed for a week or two, usually sleeping four hours at a time and coming back to the cage for the next four hours around the clock. He had had enough of that job by the time he left, but he was so kind and such a gentleman, it was a pleasure to have him help me. He remained a good friend since then and has come out to see me several times with his family.

*   *   *

We planned the Nevada Hotel's grand opening in April on my 49th birthday. I hired a Dixieland band to play out on the street to get attention. Inside, we had a singer named Jimmy Guy who was a comedian and a one-man band, whom I had hired for a week. He had been playing up on Mount Charleston at the lodge there. He played a portable organ with pedals, and a hat rack upon which he hung at least six hats, and he had a song for each one. On his right side, he had two stands for his clarinet and saxophone that he called the "Safe Sax." He would wear a cowboy hat and alligator boots, shining a spotlight on his boots as he pedaled the organ. A keyboard sat on top of the organ, and a

174

strap he slipped around his head to play the harmonica. That wasn't all! He also had a rack with a guitar and a cymbal on the side. Whenever he played a different gig he had to carry all that equipment in and set it up. When he played for us for a week or two, he was glad to get a hotel room at a reduced rate. After two weeks, everybody loved him and he loved the fact that he did not have to move all his equipment around. He was really comfortable there, so I extended his contract and he wound up staying for two years.

At the front desk I had a manager who was supposed to handle any problem, and only when a customer was irate and would not accept what he told him, he would call me in. One day he came to me and said, "We have a customer who is furious because he didn't receive a wake-up call, and he missed his ride to San Diego where he was going to get a job." I went to see the young man who explained all that to me and, since he'd missed his job opportunity, he asked me what I was going to do about it. I thought that with 130 employees, we had a lot of work, and maybe I could give him a job. I asked him what he did. He told me he was a clown! He had a complete outfit, and I got helium balloons, so I hired him to carry balloons around, wearing big Ronald McDonald shoes. He handed out change to the slot machine customers, and paraded up and down the street at the grand opening. He even got his picture in the paper in front of the Hotel, which was really nice. Now we had a clown.

There was also a singer named Adrianne Harris, a beautiful girl from Prescott, Arizona. Adrianne and her husband came, and she sang at the grand opening. They stayed for a while, and she sang for free, just for the joy of it. They had been in the hotel business in Prescott and they left it for their children to manage while they had a nice getaway, enjoying the lights of Las Vegas.

My musician cousin from Pennsylvania, Diana Sippl, came with her partner, Steve, and a musical entourage. She had bought new musical equipment for the occasion. They, too, stayed for a week or two. Millie Whitehead, a girlfriend of mine, brought a whole group of people down.

We had eight department heads who all wore rented tuxedos, and all the staff women wore cocktail dresses. It was all very festive. Jackie Gaughan came and we had photos taken together. The staff presented me with a gift of luggage. I guarantee you that luggage was not used for the next two years.

The grand opening was my fifteen minutes of fame! The Review Journal had published a very big article on April 15th that they used for their piece on the grand opening. They had published an article in 1984 under the title, "Meyers parlays misfortune into a thriving career," in Today's Woman's section. I was very honored that one of our bar customers who was with the Review Journal wrote that complimentary, beautiful article about me.

Both my girls were in college at the time, and only Bridgett came to the grand opening. Leah was at Bradley in Peoria, Illinois, working on a bachelor's degree in psychology, then later on she went to the University of Chicago to get her master's degree in sociology. Leah ended up in a life-long relationship with her first love, Greg Golden. Bridgett was in Tucson at the University of Arizona. At the time, she was an arts major in drama, creating stage settings and studying the history of costumes, then she started equestrian training. She went to college for six years, first acquiring a Bachelor of Fine Arts Degree in Theater Design in 1985, before deciding to become a physical therapist. That required two years of chemistry and biology courses before she could get into the physical therapy school where she went for about three years. She then earned a Master's Degree in Physical Therapy in 1993 at the University of Arizona in Flagstaff. I believed she would have a great future in that field. Needless to say, I felt a deep satisfaction in my girls' academic achievements. They compensated, in a way, for my own lack of education.

Bridgett had driven from Tucson with a friend and stayed only a few hours for the grand opening before returning. I commissioned an artist to do a three-dimensional freeze of her high school graduation picture, that I put onto our gaming tokens. Besides Benny Binion, we had the only gaming tokens with an image of a person. I was very

176

grateful that she came to the grand opening, and was thrilled about that token, though she was rather offhand about it. I used the tokens like a business card, with our local phone number and the 800 number on it, and I loved handing them out. It also had a dollar value if they put it into our machines. I had to buy 10,000 at a time, but they were only 23 cents apiece.

I had already created a token for The Queen of Hearts, done by my friend, Gary Darwin, who drew caricatures. He was the best customer I ever had in the bar, effervescent, even when inebriated, always wearing a beautiful suit and holding forth as if he were conducting court. He was head of the Magic Club and he would come in and perform magic tricks. In his pockets he had everything that was necessary to do a complete show. On Wednesday nights, the Magic Club met at midnight. The magicians, including Siegfried and Roy, would go to those meetings and afterwards come and drink at my bar. I met Gary one morning when I came in at eight o'clock, and found him still there from the previous night. He was on center stage in the bar, doing magic tricks and drawing caricatures of people, plus he tipped the bartenders handsomely. If I had had to pay for an entertainer, I could not have done as well as this man was performing for free. He drew a silhouette of my face and I put it on The Queen of Hearts' token. On the other side, I put the complete address and phone numbers, so that I could also use it as a business card. It was unique and effective, and I loved its originality.

*   *   *

After the grand opening, I moved into the hotel. I worked every hour, sixteen hours a day, and almost never went home, and scarcely ever slept. As a matter of fact, the first day I went home it was a Sunday and the house was so still. Chuck and the girls were gone, and I felt their absence like an emptiness in my heart. I went to the grocery store, cooked myself a meal, and then most of the day was gone, in almost total silence. I didn't adjust easily to my new life style.

On that quiet day, I was also feeling guilty, because we had bus tours that came in and we paid the bus driver a fee for each person they brought into the casino. What I felt guilty about was that I knew that on Sunday nobody on the bus had any more money left. In addition to guilt, I felt ripped off, because I was paying five or ten dollars a head, and I knew we weren't going to get five dollars apiece from those people. I would walk into the ladies' room and women would be sitting on the floor waiting for the bus to leave. I also felt guilty about taking off a Sunday. But if I didn't take off Sunday, then what day would I take off? It was very difficult for me to justify taking time off.

*   *   *

I continued to own the Queen of Hearts. That half-a-million-dollar balloon loan came due after I bought the Nevada Hotel. I was running around trying to find somebody to cover that loan. No bank would give it to me, but somehow it came up in front of Jackie and he offered to carry the loan for me. I cannot tell you what a relief that was. Jackie sent me to his attorney to write up another half-million-dollar loan, and he carried it at eight percent. Jackie was a great businessman. I saved some of the many articles about him, because he never spoke about himself, never divulged personal information, but said only what was absolutely necessary. Maybe for that reason, there was power in his words and whatever he said had weight. In later years, when he realized that he sometimes repeated himself, he refrained from speaking almost entirely.

Jackie had two sons. Michael Gaughan owned South Point, and Jackie Junior passed away in his forties. Unfortunately, I think he had might have had substance abuse issues, because his death was hushed. Jackie Senior ended up living on the top floor of the El Cortez. He eventually sold all his properties downtown, including the El Cortez, but he remained the mascot there. A lot of people didn't know that he had sold it because, in his eighties, he still showed up in the poker room downstairs, where he rarely carried on a conversation and would never sit for an interview. He was the downtown Howard Hughes. I hadn't seen an article on him in quite a few years and I think that he'd like to keep those beautiful articles of the past as they are.

Jackie, Benny Binion and Sam Boyd were the three big men downtown. They helped each other, especially on the weekends, if they needed cash. Sometimes, if they had a big winner, they would lend each other money. After 1980, the Gaming Board involved itself in those kinds of transactions. As for me, on weekends when I was short, I'd write a $5,000 check, take it over to the Union Plaza to the cashier's cage, and they would cash it for me. The last time the Gaming Control Board came in to do a surprise investigation, they came to both my hotels and froze everything that was happening at the cashiers' cages. They conducted a complete countdown, plus they counted the drawers and estimated what was in the slot machines to see if I was short of money as, of course, I always was. My quick fix was to run over to the Union Plaza, then I'd throw the money into the cage so I wouldn't be caught short. Unfortunately, that proved to be black mark against me in an investigation. As they say, though, desperate people do desperate things.

Unfortunately, one of the negatives that the Gaming Control Board found out about me was $1,200 in bad-check charges from the bank a year before, and that didn't make me look very good. I had always paid all my bills. The last day the utility bill was due before a late fee, I'd calculate precisely to be sure that my check would clear in time. As technology became a little faster, the checks went through faster, but paying my bills was always a balancing act. When I had an extra $500, the decision about how to spend that extra money was tough, because there were so many needs.

*   *   *

In life so many times you hear "do what you enjoy doing." I think that's wonderful advice. If you're able to get an education and do what you enjoy doing, that's great. When I was young, that didn't really work out for me, because I was constantly worrying about where the next paycheck would come from for food and shelter to take care of my two girls. After Leon left me, I never received more child support from him than what I paid attorneys to collect. Two hundred dollars a month for two children was hardly enough to help me in the early 1970s, but it was something, and I shouldn't make small of it, because every dollar meant so much to me. Once I came to Las Vegas, I never wanted to hear from him again, and I never collected another nickel.

179

I suppose I retained the mind set of a poor person for a long time. One of the things I found amazing when I came to Las Vegas was that real estate agents who drove me around would spend three dollars a day on valet parking, maybe two or three times a day. I couldn't help thinking that three dollars a day was once my food budget.

Finding a way to have tenants or hotel guests pay my mortgage and contribute $100,000 a year was my goal, a way of securing my future. In my mind I was always on that tight wire alone, with no safety net below.

Even today I still think of how to stretch every dollar, even if I give it to someone else, which I sometimes do, because I'm a giver and I love being able to help other people. Sometimes my friends would ask me to go out to eat. My first thought was that it might cost a minimum of $50, and I'd calculate how many groceries I could buy for $50 and how many people I could feed. Even now, when people suggest going out, I'll say, "Oh, come on over to the house and we'll put something on the grill. I always make it sound real simple, and though I feel it's important to serve an appetizer, I finally stopped making dessert. I usually buy something, and pray that my guests take it with them, because otherwise I'll eat it all.

I've thought a lot about doing what I enjoy, and decided that I learned to love what I did to make a living, to make the best of what I was doing. The reality of my career is that, after twenty-eight years, I could never say I disrespected the gambler, because that was my business. I did not respect the alcoholic and the smoker, however, who can't afford to go out on the town, but do it anyway.

As a child, my family was poor among many people as poor as us, but we never saw crimes among the poor. We all had higher values. I never saw anyone get drunk or fight, or deliberately break the law, except for stealing food when we were starving. As a result, I was not afraid of being among poor people, but I did have a problem with pimps, prostitutes, drug pushers, or criminals who always shocked me in Las Vegas.

I believe the old cliché -- if life hands you a lemon, make lemonade. Someday you might be lucky enough to do what you really want to do at a point in your life when you're able to afford it, which I did years later after I sold the hotels.

By the way, when I calculate what I actually earned over all the years, I figure I made a thousand dollars a day every day from the time I arrived in Las Vegas. Not in cash, but in equity built up in real estate. There are windows of opportunity when you might be lucky enough to cash that in. In selling hotels, you have to use a 1031, which is a tax-deferred government regulation that gives an opportunity to reinvest and pay the taxes at a later time. But that's not cash and it's hard to believe that it was necessary for me to continue to struggle when I had money in an untouchable savings account. No bank would loan you money on it but, in the end, I thought it was wonderful that I was forced to accumulate those funds and then I was able to cash in when it was time. Eventually, though, I thought that maybe I should allow myself to get a line of credit for half a million dollars, so I did. Then came the temptation to buy a country club property. It had a million-dollar mortgage on it and was selling for $350,000. I thought that was a super deal. I paid $350,000 of borrowed money for that country club property, because I was able to pay cash. I didn't have to wait for a loan, because I had a line of credit. As it turned out, that country club property is worth $100,000 less now than the $350,000 I paid for it. I never could figure out why there was a million-dollar mortgage on it. That was an example of the bank over-extending a mortgage to a borrower. Everybody who lost their home in the last recession has to take some responsibility, but can certainly share it with the government or a bank, whoever the entity was that gave them that loan. I think a lot of people learned a lot from that sad experience. I personally know that I shouldn't have bought that country club property with borrowed money.

*   *   *

Jimmy Guy, our one-man band genius at the hotel, gave me an album with his picture on it that he had recorded, on which he wrote, "Dear Ann, This is something money can't buy." And don't I know it! Music is priceless. I always felt like somewhat of a failure, because I didn't become as good of a musician as my brothers did, but I think I made up for it by learning ballroom dancing, which I eventually did competitively. I'd dance three times a week for almost two hours straight, which is wonderful exercise and releases endorphins. I called it my "cocktail." I'm an avid fan of "Dancing with the Stars." For the average person, it's difficult to see the specific dance moves, or whether a couple is doing a samba or a cha-cha, but I watch every step and can barely sit still in my chair. I also got involved in USA Dance, LLC, which was the local ballroom dance association, affiliated with an international association that we belonged to and I was treasurer of that. We'd have a dance once a month, sometimes at Harrah's. Professional dancers would come from out of town for competitions. I'd either be at the door collecting money with two or three other people, or when we had it at the Charleston Art Center on Brush Avenue, I'd volunteer to bring food, which was a big hit. I was accustomed to having a lot of parties and entertaining, so it was no big deal for me.

I get goose bumps remembering the ballroom dancing at the Nevada. I hired a guy who said he knew how to lay laminate flooring for a dance area. It was fairly small, maybe twenty-five by twenty-five feet, and I wanted it to be round, but the workman was upset, because it was more difficult to cut a round dance floor. To me, from the time I was eleven and cut that circle of fabric to make my own poodle skirt, I never thought making circles was that difficult. In the end, though, he did it and it was lovely. Booths circled around a bead of lights, with a little stage area on the side. I hung curly ribbons from the drop ceiling that had painted metal dividers. I had bought used vinyl booths and had them reupholstered in three different fabrics, all the same colors, but with three different weaves, and the cushions were different. I actually had help with that. I made a deal with an English designer named David, who did all the decorating for Big Dog's Brewing Company. I invited him to stay in my hotel and I gave him my little MG red convertible to run around in, and he helped me choose colors and designs. I'd been in every single Big Dog's, so I understood what he was doing. It was great fun! At the Las Vegas Athletic Club the doorposts that you would expect would be made of marble were painted in cow colors, black and white, with bright pink trim. He had a wonderful imagination. I missed him after he passed away.

My lovely little ballroom area looked like New Year's Eve ever day of the year, and I loved every dance there.

*　　*　　*

At the Queen of Hearts we'd have a staff meeting about once a month, but at the Nevada Hotel we met once a week. It was difficult to get staff to stay for a meeting, so I'd schedule them at the change of shift, usually at the front desk. Discussions would be more personal than practical. I told them about an Italian philosopher and economist named Pareto, who defined the 80/20 rule, that is, success is achieved by 80 percent attitude and 20 percent knowledge. I had several of Pareto's books. I posted dozens of signs like that around the hotel. I'd tell people that they were already 80 percent if they had a positive attitude, and that I had 95 percent attitude and 5 percent knowledge, because I didn't have an education.

When I moved into the Nevada Hotel, every hour I was not sleeping I was downstairs. By 10:30 in the evening I was really dragging, and I'd sneak up the back elevator and disappear, because I did not want staff to know I was leaving, but the security guards would pass the word quickly. She's gone.

I would frequently go into the bar and talk to customers. I knew most of them by name. Many would come in at eight o'clock in the morning and leave around four or five o'clock in the evening. We offered free popcorn and hot dogs, but they didn't eat. Heavy drinkers made a career of drinking, having nothing but alcohol all day and then they went downtown to eat. I would talk to some of them who I knew very well, who were nice people basically, and I'd encourage them to go to AA. Some had the desire to quit, but I guess they weren't ready. They cared about me and I cared about them, but sadly I had no influence on their drinking habits. Sometimes they'd go down the street to drink, because they didn't want to disappoint me. Whenever a person did not come back, I'd feel as if I'd lost a friend.

One of the people I hired as a front desk clerk was called Jim. He came from a Polish family and lived with his mother until she died. He had probably inherited a little money and was able to come out to Vegas, then lost it and wound up on my doorstep looking for a job. Jim was very polite. He was gay and —forgive me for stereotyping —he had the very polite mannerisms of many gay young men. I found it very appealing to have someone so courteous and friendly, prim and proper, who never used four-letter words. He was a perfect candidate to work at the front desk and live in the hotel.

An advantage of having staff living in the hotel was that they were often available in case someone else did not show up. They were also often willing to work either a swing shift or a graveyard shift -- the more difficult positions to fill, especially with a family type of person. Almost everybody wants to work a day shift.

Jim worked very faithfully with me at the front desk for many years, although he didn't have much common sense and was, perhaps, too eager to please. It was not surprising that one day I was tipped off that I needed to go into Jim's room on the first floor. When I opened his door, water splashed over the threshold at least an inch above the carpeting. I waded into the bathroom and found that he'd left the bathtub plug down and it had overflowed. As soon as I let that plug up, the water started to drain. When I asked him why he had not thought to lift the plug, he was so horribly embarrassed and intimidated that I had to back off. We soon got over the mishap.

I never wanted to put a hold on a room. If a room is blocked, it's possible for someone to use it for ten minutes on the night shift. Some people would come in to rent a room and try to bargain. "Well, why don't you just let me give you $10 or $20 and I'll be out of there in ten minutes?"

I did not condone that. I didn't want that reputation, but I could not always control what my employees did. They wouldn't want to tell me negative things, they never wanted me to be upset with them, because that kind of confrontation is like a bad smell that lingers. None of us wanted that. At our staff meetings with eight different departments, we'd discuss their work and their communication with me.

*   *   *

All of Las Vegas looked forward to New Year's Eve, the biggest holiday of the entire

184

year. Hotel/casinos made the most money at that time. I usually had a New Year's Eve party, with a dance and great decorations and entertainers. A lot of people would come, sometimes my own friends from out of town. Dr. Bob Jones, a dentist from Michigan, used to come. At midnight I would take my personal guests to the roof, seven stories high, to watch the fireworks downtown and on the Strip. All the fireworks displays were coordinated so that similar colors and configurations would explode at the same time. I couldn't wait for that moment, not because I was so enthralled with how beautiful the fireworks were, but because I could go to bed soon afterwards.

I'd set my alarm for five o'clock next morning. The first thing I did was go to the laundry room, because if the maids did not have sheets or towels to turn over rooms, we could not re-rent them, or customers who had paid a slightly higher price would be irate if their rooms were not cleaned and changed next day. Actually, on New Year's Eve most of my maids and janitors and laundry person got drunk, so they might not show up for work. I learned to prepare myself for that eventuality. Most New Year's Day I spent ten hours in the laundry by myself, with a few maids or janitors who would come in and out. Though I could smell alcohol on their breaths, I wouldn't say anything, I was just happy that they showed up. I prayed that my regular employees would come in, but I understood that they were celebrating, too, and didn't want to wake up in the morning.

Part of keeping my employees motivated depended on how I related to them. They knew that once I had been on food stamps, I had worked for minimum wage, I had no education, just like most of them. Motivational speakers had lifted me up and helped me constantly. I took a lesson from my own experience, and designed signs that I hung everywhere. The most popular was the "80 percent attitude and 20 percent knowledge" motto. I felt that everybody needed personal affirmations to keep going. We'd get "cold and pricklies" every day, so it was good to have a bit of "warm and fuzzy." I composed my own motivation motto, too. "Whether you call it work or play depends on your attitude." I realized that at the end of each day, when I was tired beyond my strength, I was also happy to be working hard at something I had come to enjoy.

185

There is no such thing as a self-made millionaire who's not extremely frugal and fastidious, willing to do whatever it takes, working sixty to eighty hours a week. If you observe extremely successful people, you'll notice that they're neat and clean. They don't mind cleaning after themselves or someone else and I was no exception. When I arrived in the morning in the parking lot of the Nevada or at the Queen of Hearts, the first thing I did was pick up trash. By the time I hit the front door, my hands were full. I'd check the back entrance of the Nevada Hotel, an area I tried to spruce up, because many customers who parked across the street at First and Bridge came in that way. We put in some turf carpeting and beautiful pink mirrors on the side. I'd often get to that back door that we tried so hard to keep attractive, and smell the urine, and the stink of cigarettes. There were maybe only ten percent of management staff who didn't smoke, so I had to put up with it. I tried very hard to have the exceptional non-smoking room, but it was very difficult. After a while, every sheet had a burn hole. We became experts at using the straight-edge razor blade to cut burn holes out of the carpets, but once that burn melts into the carpet, I could only pray that it hadn't burned all the way through.

Next, I'd head down to the front desk. The first thing I'd check at the front desk was the number of dirty rooms. Each room had a colored card. If it were turned one way, that would indicate that it was clean, turned the other way meant it was dirty. I would look at the rooms that were dirty, then I'd look at the night audit. Sometimes I noticed that there was no revenue collected on the rooms that needed cleaning. I always had a master key on me, so I'd make a quick note of suspicious rooms and I'd inspect them. Sometimes the room was completely used, and sometimes there was only one washcloth that had been used. I had to be my own detective and figure out why a card indicated that a room was clean. Did the desk clerk take ten dollars and pocket it and let the person use it for ten minutes? Was the key returned? Did the person who used the room have a key from a previous time? We had old-fashion keys, not cards. I could not afford the price of $250 for every single door for that system, but we had solid core, good quality doors with decent locks. I'd try to figure out what had happened and on

186

which shift. More than likely, it was after I was out of sight, maybe after five or six o'clock the previous evening

I didn't just check dirty rooms, but also rooms that were supposed to be clean. It was also always possible that the maid marked that she had cleaned it, but had not. I usually guessed that somebody had got into a room who had a key. The maintenance man wouldn't change a lock unless he were instructed to do so. There were so many possibilities. After I finished checking rooms, I'd go into the bar. Every eight hours there was a bar report made. There were numbers, and we had a metered gun. There were dollar drinks, dollar-fifty drinks and two-dollar drinks. At the end of each eight-hour shift those meters were read and the amount of money collected was recorded. Of course, there were a certain amount of complimentary drinks that were always difficult to justify. Since we had slot machines, whenever a customer bought ten dollars in quarters, he got a free drink. Sometimes there were hardly any quarters that had been used or sold, but a certain amount of drink money missing. I'd do my best to account for discrepancies and questionable room maintenance, but sometimes I felt as if I were sticking my finger into the proverbial dike.

Most customers drank more than they ate. In our coffee shop I only wanted to break even, but there were thousands of dollars of losses there all the time. Based on food costs and menu prices, we should have made a profit. I had to be vigilant about food handling, too. Rotisserie chicken was one of our specialties, a half rotisserie chicken that would be stored in brine in a fifty-five-gallon bucket with lemon juice and salt, natural preservatives. It would have taken weeks for that chicken to begin to go bad, but I would find buckets in the refrigerator that would take your lunch away when you smelled it. Employees didn't take responsibility for such details. I'd have arguments with them about a plain old potato. We served a large free breakfast. I'm not sure that was a good idea, but with a hotel room we had to provide a free breakfast buffet with home fries and scrambled eggs, bacon or sausage. I can tell the difference between a potato that has been cooked and reheated and a freshly cooked one. Cooks came in at four or five o'clock in the morning, and there was no reason they couldn't cook fresh potatoes. But time and time again they would boil potatoes at midnight or on a graveyard shift and reheat them in the morning for home fries. It seemed so simple to me, to do the job right, but they chose the easier way.

The devil is in the detail, and I must say that there is no successful owner of a hotel or any property who doesn't go through the hell of such details. I had to constantly be wary of theft, while never letting on that I suspected anybody. When I first bought the hotel in 1976, I remember my Hungarian friend, George, telling that most people will steal if they think they can get away with it, especially when they need just enough money to buy another pack of cigarettes, or a gallon of gasoline. I did not believe it at that time and I hate to believe it today, but I learned that anyone in business has to be aware of the probability. I walked a fine line with my employees. I did all my snooping carefully, so as not to offend them, but in some cases, employees actually brought transgressions to my attention, sometimes unwittingly. One example was the roulette dealer who seemed to be open and friendly.

"I can hit 29 on the roulette wheel every time," he told me one day.

I pulled out a hundred dollars and said, "Here, I bet you can't; this is yours if you can."

We went to the roulette wheel and, on the first spin, he didn't hit 29, but he did every time after that! I was so shocked, I actually started shaking. I wondered what to do, call Gaming Control? I couldn't sleep that night, casting about for someone I could talk to, and I thought of Bob Stupak, whom I trusted, but then I decided not to. I came to the realization that roulette dealers work forty hours a week, fifty weeks a year, for years and years. Probably more than fifty percent of that time they have nothing to do, but are supposed to be showing some action, spinning that ball and wheel. They have all that time to practice spinning the wheel at a certain speed and dropping the ball at a certain place, so they could become proficient at hitting a specific number. I let it go. I didn't call Gaming. I told the dealer, however, that he had better not do that; I'd be watching him. That was another hard lesson in discovering something I had to deal with and not knowing who to turn to or what to do about it.

Then there was George Moore, my assistant casino manager, a good-looking. flirtatious guy. Customers would come in asking for him. He hired many Asian girls, probably because he had been in Vietnam and was familiar with them and thought they had an innate sense of loyalty. He pretended to have an intimate relationship with me. When George would flirt and joke with me around the girls at the pit, I thought nothing of it. He was flirtatious with everybody. What I didn't realize is that the girls believed that he was having a relationship with me, so if anything went wrong, they would never come to me, unlike white girls who were dealers who would let me know about sexual harassment. None of the Asian girls did that. Did George harass them? I hoped not. They were afraid, and they didn't understand our culture.

One day, George showed me his skill with cards and demonstrated some card tricks. He took out a brand-new pack of cards wrapped just like a cigarette pack with a little red bead around it. He tore that off, then the plastic, then took the cards and plucked out the top and the bottom ones. I think there was one blank and one joker, which he took off and handed the pack to the dealer, who fanned out the cards and then turned them upside down and checked to see that all the cards were there. "Okay, they're all there."

George held out a king of hearts. "What about this one?"

I had stood there and watched him open a new pack of cards that he handed to the dealer, who checked them, both sides, verified that there were 52, and then George came up with that card. He had removed a card with both of us watching and we never saw it. That trick worried me, because he was obviously an accomplished gambler. He also pushed me to get black hundred-dollar chips. I found out later that he could hide a chip in his palm through sleight of hand, and probably stole more than I'd ever known. Whatever he was doing, he had fingers like a magician. He scared me, but what could I do? He was only the assistant manager, because he wasn't good enough to be the manager. It was very difficult to find a competent, honest manager.

I hired one guy who had been a manager at the Indian Springs Casino. I spoke to the owners there and they recommended him highly. He was earning $75,000 a year. I figured that if the owners said he was very good, and paid him two or three times what I paid my guys, he must be fine. But he did not have a real presence in the casino, he was not personable enough, so he didn't stay very long.

I hired another guy who must have weighed 350 pounds at six-feet-two, smoked a big, fat cigar, and used a lot of four-letter words. I have a tough time with four-letter words. It's one thing when you have to put up with your customers using them, and I even corrected them many times.

"You know, I'm really not comfortable with those words," I'd whisper, and they'd be surprised but usually tone down.

In a casino and drinking atmosphere, maybe I should have been more tolerant of that, but I would not allow my employees to use that kind of language, and I hated that stinky cigar. He had no class. Maybe he was good for the pit, but I could not stand him. I had employees before that I couldn't stand, but sometimes they did a wonderful job. I had a bartender who hated me, and I hated her, but I kept my distance, because the customers loved her. I tried to do this with the cigar-smoking casino manager, but I couldn't put up with him for long.

There was a girl named Porta who was initially a bar customer. She had a beautiful face and was tall, with lanky, lovely legs and she wore shorts a lot. I wound up hiring her as a bartender, but the poor girl couldn't count. I truly believe that Porta's mistakes were not from theft, but from ignorance, and she sometimes had a drinking problem. I fired her for that, but she'd still hang around like she was family. When she told me she was headed for the streets unless she got a job, I asked her if she was willing to clean rooms. When she said she was, I made her an offer.

"I'll tell you what; I'll make a deal with you. You quit drinking and I'll give you a job cleaning rooms, plus I'll give you a free place to live and I promise you that you can

190

count on this job as long as you don't drink."

We agreed to my terms. I think she actually had a bit of a mental problem, because she could handle only so much tension and then she'd fly off the handle and offend people. She started to develop little growths around her mouth, then all over her face. I took her to a doctor. I was willing to pay to have them removed, but the doctor wouldn't touch them, because they were cancerous. Every once in a while, one would fall off and then more would grow. I felt sorry for her. I couldn't fire her, yet the customers couldn't stand to look at her, but I kept her on. The last two years she was there she hardly worked at all, because she looked so awful, and she wasn't able to keep her cool in any kind of a job, but I had promised her that if she didn't drink she'd have a free room. I had to keep that quiet, because if other employees or customers knew, it would be like being in a foreign country when you give a dollar to one kid who's begging, then they all come around begging. Nobody except the accountant and me knew that Porta had a free room. It wasn't the finest room, but at least she wasn't on the street. A few years after she finally left, I got a call from one of our former employees who told me that Porta had died. Old-time employees often called me to tell me someone like Porta had died. They knew I cared about them. I was sad that I was not able to attend her funeral.

Then there was the pretty cocktail waitress who came to me from a half-way house. She was as cute as any waitress you'd find at the high-class hotel/casinos. I had never heard of half-way houses before I met her, and I wanted to know why she'd been in one. She told me she'd been arrested on drug charges, and that she was on probation. I decided to take a chance on hiring her, hoping she would not do anything illegal, because she had too much to lose. She got a lot of tips. One of the ways she attracted so many tips is that she worked bra-less, wearing a loose jersey, and a customer would lay down a dollar or more on the bar and she'd loosen her top and pick up the bills with her breasts. Customers loved that trick and laid down a lot of bills to watch her do it. I'd never seen such a thing. I actually wondered if it was legal. She moved on to another bar where she probably picked up $20 bills instead of dollar bills.

*   *   *

In 1995 I had a once-in-a-lifetime visit from my cousins in Vienna, a husband and wife who stayed at the Nevada Hotel. I wanted everything to be absolutely perfect for them but, as luck would have it, I got a call that there had been a drive-by shooting at the Queen of Hearts, somebody had sprayed the front doors with bullets. The doors had been locked, but bullets had broken the glass, and a man had staggered into the lobby, collapsed and died there. It was all over the news and I was so afraid that my cousins would see it on television. I couldn't imagine who the dead man was, but I found out when his African-American family from Henderson came to me and complained that they did not have the money to bury him. I had nothing to do with his murder or the fact that he died in my lobby, but people sued me for the most ridiculous things, I was concerned that somehow they were going to accuse me of being involved in his murder. I gave them $4,500 for the funeral and had them sign a release that they would not try to sue me. I later found out that the deceased man had hung around the neighborhood quite a bit. I wanted to know who he was, whose funeral I had paid for. An African-American man was working in my restaurant and I approached him.

"I need you to help me out with something. Would you take off your apron and come with me?" Once he got into the car and we took off, I said, "You know that man who died in our lobby; he was laid out at Bunker's funeral home and I need to see who he was, but I can't go in by myself as a lone white woman."

"No, no!" he yelled, "I'm not going, I'm not going; you can't do this to me; I'm not going."

"You have to help me; you have to go with me. I can't walk in there alone."

We walked into Bunker's and I looked at the man in the casket. I recognized his face, held up my camera and took a flash picture of him. That family roared up from their seats and went after me. We took off, hearts racing, jumped into the car and sped away. They say that "curiosity kills the cat," but I didn't care. I now knew who the man was. As there were a lot of drug dealings in that neighborhood. I'm going to guess that a drug deal had gone bad. It happened outside on the sidewalk, and the guy was looking for refuge; he would have run into any door. It just so happened to be mine.

Television coverage was broad, and I hoped my relatives were not watching TV. They never found out, to the best of my knowledge. If they had, I hate to think what they would have thought of my life style.

As I look back at harrowing moments when my life was in danger, the one that scared me most was when the restaurant and the main part of the casino was closed at the Nevada Hotel, and we just had the bar open, serving a little food in there at the time. I walked into the restaurant in the back and heard the hissing of gas and smelled it. I looked behind the stove and I could see a half-inch pipe with its cap removed, and gas was gushing out. I picked up that cap and screwed it back on. I realized that if I called the fire department, they would evacuate the whole building. But we had so many smokers around, including employees and customers, that I worried about the gas leak being close to the bar where people smoked. I screwed that cap on with my heart beating out of my chest, fearing that maybe the metal on metal would create a spark. I'd go up in flames with the rest of the place. That would be the end of me. I capped the gas, and nothing happened, but it was a while before I could breathe a sigh of relief. That was the scariest split-second decision I ever made.

*   *   *

At a Viennese ball in one of the hotels I met one of the most important people in my life, Dr. Ivan Perkovic. He was of medium height, very handsome, with pitch black wavy hair, and hazel eyes. He was astonished when I guessed from his name that he was Yugoslav. I was there with a date, but he was alone, and he loved Viennese waltzes as much as I did. He was agile, limber, and danced beautifully. I had heard that he was a medical doctor and a holistic healer. After that encounter, he would stop in at the Nevada to see me, and often invited me for Sunday dinner when his father was visiting from Croatia with his lady friend, who cooked a fabulous traditional dinner.

Ivan was so dedicated to his work that he worked eighteen to twenty hours a day, and needed only four hours sleep. He took patients who were deemed terminally ill into his home and cured them. I once saw a man on his exam table who had cancerous wounds on his legs that Ivan treated with a holistic paste and strict diet. Healthy tissues regenerated. He was a true healer, unconcerned about money. One day he showed me a brown paper bag full of bandages, and told me he earned barely enough money to buy them. I helped him with business matters, which he sorely needed. I was working sixteen hours a day, so we didn't see each other very often, perhaps for occasional dances on Sunday afternoons. Neither of us had play time, and so we slowly drifted apart.

After two years of living in the hotel I had a health crisis. I was breathing cigarette smoke constantly in the early 1990s, as the air in the casino was totally polluted. I became so sick that I couldn't leave my room; people brought checks to me to sign in my bed. I couldn't sleep, because of intense abdominal pain. I was reluctant to bother Ivan but, in the middle of the night, when I thought I was dying, I called him. He summoned me to his house immediately, and I was somehow able to drive the short distance to him. He examined me, probing and palpating, and concluded that I had appendicitis. Typically, all I could think of was the cost of surgery, the time I'd have to take off work, etc. But Ivan assured me I would not need surgery. He gave me chamomile flowers with which to make tea with boiled water, and instructed me to make at least two gallons and drink only that for the next twenty-four hours. I made it back to the hotel and crawled into my bed with the gallon of tea and slowly drank it over the next few hours until I fell asleep. I awoke in the morning not only pain free, but refreshed, though still very weak. Chamomile is a natural anti-inflammatory that cured me.

Ivan was the most brilliant man I have ever met. He would tell me things that I'd hear later on -- announcements ten years later on television about "scientists have discovered …" -- and it would be something he was already doing in 1992.

Among his other diagnoses, when I was crippled to the point of walking bent over at a ninety-degree angle, and my hip felt like there was a railroad spike in it, Ivan told me I had severe arthritis in my hip. I was shocked. "I'm too young; I'm fifty years old. How could I have arthritis?" He explained that it was probably caused by a combination of all the hard work, stress, no fresh air, an unhealthy life style. That was a blow. I thought I'd never dance or ski again.

He had created a six-week diet he called "The Onion Diet," based on the idea that we imperceptibly shed our skins every six weeks and the body renews itself. If you could eat that diet, you already had a lot of strength, because I certainly had a difficult time with it, while Ivan lived on it. I had to start the morning with a raw yellow onion, not a red onion or a Vidalia or a sweet onion, but the one that makes you cry when you peel it. I would eat that with a baked potato. He also recommended raw garlic, half a head each day. He also prohibited alcohol, which wasn't a problem, and caffeine, including sodas as well as coffee, no sugar, salt or fat. After a day or two I was able to add sauerkraut with salt only, no chemicals. There's something about the acid in sauerkraut that is very beneficial, just like apple cider vinegar, which is also a stimulant. I couldn't imagine that I would ever use my leg again, but in six weeks I was up and about and even took a skiing vacation with my kids. And I'd been thinking I'd never ski again. That was more than twenty years ago and today I can still kick my leg almost as high as my head. What's amazing is that I've only had a couple of recurrences when a slight pain would return because I'd eaten pork or prime rib. I decided to stick to chicken and fish.

Not only did Ivan cure me, but he had saved Chuck's life. When he was forty-five, he had suffered a heart attack and almost died in my arms. How grateful I was that doctors brought him back! That heart attack had been stress related, and I'm sure that not getting enough exercise was also part of it, and he was slightly overweight. After the heart attack and a five-way bypass operation, the doctors didn't expect him to live very long, but their prognosis was wrong. When Chuck was 61, he kindly came to help me with a structural problem at the Nevada Hotel. I inquired about his health and he told me he was scheduled for another bypass surgery. I urged him to see Ivan, who treated him with his holistic cures, including the Onion Diet, that unclogged veins and arteries, and Chuck never had to have surgery again.

*   *   *

After I recuperated and went back to my daily work schedule, one morning my head housekeeper came to me when I happened to be speaking to Jack Keiser, the banker who lent me the $50,000 that saved me in 1976. I had not seen him for years, and he had just come into my hotel/casino to say hello. I was so delighted to see him, but my head housekeeper interrupted us.

"Excuse me, I need to speak to you."

"It needs to be very important," I replied.

"It is."

I excused myself, and we got into the elevator, headed for the seventh floor, and she warned me that there were police there regarding a fellow in Room 720. I was shocked, as I'd been staying in 723. The man in 720 was a good customer, a high roller, someone who would play a hundred dollars a hand. I had introduced myself to him, and he joined me to listen to Jimmy Guy playing in the lounge area only twelve hours before. He was interested in how one gets a gaming license and I explained some things to him. He made a point of telling me he was not gay, though I had no idea why he would mention that.

When my maid took me into the elevator, I remembered assigning him to room 720 and telling him something about gaming revenues. The Gaming Control Board published a report on income of the quarter machines, the nickel machines, and different games. Since he seemed so interested, I told him I had that report and I would slip it under his door. His door was across from the elevator, and next morning I noticed that the report was gone. Not thinking anything of it, I continued downstairs.

When the maid and I got to his room, the door was wide open and I saw police

196

and private investigators everywhere. The yellow bedspread from the king-size canopy bed covered his body on the floor. He had been stabbed to death. A cold chill came over me, remembering grim movies I'd seen with such scenes. I wondered if I was the last person to speak to him, because after our conversation I had gone off to bed and I assumed that he did, too. The police questioned me about whether I had been with him the night before, and they wanted me to identify the body. I didn't want to walk close to him. Shocked, all I could think of was my bedspread, my bed, my carpeting, and he was laying there dead on it. When they pulled back the bedspread and I saw his face, I identified him as the same gentleman I had spoken to the night before. I was terrified that they might somehow blame me. I accompanied an investigator into 723, my room, and he asked me a few questions and left. By then, the place was surrounded, and I decided I needed to escape out the fire exit. I went down the back stairs, ran all the way to the fire exit door, ran to my car and got out of there, shaking. In the meantime, people were already beeping me. The press wanted to talk to me. I called an FBI agent I'd met once who had been very nice to me about another case. There was no answer, so I could only leave a message. I was so distraught, I needed to speak to someone, so I called Darrel Wayland, my former casino manager. Darrel happened to be at a bar someplace in the middle of town, so I met him there. I could hardly stand. I sipped a glass of water and told him what had happened. In the meantime, my phone beeped continuously from different news media and the front desk. They all wanted a statement from me. Finally, towards the end of the afternoon, I calmed down and decided that not speaking to them was worse than telling them what had happened. When I called them, they told me to stay where I was, they'd come to meet me. They came to interview me, with all the lights and cameras, and the manager of that bar was totally upset with me.

What bothered me is that after the police left, I didn't hear a thing afterwards. Some time later, someone showed me an article in the newspaper where I read that they had caught a German backpacker who was suspected of having killed the man. One of the investigators informed me that the victim was gay and so was the backpacker. I

197

remembered how strange I thought it was that the man remarked to me that he was not gay. I imagined all sorts of things about the backpacker, but actually I had no idea what happened. My assistant told me he had seen him in his own room throwing knives into the drywall, using it like target practice, then she saw him again in 720. I assume he was convicted for that murder, but I was never contacted again.

Murders and suicides often happen in hotels. One of the biggest pressures in life includes going on vacation. People are away from their comfort zones, without friends or support around them, in a strange environment. Can you imagine that people bring their life savings here and lose it all because they think that they've got a lucky formula? How many stories have I heard like that! It's unbelievable. They lose all their money, so they decide to go to their rooms and slit their wrists.

In Room 101—an especially beautiful room -- the maid went in and found a guy bleeding to death from both wrists. After the ambulance took him away, I knew I had to go in there and clean up that blood, because the maids would not. In this case, most of the blood had flowed into his brief case, so I threw that out and it saved me a little cleaning. I left the door open so that the maids could see me working. When that happens they usually offer to help me and, if I'm lucky, they'll finish the job.

One day we had a regular customer who was drinking a lot. He was staying in Room 116. After a few days, there was a horrible smell coming from the first floor hallway near that room. No one had seen the man for a couple of days, so we decided to go in. Sure enough, he had died, his body all blown up, maybe from alcohol poisoning.

An Asian woman once checked into Room 107, close to the front desk. All of a sudden, we saw smoke coming out of the room. The door was locked, and we couldn't get in, so we called the fire department and they broke through the door. The woman had chosen to commit suicide by putting a few dozen candles around her on the bed and then she lit them. I saw her charred face when they took her out on a gurney. We later met her next of kin and found out that her husband had left her, and she didn't want to live anymore. It's so sad that people often choose to die alone in a hotel.

In 1994 I'd had the Nevada casino for two years. The Gaming Control Board had given me a license to review and/or renew after that period, when they have a choice of not renewing, of denying my license. It could be denied if you did something evil, committed a felony or something like that. On the other hand, there are many reasons for not being renewed, like not having enough money for the cage. Gaming Control audited regularly, looking for infractions. On an hourly basis, a coin-operated slot machine could only carry so many coins; if someone hit a substantial jackpot and the machine could not pay out the full amount, an attendant would pay off the balance. The lucky customer would sign a hand-written receipt for the sum, and all three copies had to be initialed by two employees. If $1,000 or more was involved I would also sign it, though that was not required by Gaming. There could be many minor infractions in that process, for example, if something on the receipt was crossed out, two employees had to put their initials next to the crossed-out item. The receipt that the customer had signed and one copy remained in the machine in a locked box accessed only by my CPA. If there were not initials of two employees next to a cross out, that would constitute an infraction. I heard about Bob Stupak who had three hundred or more infractions. They were public knowledge and published in newspapers that would sensationalize them without specifics. Readers, including the Gaming Control Board, would not understand the level of intensity of the offense, and it would look bad, though it could have been a very innocent mistake.

The internal controls required by Gaming Control are as much of a blessing to us as a stop sign is on the road, because it keeps the gaming clean and protects customers. How quickly gaming would deteriorate if things were not done up according to standards. My casino's internal controls were written by George Zakilyanis, who was required to serve as an outside accountant for the gaming portion of the hotel. I had to pay him, but his first obligation was to Gaming Control. After we made drops, all the paperwork went to George, and occasionally he paid a surprise visit and would sit in on the audits and make sure that we were following the proper procedures that Gaming Control and our internal controls required. The internal controls described how we would do our drop. George wrote them before I was licensed, also for my property at the Queen of Hearts where I had an uninterrupted non-restricted license for twenty-five years. Internal controls help you to protect yourself against potential theft. In the same way that Gaming tries to make sure they get their taxes and nobody is cheating, at the same time, as an owner it's beneficial to require employees to stick to guide lines, which keep them from stealing. Of course, theft is possible in any kind of business. You have to be vigilant. In fact, justice is for the vigilant.

As this was my first experience in having live games and so many employees— 130 who were constantly turning over—we had a thousand W-2s that went out each year. The local dealer school would send their dealers to us, but they were learning and they made mistakes at our tables. As soon as they were good enough, six weeks later, then somebody else would hire them where they would get benefits that I couldn't afford. I tried paying for different benefits, like fifty percent of health insurance premiums, and I tried different retirement plans, but with the minimum wages that my employees received, they were not able to contribute even their small share.

The Gaming Control Board has thousands of undercover agents and they sometimes conduct sting operations. I would guess that there isn't a casino that doesn't have a dozen undercover agents in it at all times. For example, there was an incident at the Queen of Hearts when a heavily bearded young fellow asked for a drink and ten dollars in quarters. J.J., the bartender served him, but he was concerned about the customer's age, because when he asked him for a driver's license, he told him he didn't have one. J.J. asked the front desk manager if he ought to give him the quarters, and he told him to go ahead, so he did. The fellow took out one quarter, dropped it in the machine, walked out the door, and two agents came in flashing their badges. It was a sting! They wrote us up for serving a minor, and allowing a minor to game, and put both the bartender and the manager on probation. I was concerned that they would force me to fire them, because J.J. was one of the most honest employees I ever had, and so was the front desk manager.

The reality was that an undercover agent usually talked to alcoholics at the bar, usually in a stupor, and the agent or attorney couldn't write fast enough. None of those agents ever spoke to me, because I obviously had a totally different attitude and conducted myself respectably.

Judgement Day

When it came time to apply for renewal of my license, I had to leave at five a.m. to fly up to Carson City where the Board met. Whenever I went before the Gaming Control Board, I was so intimated that I'd be sweating and feeling sick. I had always worried that Gaming would test me on whether I knew the games or not, because I didn't. I never gambled. Fortunately, they never inquired about my knowledge of gaming.

When I arrived at the Board meeting, I was told that my case had been delayed, and they couldn't say how long I might have to wait. By four o'clock in the afternoon they had not decided what they were going to do yet. Fortunately, Jackie Gaughan was there as well. They finished with his hearing and when Jackie walked down the aisle, I leaned over to him and begged him to stay with me until my hearing was finished. Jackie slipped in right next to me and when they started, I sensed that they were being a little kinder because Jackie was there. He gave me moral support. He was carrying my mortgage, and was a character witness for me. He was a real emotional life-saver, especially when the Gaming Control Board finally announced that they would not renew my license. I couldn't believe it! I was devastated.

They stipulated that I was to close at midnight. I had 130 employees, and I would have to fire about a hundred of them by midnight. I had to empty every slot machine and close every table. We had approximately $75,000 in the cashier's cage, which I had to close. I was exhausted, having been up since dawn, and went through all that pressure with no attorney. I flew back feeling totally defeated.

Back at the hotel, I walked up to Jimmy Guy, our entertainer six days a week for the last two years.

"I'm sorry, Jimmy, but they didn't renew my license and we're going to have to close the casino."

He glared at me. "I'm fired? How dare you!"

I was feeling desperate and in need of a kind word and comfort, but the response from most of my employees was exactly like Jimmy's, as if I had done something deliberately wrong and they were losing their jobs through my fault. I never expected I'd have to close the casino. I treated my employees like my children, cared about them, and tried to set a good example. For them to respond in such a negative way, was very, very hurtful. I never said an unkind or improper word to any of them, in spite of the stress I was suffering, because everybody was on edge.

Kusala at the front desk was one of the few kind people left in the hotel. She was an Indian woman whose husband was a psychologist.

"You can cut the tension with a knife, just relax," she said.

I told Kusala I didn't know it showed but, obviously, it did.

It took us a long time to do the drop, because it started at midnight when we closed and went on until 2:30 in the morning. The regular employees stayed, but there had to be ten Gaming Control agents in there watching us do it. Whenever they close a place like that it's almost as if they're afraid you're going to do something drastic. Somehow, I kept myself and the work under control, and we got through it.

I could not get over a heart-breaking feeling of rejection, failure and despondency that lasted for years, even after I sold the hotel. One day I saw Augie Gurolla at the Las Vegas Country Club. Augie was a civil engineer who had replaced Kenny Gragson on the State Gaming Commission. He had also been Chuck's boss for several years, and I would see him, as well as Chuck with his new wife, Barbara, at parties. Augie was single and I was single and we started to date. He was a handsome man with a high forehead, mischievous dark eyes, and a ready smile. He was smart, and a wonderful politician, but I could never get close to Augie, because I felt that he had something to do with my license not being renewed, as he had excluded himself from that vote. I tried to explain how I felt to Augie. hoping he'd understand why I was so cool, why I could not warm up to him. It was a matter of trust. His response was, "We thought we were helping you." We thought we were helping you! That sounded to me like a big

203

daddy saying, now, little girl, you know this is too big for you to handle, so we're going to do you a favor. I was outraged at the thought that they would dare to judge me, to underestimate me so. I'd done very well. In fact, I did better than Augie. I did better than a lot of those people who did not start with nothing, including an education or connections that they all had. Obviously, I am not the kind of woman who would consider such a comment endearing.

*   *   *

Some time after that dreadful day, I went to a self-hypnosis seminar. I believe that we can make ourselves think and believe whatever we need to survive. I arrived at that seminar without saying what had happened. I had experienced a horrible disappointment and I was struggling with it. I didn't know how to either meditate or hypnotize myself to follow through and accept it. The seminar leader commented that when you accept what has happened you'll be free. I thanked him, sat down, waited for the intermission and left the seminar. I knew he was right and his answer was correct, but I felt hopeless, because I didn't know if I would ever have another opportunity again. There was no hotel/casino that ever stayed open once the casino was closed. There was rarely in all of Las Vegas a hotel/casino owner whose gaming license was not renewed who was able to survive with a hotel only. I am one of the few who was able to do that.

*   *   *

One day, joyful news reminded me that there was, after all, life outside Las Vegas. I still had relatives in Austria, one of whom informed me that my cousin, Renata Koren, was sending her sixteen-year-old daughter, Veronica, to be an exchange student in Mississippi. They had helped us after the war and were dear to us. They had never been to the United States. They're a very proper family and I thought it was all wonderful, but I worried about the family traveling on their own. I felt obliged to go to Mississippi to see the family that Veronica would be living with. I didn't have much time, so I flew there and, because of the short notice, I paid $880 for the trip. When I arrived, the host family met me at the airport and we went to see their house and the room Veronica

204

would be staying in. The window was only a couple of inches from the floor so that it could actually be used like a door, and there was no lock on the window. That worried me, and I kindly asked if they would please put a lock on it. They were a southern family who seemed very respectable, and they even had a little party to introduce me to some of their friends, but they were somewhat offended by my request. However, I trusted they would do it. I was overjoyed to be with family members again, and to meet Veronica, a polite, lovely girl.

The day they took me to the airport we stopped at a beautiful lake and ate fried chicken at a restaurant. By the time we arrived, I started to feel sick, and suspected it was the chicken. I had to change in Atlanta, at Gate 23, and the gate right next to mine was going directly to Las Vegas. Though that was not the flight I had booked, I couldn't understand why I couldn't get on it, why I should wait for my later connecting flight. I got into the line for the direct flight, handed the agent my ticket, which he tore off as they did in those days, and I boarded the plane. Nauseous, I went directly into the bathroom to relieve my stomach distress and freshen up. When I came out, my seat was taken. Of course, I knew why it wasn't available, but I hadn't considered that possibility. I thought, oh, my God, what am I going to do? I went back into the bathroom until they knocked on the door and said I had to go to my seat, but I didn't have a seat on that flight.

They called me a stowaway, though I tried to vindicate myself. "Please phone down to your people and you'll see that I paid $880 for this ticket." The attendants were at fault for allowing me on that plane without checking my ticket more closely, and they did not want to be held responsible. They called ahead to Las Vegas to report a stowaway. When I got off the plane, a police officer was waiting for me.

"I know who you are; you lost your license at the Queen of Hearts."

"No, sir, I never lost my license at the Queen of Hearts."

It was at the Nevada, but I didn't say that; I very politely said that I never lost my license at the Queen of Hearts.

"Could we go down to Delta Airlines?" I asked. "We can clear this up very quickly if we just go down to Delta. They can confirm that I paid $880 for my ticket." But he didn't want to hear that.

It was Sunday night, and he took me into a room for questioning, wrote a citation, and kept me there for two hours. He called the FBI and didn't find a record, and then he called the local police, but there was nothing. He was waiting for his supervisor to leave. It was ten or eleven o'clock at night and, once his supervisor left, he was in charge. After he left, the policeman turned to me.

"We're going to take you downtown and book you."

A car came for me with a girl in the back seat who was handcuffed. They put me in the front seat, and the girl said, "Why doesn't she have handcuffs on and I do?" The policeman handcuffed me apologetically. "I'm sorry." They took me down and booked me. It was late at night, and I wouldn't get out until morning. The room was full of benches, with some people sleeping on them. There was no way I could sleep, I was too upset.

Next morning, my manager bailed me out and I called my attorney. The incident had to be reported to the Gaming Control Board. I paid a few thousand dollars to the attorney to investigate. When he called the police security department at the airport, before he ever told him the name of the policeman who had arrested me, his supervisor said, "There isn't anything you could tell me about this officer that would surprise me." That's all my attorney needed to hear. The whole case ended in a big apology, and they expunged my record.

But that incident had to be explained to Gaming Control. Steve DuCharme had the audacity to say, "Well, that wasn't really the gate right next to where you were supposed to board."

"Yes, it was," I insisted.

They wanted me to admit that I had deliberately got onto the wrong plane. The only thing I would admit is that I should not have gotten onto that plane.

206

I told my daughter Bridgett and her husband what had happened, but the rest of my family never knew what I did, all in the cause of helping my cousin's daughter. As it turned out, she stayed with the family in Mississippi for one year and then came to Las Vegas to spend a few days with me. I asked her if she'd like to go see the Grand Canyon or Hollywood, and she opted for Hollywood, so we drove there and up the coast to Santa Barbara and Venice Beach, where all the crazy people skate on the sidewalk in their crazy costumes or work out on Muscle Beach. That little trip was her dream come true.

Since then, Veronica and her brother, Max, have also come with four or five friends to stay with me for a week or ten days in the summer. It was such a joy to see them bouncing around my swimming pool, which are not very common in Austria. Fortunately, I didn't have to do a lot of entertaining with them. They'd go out late at night and roam up and down the Strip. They were all just over twenty-one, so I didn't worry about them, as I would about younger people.

*　　*　　*

Fortunately, I was able to reapply for a casino license after two years, and I did get permission for slot machines, but I could not operate them. I had fifteen slot machines in the bar with a route operator, someone who installs and operates the machines, making rounds among different casinos. To me that was such a slap in the face, the assumption being that I couldn't operate fifteen slot machines. I already had a non-restricted license with more machines than that a block away. His presence humiliated me. There were so many painful things that I had to put up with, but I had to continue to have slot machines, and the liquor license and food service license, because if I ever lost any of that, I would have so many other bundles of trouble that I might as well give up.

Reapplying is exactly the same as the first time you apply, when the stack of paper work might be an inch high. When I reapplied, and they brought my files out in front of the Board, they were a couple of feet high. They wanted to keep that route operator in the Nevada, even though I continued to maintain a license at the Queen of Hearts. It was a horrible insult to me that they didn't allow me to run my own machines. I felt helpless.

I couldn't help thinking about people like John Woodrum, who owned the Klondike. John went in front of the Gaming Control Board and he demanded that they not set a time limit on his license the way they did the two-year license for me. He demanded it! He had a rough, aggressive voice, and was a super salesman. He wasn't accepting anything from the Board. They gave him that license, approximately the same time as mine, without the two-year limit. I couldn't believe it. In the meantime, his daughter was involved in an armed robbery, and his son had got into trouble. Finally, with the sale of the Klondike, something happened and they lost all their money. I never knew what the details were, but I remember him saying so long ago that his biggest problem would be keeping his son out of jail.

What I carried away from my hearing was the conviction that, even though I might be a better person than him, I did not get what he did as an aggressive male who demanded it. I didn't have the guts to demand anything.

I was reminded many times that women in Las Vegas are treated very differently from men. For one thing, you hardly ever have a woman in front of the Gaming Control Board. When I went in front of the Board the first time for a non-restricted license, it was in an air-conditioned auditorium, and I was in the back with my accountant and my attorney. The Board members calmly and quietly took care of whoever was before them, but when they called my name, I went up to them and the news media -- Channel 8 and Channel 5 -- turned the cameras and lights on and recorded everything I was saying, which was very intimidating. I was walking towards them with my attorney when a camera man leered at me and commented that I must be awfully popular. I didn't respond, but I didn't appreciate it. I lived my life as though I was on stage all the time.

When my license was not renewed, the head of the Board at that time said, "Well, with all these lawsuits, it looks like you're using them to avoid paying your bills." When someone on the Gaming Control Board says something like that you don't want to argue, though I'm sure my eyes were defiant. Many times, attorneys are afraid to speak up to Board members. Attorney Ferrara got himself in a lot of trouble when he spoke up for Ted Binion while defending him, which is what I thought he was supposed to do. My attorneys never spoke up for me. As a matter of fact, they told me sometimes to be quiet and allow the Board to scold me. For example, when Mr. McAllister was a commissioner, my attorney warned me to keep my mouth shut when a Board member was rattling off all kinds of lies about me. I kept looking up at my attorney, but we were not allowed to say anything, and all those untruths went into the record. I have no idea what was behind it, but I knew that I had been wronged, and I never forgot it.

In preparation for the two-year license renewal, when they were doing all this sting action and so on, they brought the Labor Board in. Oh, they bring every agency -- the Health Department, the Building Department, the Fire Department, and OSHA (Occupational Safety and Health Administration). A beautiful, well-dressed girl from the Labor Department came and talked to me. We were walking from the casino through the lobby when I picked up a piece of paper and threw it into the trash.

"You shouldn't do that," she remarked.

"I 'm setting an example for my employees," I replied.

"Well, you shouldn't do that."

After the woman's visit, the Labor Board went through my records and noticed that I did not allow overtime. We had three eight-hour shifts a day, with appropriate breaks, but employees were not allowed to work overtime. I knew what the laws were, but it was very difficult for me to get my employees to quit on time. They would dilly-dally, socializing, before clocking out. Sometimes when a shift was over in the restaurant, an employee might not have had time to get food to take out which, incidentally, was not permitted, in principle. I had big problems with employees stealing food. Bartenders would also give free drinks for a dollar that often went into the tip jar. Then they'd chat at the time card machines for an extra ten or fifteen minutes. I was required to pay for that time and, after eight minutes, I had to pay for fifteen. The Labor Board ended up fining me $75,000 for unpaid overtime.

"The First Thing We Do Is Kill All the Lawyers"

(Shakespeare, Henry VI)

Having hired almost a hundred lawyers in my lifetime, I learned that their absolute priority is assessing how much money they will make in each case. Lawyers scrutinize the person sitting across from them, calculating whether that person might give them a hard time or if they will have difficulty collecting their money. Lawyers have "old boys clubs." They play golf and have dinner together, they do favors for each other. With most communication and transactions, especially in business, I, too, want to know what's on the other person's mind. If it happens to be money, then I'd rather satisfy that issue first and then talk about my own needs.

I happened to know an attorney to whom I said hello on the streets many times, but when I asked for his counsel he refused. I was not rich enough. There were many smaller attorneys who had covered me when there were only 250,000 people in town, but as soon as the population reached a million or more, they only wanted to represent the big hotel/casino owners. I could no longer afford them, and they would tell me that up front.

Whenever I needed just an hour of an attorney's time, I figured out what to do. One case happened to involve Chuck Deaner, from whom I needed some real estate advice. I took $200 in cash, went into his office, asked if I could have one hour of his time, and laid down the $200. At the time, he probably only charged $150, but who knows? You never know how they're billing, because you can't justify their bills. Even though they may advertise themselves as half-price attorneys, it's not what they charge an hour, it's how they bill you. You have absolutely zero control over that and if you try to question a bill, that when the attorney loses interest in you. You've got to expect it's going to cost you twice what you think. But when I laid $200 on Deaner's desk, he

211

looked at the clock.

"Okay, I don't have an appointment for another hour, this is pocket money," and he took it and talked to me for an hour.

I had other similar situations of going to attorneys I knew and offering a set amount of cash for an hour. Sometimes it's easier because they might be paranoid, thinking maybe you're part of a sting operation. Immediately relieve them of that worry, so they can concentrate on what your own worries are. That's my formula for getting one quick, honest hour of an attorney's time.

Attorneys are always thinking of themselves first. If you listen to them carefully, you'll realize that they might want to draw a case out as long as possible, because that means more money for them. When it's costing $250 an hour, they'd like to keep a client on a lucrative string. Today it's probably more like $300 an hour. At least, for a really good attorney. You're always going to be much better off if there is any way to shorten the case. You can try to convince the lawyer that you have no more money and have to wrap up the case, or you can offer a flat fee of $2,000 or so to finish it. Try to contract a price, insisting that you don't have the time, energy, or money to drag on your case. However, you have to have a degree in rhetoric to negotiate with an attorney. Clients don't have their extensive training; they know so much more than we'll ever know. If you're suing someone, hiring attorneys on a contingency of having them take a certain percentage motivates them to work more quickly and diligently. Also, it's the best way to receive a set amount.

In probably fifty lawsuits that I've been involved in, I did not initiate most of them. As a hotel owner, I was prey for predators who make a living suing people. They find me in the phone book as a hotel owner and think of a way to sue me. It's that simple. They'd assume I was very wealthy and they'd go after me. Most of them were what they call nuisance suits, where an attorney would tell me that I could either give him $500, or give the plaintiff $500 to end the suit. I used a pre-paid legal service that covered a certain number of law suits. During that so-called free service, the best I would get is exactly what the attorney told me, either pay him or the fellow who was harassing me. The legal services I experienced were not worth the money I pre-paid.

Another thing I learned is that whenever somebody threatened to sue me, they never did. The people who sue you are the ones who never tell you their intentions. Someone who serves you a law-suit subpoena is supposed to walk up to you, ask your name or know who you are—they usually have a picture of you—and hand you the paper. I've had situations when a server threw the paper onto the front desk as I watched him from the back. The guy obviously knew who I was, but I didn't know who he was and I didn't identify myself. I've had them on the other side of my back door, hearing them say, "Ann Meyers, you're served," and drop the paper in front of the door and walk off. In both of those situations I asked my son-in-law attorney, Ed, whether that was legitimate service, and he told me that it was not, so I'd ignore it. As a result of such negligent service, some frightening things happened. Once, when I was spending six months a year in Tahoe and came home to Las Vegas, I received a letter from Bank of America stating that there was a judgment on my bank account of $4,250,000, and that I had ten days to do something about it or they'd release the money. At the time, I had $2,000,000 in the bank account. Fortunately, I had made it back within the ten days and I called my son-in-law again, who handled that part of the case to stop them from emptying my bank account. They froze my account, but the letter I received was not certified. In other words, the service was not legal. If that money had been released, I would never have had a chance to get it back. It would have been gone. Attorneys would have eaten it up or the person who was suing me, Scott Burton, would have gambled it away. I was told that people who get fast money rush to the gambling tables or the races to spend their ill-gotten funds. The alleged reason Scott sued me was that while he was sitting at my bar and had his legs twisted around the bar stool, playing around, teetering back and forth, he fell and broke his leg. That was the first time he sued me. The second was when he was upset at the bartender for serving his girlfriend a drink against his wishes. He took all her clothes from their room and threw them on the floor in the bar. We had a policy that we tried never to call the police, but he came to me at the front desk.

"I told the bartender to call the police and get her out of here, but he wouldn't. Now I want you to call the police."

"We don't call the police unless there is a life or death matter," I replied.

But there at the front desk he called the police himself, who came. It turned out that there was a warrant out for his arrest, so he didn't get far with that dispute. That was the last time I saw Scott Burton. I found out that he'd been doing drugs as well as alcohol and he had been using an alias name. Then he sued me from jail! He actually studied law in jail. It cost me $75,000 in attorney fees over a year and a half, during which time I hated those monthly bills coming in from the attorney. I tried to negotiate with him, knowing he would charge me up to $5,000 every month, so I asked if we could just pay off Scott to make the law suit go away. The attorney wouldn't tell me how many more months it might drag on or how many more thousands of dollars I might have to spend to make it go away. An attorney will usually tell you that your fee will be less than a thousand dollars, but it never is, I guarantee you. I actually paid him $12,000 to drop the case. A few months later, my attorney called.

"I've got some good news and bad news. Scott Burton died last January."

It was August. I'd been billed all those months and he never let me know that Scott had died in January.

"Well, then the case is over."

"Oh, no, the case still goes on. His girlfriend is going to continue with the lawsuit."

"She has nothing to do with this lawsuit."

"Oh yes, she does; her clothing was in the room they stayed in."

He told me he'd have to file a request for closure of the case.

"Okay, how much?" was all I said. I was defeated.

The only winners in lawsuits are the attorneys. Anyone who thinks that law suits

214

are the answer, I can tell you they've never been the answer for me. Never.

Bottom line, no attorney is interested in your case unless he can make money. It's not a love affair; it's a financial agreement. On the other hand, it could be a love affair. The ninth attorney I approached to handle my divorce from Leon, who emptied our bank account, sold our house and ran off with another woman who was pregnant, that attorney was interested in romance. The reason I had such a hard time hiring an attorney was, obviously, because I had no money, but finally I found Max Ziskin. Max was an extremely intelligent man, financially well off, and he really liked me. Even though he didn't get me a super settlement – I got fifty percent of what was in our bank account and so did Leon -- at least it was done and I could get on with my life. I tried to get over the fact that I came into that marriage with $6,000 for a down payment on a house, and the fact that it cost me as much in attorney's fees to collect child support payments of $200 a month. Once I arrived in Las Vegas, of course, I accepted it; I didn't chase it any longer, and I didn't get any money after 1976.

Max hinted that he'd like to have a romantic relationship with me. Legally, he didn't do any more than anybody else would have, but he didn't charge me, he worked *pro bono* for me. He was a fantastic attorney, and having him on my side was crucial. I never said no to Max unless I absolutely had to. I let him know that I had a boyfriend, Chuck, but that didn't deter him. One day, I finally agreed to see him for a date, because I was scared to death that he might drop my case if I disappointed him. I couldn't sleep that night, and called him first thing in the morning to cancel the date, because I felt like I was prostituting myself, and I could not handle doing that. When you have strong principles, there are some lines you do not cross.

Having said that, I must add that sometimes you wind up right at the edge of doing illegal things yourself, because you're trying to survive. I'll give you an example of how I broke the law.

It's no secret that on the corner of First and Lewis where the Queen of Hearts was, there were a lot of street people, and also a lot of crime. When I took over the Queen of

Hearts, we didn't have more than a handful of TVs and it was almost impossible to rent a room without a TV. I would have rented a room for myself without a TV, if it meant paying less for it, but I'm not the typical American. I realized how important it was to get TVs into the rooms, and when a guy came to the front desk offering to sell used TVs cheap, it was very hard to resist the temptation. I was like a hungry dog, drooling when I saw those TVs for $30 each, but I didn't buy them. I knew they had to be hot. Once again, I was shocked, because I'd never been offered stolen merchandise in my life. I never bought a hot TV, but for all I knew they might have been offering me one of my own TVs they had stolen from me!

We had an alarm at the back fire exit that we could hear from the front desk. It would go off often. If you only have one person at the desk and that alarm goes off, that person would be inclined to run down to see what was happening, leaving the desk open to a robber. My own TVs would go missing through that fire exit, so I decided to lock it. That's against the law, but it was the only way I could stop thieves from escaping with hotel property. Crafty as they were, they would report me to the Fire Department for locking the door. What always amazed me was that thieves knew the law better than I did. I locked the door and put the key in the cash drawer with a label, "fire exit door." During the course of the day, if we had a fire inspector walk in, the first thing we did was grab that key and go unlock the door. I actually believe that, in some cases, the Fire Department understood what we were doing. They could not legally condone it, but they sometimes turned a blind eye. A fireman might find the fire exit door locked, but we would go back to the exit and he would push on the door, and it would open. He'd say, "OK, it's working as far as I'm concerned," and he would leave. We prayed that we would have enough time to go unlock it, because that didn't always happen. If the door was locked, and the fireman warned me that it was a violation that needed to be corrected immediately, I would rush back and unlock it and he'd write, "While I was there, they corrected it." But many of those reports went to Gaming Control. I learned that every business, large or small, has something to steal, and if a business has more than one door, it's something to think about.

I made some terrifying decisions, and I made big mistakes. The biggest mistake was with the IRS, which you don't ever want to do! It was about employee taxes that I had to deposit with the IRS within a certain number of days or face severe penalties. In my case, as usual, I was short of money, and I didn't have enough to pay the IRS and keep my doors open for gaming with enough money in the cage. I decided not to make the tax deposit as I usually did -- directly to the bank from which it was transferred to IRS -- within the stipulated number of days. It didn't take long for IRS to come in and present a seizure notice. First, they demanded all the money in my bank account, so I had to go a couple of blocks away to Bank of America, empty my bank account and give it to the IRS. After that they demanded all the money in the cashier's cage. As soon as they took the money out, they wanted all the money inside the slot machines and at the front desk, and I had to close the doors. They notified Gaming Control. After they did all that, the IRS agent told me he wanted more money.

"You owe us more money; we want it right now."

"But I gave you all the money I have. I don't even have money to make change for a hundred-dollar bill at the front desk."

He must have thought I had a special stash somewhere else, but I didn't. They even took the personal money I had on me. They took everything.

Within a few days I made arrangements for a loan at a high interest rate -- about 16 percent -- and I gave the IRS agent a copy of the papers and promised to deliver money to the IRS through that loan, which would have gone through in two days. But five or six big guys came in a day before that and put seizure notices all over the entire outside of the building. I was so intimidated I went to my office and called Jackie. He gave me the full amount of money I needed and added it to my loan and didn't increase my monthly payment!

I can't say enough about how much I appreciated Jackie Gaughan. When Jackie and I made a deal about property, we never had any inventory lists. With some people they'll haggle over a chandelier. There was not one list of inventory of the Nevada Hotel when I bought it. Our deals were sealed with a hand shake. That's unheard of today.

Whatever problems I've had, my response has always been, "And this, too, will make me stronger. What can I learn from this?" You have to talk to yourself and do the very best you can and pat yourself on the back for what you've done, because nobody knows the personal struggles that you have gone through.

Disaster in the Desert

And then 9/11 happened! The country was in shock, in the throes of the worst disaster of our history, feeling deeply vulnerable in the wake of the first major terrorist attack on the United States. We were sobered by the loss of that sense of security we thought was our birthright.

I had been working around the hotel, one eye on a television screen, the other concerned with tasks at hand. When I saw the planes explode into the Twin Towers, I thought I was watching a horror movie, and barely paid attention. Then my cousin, Veronica, called me from Austria. She sounded very upset, telling me she was sorry about something I didn't comprehend. Oblivious, I told her not to worry -- everything would be all right. Finally, I registered the scenes playing out on the TV screen, as staff gathered round to watch in disbelief as the reality of that catastrophic morning slowly sunk in.

Las Vegas turned into a ghost town. No one walked the streets; everyone was glued to television screens. No airplanes crossed the sky, and I noticed an eerie silence. People who had driven into town fled in their cars, anxious to get home, as one is during a crisis. Traffic exiting Las Vegas was bumper to bumper. I watched television reports, mesmerized, to see car rental agencies and the downtown bus station mobbed by visitors stranded by the closure of McCarran Airport, grounding about seventy local flights, and clearing 10,000 travelers from the airport. Almost all hotel bookings were cancelled. Local car dealers were besieged by desperate travelers wanting to buy a car, drive it home and sell it. Overnight, tourism and business dried up in the desert of Las Vegas, and thousands of employees were laid off.

For weeks, I had nothing to do but sit around my empty hotel all day, worrying about how I was going to pay the bills. In the evening I'd go to bed at eight o'clock. I finally decided I needed to get out and be with other people, so I went to the Dunes and sat at the bar. I ordered a soft drink and a handsome gentleman sat down next to me. We started talking, and he asked me if I was "a working girl."

"Oh Yes. I've been working since I was fourteen years old. I worked as a dental assistant, then after that I worked as a bank teller," and so on. I was so ridiculously naive. The gentleman didn't leave immediately, but our conversation flagged. I found out afterwards what "a working girl" meant.

While some businesses picked up the following spring, the fiscal year ended with 6,000 fewer casino jobs on the Strip. I was so broke I couldn't make payments on my house that I had bought in 1980. I missed three mortgage payments and lived under a dark cloud of fear that my house would be foreclosed. I had no idea what foreclosure entailed, but imagined that, out of the blue one day, tough-looking guys would come to my house and evict me. I started inventorying everything in the house, and gathered precious objects just in case I had to make a quick exit. Worried that I might lose it, I moved my baby grand piano into the hotel lobby, thinking that Jackie wouldn't throw me out of the hotel, and at least I'd have my piano there. Overwhelmed with anxiety, I found a moment of spiritual reprieve one day when I looked out my front windows at the mountains in the distance. I recalled hiking through them many times, gathering wild flowers, gazing at the views across the desert all the way to the horizon. At such moments I felt as free as any bird winging its way across the sky. I comforted myself with the thought that this grand vista, this wonder of nature, would always be mine. No one could ever take that away from me.

My house was never foreclosed. I managed somehow to make mortgage payments, which always came first, then payroll a close second. Sometimes employees' checks were refused at the bank, and I would try to cash them myself. The bank often did not bounce my checks, but did charge an overdraft fee. I became so desperate at one point that I tried to procure a loan on my car, a 1998 Lincoln Mark 8 that was five years old. I was offered only a few thousand dollars, way below the value of the car, and I walked out.

I went to Jackie and asked if he would reduce the interest rate on my loan from ten to eight percent, and he allowed it. There was never a time that I asked Jackie for anything that he didn't say yes. I never called unless it was absolutely necessary, but when I needed him, I'd make a phone call and he'd say, "Okay, go see my attorney at ten o'clock tomorrow morning." I'm proud to say that we had a great relationship. Jackie was a civic leader, a supporter of the Catholic Church and Bishop Gorman High School, from which both of his sons graduated. I was not surprised when in 1987, Jackie was named Humanitarian of the Year by the Clark County Chapter of the National Conference of Christians and Jews.

In 2003, my 10,000 square feet casino remained almost empty, and I needed to make some money. A fellow named Franklin came along who operated an athletic club, and he wanted to install a similar club in my hotel. I told him the rent would be $20,000 a month. He was willing to put $50,000 up front, but he wanted to tear out the whole casino—the restaurant, the bar, bathrooms, decor, ceiling -- everything. Actually, $50,000 up front was a small amount, and he signed a lease that stipulated that he would start paying $20,000 a month after thirty days.

I was elated! I'd be able to pay my bills, and I felt bailed out. I was so elated that I went on a trip with one of the ski club groups to Bangkok. During a shopping expedition, I found a magnificent painting of the Madonna and Child. I was so taken by it, seeing in their expressions the wonder and love that mark motherhood, that I bought it and brought it home. I thought of Bridgett, who had divorced Barry, the astronomer, long ago, and married Ed Gaines, a successful attorney. They had been longing to have a child, to no avail, and now Bridgett was forty years old. When we went on our annual ski trip to Aspen I gave the painting to her, sharing my love of that moment of bonding between a mother and her baby. I've always believed in magic and was thrilled but only mildly surprised when Bridgett told me she had become pregnant forty-eight hours after receiving the painting. Their daughter was born in 2004, and they named her Aspen, as she had been conceived there.

When I came back from Bangkok, Franklin met me at the door of the casino and, to my horror, I saw that it had been totally stripped. There were no walls, no ceilings, the floor had been ripped up, the drains were filled with sand and the water fixtures had been ripped out. He was building shower stalls instead of urinals. Then he had the nerve to look me in the face and say, "I don't have any more money. I need $50,000 to be able to start building." I was speechless. I couldn't even begin to say whether it would cost a million to put the kitchen back together, and a quarter million to replace the flooring and electrical outlets. All the stainless steel in the kitchen was gone, and I figured he'd sold everything he could. I realized he was trying to scam me, and I didn't know what he'd do next. Actually, he did nothing after that. Nor did I give him his $50,000 back. Our contract specified that he had to pay each contractor, but that didn't stop the contractors from putting liens on my property. I did the lien release forms and whatever I was supposed to do legally and, after paying several legal fees, I was faced with a slew of attorney fees, a heavy heart and dashed hopes. I was so choked up with hurt and pain, not to mention anxiety, that I could hardy breathe.

Miracles Still Happen

At the end of 2003, in the midst of my frantic struggles to survive, when I thought all hope was lost, a miraculous thing happened. Someone offered to buy my properties!

I belonged to the Las Vegas Country Club, and I went there one day and saw David Atwell, who had sold the Casbah to me. He asked me if I was interested in selling my properties. Realtors ask this all the time, and it's usually unproductive, but David told me he knew a company that might be interested in buying them. Right there and then we agreed that I'd sell everything for seven million dollars. He said he'd speak to his people and convey my offer. They came back and tried to get it for six million, but I refused and stuck to my offer. On a one-page document we wrote the selling price that included the hotels and all the contiguous properties. Dave Barrick, founder of Barrick Gold Mining Corporation, bought the Queen of Hearts and the Hotel Nevada, and most of Jackie Gaughan's downtown Las Vegas real estate assets for around $82 million. One year after that lunch at the Country Club, I found out who Dave Barrick was and that, in fact, he was the man I'd been talking to over lunch that fateful day. At that point he was already in contract on several of the casinos and was making a contract on mine, too. He wound up owning five or six casinos downtown. I was not aware that he actually already had a casino in Colorado and was doing quite well with it. Of course, being the mogul that he was, he has many people operating places for him.

At the Queen of Hearts, I had to buy the bar for $80,000, which I had previously leased to Woody from Carlson Electric. They're still there on Main Street just north of Bonanza and he's still in business now. I call him occasionally to fix my home pool pump. He's an old-timer.

I had to list all the properties – two hotels and three parcels, two of which I was using for a parking area. There was a lease option to buy the Nevada Hotel parking lot, which I could have bought for a million dollars from Jackie but, in the meantime, I rented it from him for only $2,000 a month, a very good deal.

In December 2003 Barrick opened an escrow account -- "earnest money" as they'd say in Ohio -- into which incremental payments were deposited during ten months until the closing in October 2004. When the escrow people finally asked me to come down and sign the papers, I was so anxious—it had been delayed so many times— that I ran down, went into that office and signed the papers. Negotiating the sale of my properties, there were some things that I felt were unclear, for example, the parking lot was not part of the deal. I wrote that in the margins of the contract in a couple of different places. I counted how many papers there were. The Escrow Agent took them out of the office to make copies for me, but when she came back and I looked at them, my changes did not appear. She said, offhand, "Oh, Barrick's people were here and picked up the papers and they already took off."

I spent close to $70,000 trying to get that parking lot back. It was such a money maker and I did not want to lose it but, in spite of all my aggravation, I did. If I had had someone sitting next to me who could have been a witness to my note that the sale did not include the parking lot, I could have had it. I should have known that you always want to have a witness with you. As a woman, I usually had a man standing next to me. I sometimes put the man into a suit—he might have been a janitor—and asked him not to open his mouth, just to come and be my witness and not speak. I'd love it when people thought he was an attorney. In this case, at least the Escrow Agent returned my documents to me.

After he bought my hotels, Barrick kept my manager, Deon Brozen who, by the way, came back to work for me in two different office complexes I owned. He's over 75 and he's slowing down, but he's there at six o'clock in the morning, because he wants to be, not because I ask him. He could come in at nine o'clock, as far as I'm concerned. I sometimes don't get to that property but once a month, but he knows what to do and he's doing okay.

A fellow named Gadsby was the manager of the Queen of Hearts, but he did not see eye to eye with Barrick, who immediately hired someone else. Unfortunately, he took a desk clerk and made him manager, though he was not qualified. I always felt that managing a large staff was like being an orchestra leader, someone to keep everyone in tune and coordinate their solo work within the ensemble. The difference in the new operations was that the orchestra leader was gone, and no qualified person was conducting. The kind of love and attention you give a property when it's your life blood, when it is everything you've ever worked for, is totally different than someone like Barrick coming in and hiring operators. You can't pay enough to someone to be devoted and give their all to a place they don't own.

Barrick did not do well at either properties, and they wound up selling it to Tamares Group, which was acquired by LiveWork Las Vegas. In September 2008, the Los Angeles Times published a story about the owners who, in order to keep their gambling license, opened the shuttered casino for eight hours once every two years. The newspaper reported that the property at the time was valued at between $13 million and $15 million.

When I was approached about operating other people's hotel/casinos. I thought, well, what is my value? And I figured my value was a thousand dollars a day. To give what I gave to my hotels is worth a thousand dollars a day, and I don't mean 250 days a year, I mean $365,000 a year.

By the way, if I were to come to Las Vegas and start all over again, my goal would be to own a bar on a piece of land with parking around it, a nice restaurant and fifteen slot machines. Most important, I'd own the real estate. No hotel rooms. Kilroy's bar was like that. It just so happens that my friend, Michael Loudermilk, the real estate investor, built that bar and then he leased it for $20,000 a month, which was really good, especially considering that the building was only about 5,000 square feet, so it didn't cost him a lot of money to build it. It's at Buffalo and West Charleston on the northeast corner. Most people would think $20,000 a month is good income. The owner of the bar was bringing in between $750,000 and a million dollars net a year from those slot

225

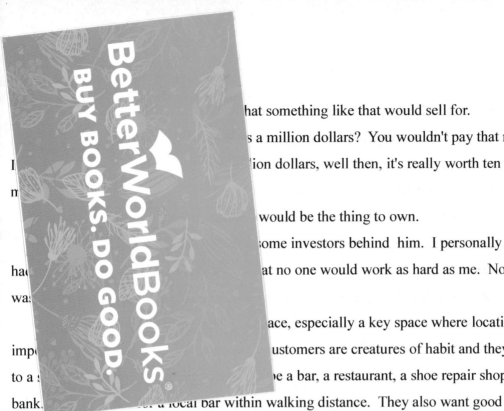

hat something like that would sell for.

s a million dollars? You wouldn't pay that much.

I ... lion dollars, well then, it's really worth ten

m ...

... would be the thing to own.

... ome investors behind him. I personally never

ha ... at no one would work as hard as me. Nobody

wa ...

... ace, especially a key space where location is

imp ... ustomers are creatures of habit and they go

to a ... e a bar, a restaurant, a shoe repair shop, or a

bank. ... ocal bar within walking distance. They also want good

simple food like hamburgers or quality guacamole and chips, not fancy food. Very few

of those kind of bars serve anything like prime rib, although Big Dogs did a great job. If

you are leasing that business, when the lease expires and you're doing well, the owner

can raise the rent so high that you can't afford to operate. I saw it happen with the health

food store on Charleston, I saw it with the shoe repair shop, and I saw it with bars,

namely, the Eureka Bar and Casino at the corner of East Sahara and Sixth.

The Eureka was leased out as a casino/bar/restaurant. When that lease expired,

the landlord didn't raise their rent or renew the lease, he took it over. He established a

wonderful casino with all the advertising and all the neighbors coming in, and then he

took it a step further. There are certain license issues about being closed for thirty days

and having to reapply. Instead, the landlord built on the outside of the casino, enlarging

the whole building. After construction, he had a bigger, more modern casino, and all his

customers, who never had a chance to go someplace else, kept coming there for their

morning coffee.

As a matter of fact, I remodeled while remaining open, and the sawdust was

flying, but the regular customers kept coming in. They would sit at the bar and complain about all the dust flying around, but they liked to watch the workers, and they were interested in the changes. I actually had more business than ever while construction was going on.

There was a shoe repair shop and Siemens Health Food Store on East Charleston, and a shoe repair shop on that southeast corner, and the owners paid their rent for years. They had a five-year rent contract with a renewal for another five years and they built up their businesses. Then when the leases expired, the landlord raised their rents astronomically, because he figured they would not go elsewhere, having worked so hard to establish their clienteles. He was right. Those businesses couldn't exist unless they stayed where they were, but both Siemens and the shoe repair shop had to move, because they couldn't afford the rent. One moved across the street, the other moved to the other side of town and then to a place around the corner from there. They lost their customers, who were not used to walking across the street. Both businesses went out of business. I was told that the Siemens parents had died and their children were taking it over, but they lost it. That was when Las Vegas was experiencing a great spike in business in 2006-07. Real estate was on the rise, so landlords thought they could ask anything they wanted. Younger people coming in did not have the experience to understand what was happening, and landlords became too greedy. They forgot that it might be better to take less than to have the place empty.

*   *   *

I learned so much during the years I was in business, not only about commercial ins and outs, but about people of all calibers. I never want to stop learning about people, what makes them tick, how to communicate with them, how to help them. At the same time, you cannot enhance someone else's life without enhancing your own. It's like the old adage says, you cannot pour from an empty pitcher. Teaching by example is probably the best way, as my parents taught me. A strong individual is taught by strong parents. Schoolteachers are second most important but, sadly, they have lost a lot of rights and power they used to have. They are walking on eggs to make sure they don't offend a student and, in the process, their ability to teach is compromised. I also think that teaching parenting should be required. We go to driver's school, don't we? Isn't learning how to raise children more important than driving? In the same vein, I think that the answer to health care is teaching healthy living, alternative medicine, exercise, diet. In certain insurance plans they already give free health club memberships. They should be provided for young people, too. I was told, however, that if we teach people how to live longer, that would put more pressure on Social Security. It's hard to believe that anyone would be more concerned about money than health but, unfortunately, I think it's true.

*　　*　　*

I love to spend time with my grand-daughter, Aspen. We would go to the county fair together, which delighted me, as it reminded me of the lovely village fairs of my childhood, though, of course, in Arizona the fair was much grander. Aspen had become an avid gardener, and I could not contain my excitement and pride when Aspen won a prize for her fantastic squashes!

I wondered how I could tell her about my values and share them with her. I came up with a way. When I visited them, I went to a ceramic shop in Tucson. They had beautiful affirmations written on ceramic tiles with floral designs, and the clerk told me I could put anything I wanted on a tile, and they would make it for me. My granddaughter was getting a new bathroom and I decided to create a wainscot of tiles with sayings on them, interspersed with flowered and plain tiles. I figured that while she was growing up she might contemplate those tiles -- "A stitch in time saves nine." "Understanding develops in degrees." I added my own personal motto: "Whether you call it work or play depends on your attitude." "Whether you think you can or you think you can't, you're right." "Genius is differentiating importance." They are still in her bathroom, permanently fixed, and I can only hope that they continue to inspire her.

To the Boneyard

On February 2, 2010, the Queen of Hearts was demolished to make way for the new city hall and downtown center. The <u>Las Vegas Review Journal</u> covered it, and there was a big celebration. Even though the whole two blocks were taken down, the news media chose the Queen of Hearts as a headliner. Mayor Oscar Goodman and I were on the front page with that story. I'm actually in a video on YouTube, where I say, "It is very nostalgic. A lot of memories come back, there are a lot of stories of things that happened in that hotel. Unfortunately, people come to a hotel to commit suicide, commit crimes, do drugs, prostitution. All of this lovely new construction and the security that will surround it is going to lift the downtown area up."

I watched as the giant claw raked the building apart in a torrent of falling walls, but the sign, "Ann Meyers' Queen of Hearts," was gently lowered to the sidewalk, and transported to the Neon Museum's Boneyard.

The Neon Museum was founded in 1996, and it's dedicated to exhibiting iconic Las Vegas signs. In 2012 the Boneyard opened at 770 Las Vegas Boulevard North. The nearly two-acre lot includes an outdoor exhibition space that features more than 200 signs from famous casinos such as the Golden Nugget, seven of which have been restored. Another fascinating aspect of the place is that changes and trends in sign design and technology are also illustrated in pieces that range from the 1930s to the present day.

You have to take a guided tour of the Boneyard, as people aren't allowed to wander around by themselves. I took my friends, Bob and Leita Davis there one year, and the tour guide was thrilled to meet me and have me tell some of my story to her group. As she said, "It's the unique stories behind the signs that are significant -- the personalities that created each casino, what inspired them, where and when they were made, and the role they played in Las Vegas' unique history."

Lake Tahoe -- New Dreams

Lake Tahoe was voted "The Most Beautiful Lake in America." It is vast, with rippling shades of blue stretching to the horizon. High snowy mountains encircle the lake and, as the sun moves across the sky, colors soften or brighten in its glow. I was so enthralled with its beauty that I could stand on the walkway for hours and watch the shadows of clouds on the water and the majestic mountains in the distance. I used to talk about living in Hawaii one day, but after I discovered Lake Tahoe, I forgot about that. I fell in love with Tahoe. My friends could not believe me until they saw it themselves. It is just amazing, especially Logan Creek. There, I feel like I'm away from the world, it's so peaceful and so stunningly beautiful. I agree with Mark Twain who wrote, "To breathe the same air as the angels, you must go to Tahoe."

I went to look at a house at Lake Tahoe with my friend, Bob Jones. The real estate agent drove us around, invited Bob to sit up front and gave him all his attention, obviously assuming that Bob was the prospective buyer, while I listened from the back seat. When I made him an offer, he was astonished, looked from me to Bob and sputtered through financial details, finally with me. But then we saw Logan Creek, and I fell in love again. Living there would be my nirvana. Logan Creek is on the east shore of the lake, where there are forested slopes, beaches and a breakwater cove, with a view across the lake to those snow-capped mountains. I made an offer on a house there, too, and so wound up with two properties. Maybe that wasn't the wisest financial decision I ever made, but I felt flush from the sale of my hotels, and gave in to the temptation to be extravagant for once in my life.

The only problem with living at Logan Creek is that I feel so lonely there by myself. At the hotels, I had lived in the midst of throngs of people, rarely able to catch a break by myself. Here, I was alone. Awed by silence and vast natural vistas, I longed to share my new world with someone. Over time, I met a few men who seemed to be likely prospects, but for one reason or another they didn't materialize. I still love to dance and wouldn't miss an opportunity to whirl around the floor. I love to travel, but not alone. I work very hard on my houses, constantly maintaining, renovating and decorating them. At least I'm no longer broke! I still hope that one day I may find someone with whom I can share my small corner of paradise. I have a lovely pillow upon which these words are embroidered: *Grow old with me; the best is yet to come.*

<u>Queen of Hearts: The Story of Ann Sipl Meyers</u> recounts the life of the first woman of her time to own and successfully manage a hotel and casino in Las Vegas: the first was The Casbah, changed to Queen of Hearts, the second *Little Annie's* Nevada Hotel and Casino. Ann Meyers socialized with the noteworthy and the notorious, gentlemen and thugs. She cared for the homeless and the derelicts and bore the scorn of the Country Club set who ended up celebrating her.

Though Ann is very well known in Las Vegas, not many people are aware of her painful childhood in the former Yugoslavia region populated by Germans (Danube Schwabians), and persecuted by Tito. She and her family survived concentration camps and the plight of post-World War II refugees, before finally emigrating to the United States.

Ann's story is extraordinary. She is an icon of womanly strength honed in hardship, who cultivated wisdom based on what she made of her experiences. Her philosophy has always been "Whether you call it work or play depends on your attitude." She rose from a child who begged for a bit of bread to a queen who built her own throne.

*   *   *

Anna Sipl Meyers' book is based on two years of interviews conducted by Claytee D. White, Director of the Oral History Research Center at UNLV Libraries.

Leita Kaldi Davis (Editor) worked for the United Nations and UNESCO, for Tufts University Fletcher School of Law and Diplomacy and Harvard University. She worked with Roma (Gypsies) for fifteen years, became a Peace Corps Volunteer in Senegal at the age of 55, then went to work for the Albert Schweitzer Hospital in Haiti for five years. She retired in Florida in 2002, and wrote a memoir of Senegal, <u>Roller Skating in the Desert</u>, and of Haiti, <u>In the Valley of Atibon</u>, along with several travel memoirs. (amazon.com). She received the 2017 Lillian Carter Award.

Made in the USA
San Bernardino, CA
09 March 2020